Animation

THE WHOLE STORY

HOWARD BECKERMAN

REVISED EDITION

ALLWORTH PRESS
NEW YORK

To the memory of

A. Kip Livingston

07 06 05 04 03   5 4 3 2 1

Published by Allworth Press
An imprint of Allworth Communications, Inc.
10 East 23rd Street, New York, NY 10010

Cover design by Derek Bacchus
Cover illustration by Howard Beckerman

Interior design and page composition
by Sharp Designs, Lansing, MI

ISBN: 1-58115-301-5

LIBRARY OF CONGRESS CATALOGING-IN-PUBLICATION DATA
Beckerman, Howard.
Animation : the whole story / Howard Beckerman.
p. cm.
1. Animated films—Technique. 2. Animated films—History. I. Title.
NC1765.B37 2003
778.5'347—dc22
2003022936

Printed in Canada

Contents

Acknowledgments

It was Eli Bauer who suggested I write a book about animation, and it was Kip Livingston who got me to begin in earnest. To Eli for striking the match and to Kip for kindling the fire, I am deeply indebted. Sincere thanks also to my editor Nicole Potter for her patience and guidance in organizing the material found in these pages, and to Derek Bacchus for adding his imaginative and vigorous design skills to the final product. My heartfelt thanks to: Lewis Cohen, Alexander Reyna, Judson Rosebush, Sonya Shannon, and Richard Sneiderman, for clarifying the world of computers for me, and to Sheri Weisz for her insight and advice. I am also deeply indebted to the yeoman efforts of recent animation historians: Joe Adamson, Michael Barrier, Giannalberto Bendazzi, John Canemaker, Leslie Carbaga, Karl Cohen, Donald Crafton, John Culhane, Leonard Maltin, Charles Solomon, and Michael Frierson for their scholarship and observations in bringing animation history to light.

To everyone who patiently gave their time, offered their knowledge, answered my questions, and provided encouragement, I offer my appreciation: Preston Blair, Gerardo Blumenthal, Tad Crawford, Shamus Culhane, George Davis, Ronen Divon, David Ehrlich, Bill Focht, Dave Gantz, John Gati, George Griffin, Lu Guarnier, Kit Hawkins, Bert Hecht, Judi Lynn Lake, Reeves Lehmann, Pat Terry Leahy, Bill Lorenzo, Bob Lyons, Nick Mavroson, Gil Miret, Allan Neuwirth, Silvie Newman, Barbara Nessim, Don Nolan, Tzvika Oren, Don Oriolo, Michael Pinto, Bill Plympton, David Rhodes, Keith Robinson, Fenton Rose, Ronald Schwarz, Miriam Sherry, Adrian Sinnott, Tom Sito, Mara Sneiderman, Cecile Starr, Gunnar Strom, Ed Summer, Beth Tondreau, David Tung, Maureen Volpe, Becky Wilde, Richard Williams, and Amy Zarndt.

Last, but not least, I must thank my wife, Iris, whose artistic talents helped me appreciably and whose abiding faith and sense of humor carried me through the long months of writing and drawing.

Foreword

Animation is a highly competitive field where each project poses a different style and technique, but where, surprisingly, there is often a lack of creative freedom. Though devoted to fantasy, the animator must confront many realities. No one is more aware of these pitfalls than Howard Beckerman. He had a brilliant career as a writer, director, and animator of theatrical shorts at Paramount Pictures, and when its cartoon unit closed, he opened his own studio to do television commercials and educational films.

Readers will find this book a font of information, and the enthusiastic artist or writer will discover valuable tips on how to succeed in this challenging field.

Shamus Culhane

Shamus Culhane
Animator, director, producer, former
director of animation, Paramount Cartoons

Preface

Animation is a compact medium; its strength is its conciseness. It's like a fruitcake, embracing many wonderful things in one tight space, and, like a fruitcake, it can be very nutty.

The animated picture goes beyond the scope of live-action film and television, there is no other graphic art that so stretches the imagination to get a laugh, display an abstraction, explain a method, or sell a product. It is the ultimate fantasy medium, twisting time and distorting shape. Yet even as it amuses and soothes it also describes and instructs. It is an excellent tool for expressing ideas. It is also fun to do, and you don't have to like fruitcake to do it either.

When I was asked to teach animation after years of working in the field, I found there were few texts available to guide serious students. This book is the result of hundreds of hours of instruction at various levels. As an animator turned teacher, I discovered that students' difficulties with drawing, animating, and storytelling were exactly those that I had grappled with when I was starting out. My classes derive from my personal experience in approaching problems, and these encounters have become the basis for this book.

Animators are honest people who take their work seriously, and they know you can't fake it. To get good results takes long, hard, careful effort. To arrive at a point where you know what works and what doesn't requires experience. Traditionally, individuals learned animation by working in one or more studios under the pressure of deadlines, in the presence of intractable artists who were not always forthcoming with their advice.

When I started out in the field I was fortunate to be able to work with veteran animator Irving Spector. "Spec," only too happy to take a break from his own tasks, welcomed the opportunity to offer guidance. He was a writer as well as an animator and his work was full of invention. There was little evidence of struggle in his drawings of characters and the worlds they inhabited. I was all of nineteen and he, fifteen years my senior, had put in considerable time at studios in Hollywood and New York. He understood my clashes with the complexities of the medium and that it would take time and patience for me to achieve my goals. His response was, "When you're thirty-two, you'll know how to do it."

My purpose in this book is to tell the whole story of animation for people truly interested in the medium, to help fill the gaps in their knowledge—no matter what their age.

Basically, to learn animation, *do* animation. Cast yourself in the roles of director, writer, animator, and camera operator. Decide which events will occur in the story, and create the characters that will act in it. Choose the technique you are most comfortable with, be it drawing on paper, cels, clear movie film, or using cutouts, clay, sand, puppets, or computers.

Whichever direction you take, you'll find that drawing is basic to animation. From the creation of storyboards to the designing of characters and settings, from the planning of special effects to the preliminary plotting of computer images, the pencil is the foremost tool. To draw, you must first learn to see, to observe how people and things look, and then to quickly get your impressions down on paper.

Drawing, however, is a means to an end. Pictures on the screen move in time and, unlike pages in a book, are not meant to be studied individually. This matter of time directly relates to the spaces between drawings and their duration in a sequence. Time is the soul of animation, and it is animators'

respect for timing that casts them as actors.

But before there is any animation there must be a story. How do dislocated ideas and gags become a series of smooth, flowing scenes? It happens by making a storyboard, a method used by animators around the world in which small sketches are arranged, rearranged, discarded, or changed before any animation is begun. With a storyboard, a continuity is formed and a progression of actions and events is given a structure. Once the storyboard is complete, the characters and locations are detailed in pencil or on computer. Though computer animation is a much-used technique, it is only briefly touched on in this book. With the speedy changes and upgrading in that sphere, everything written about it is obsolete before the ink dries. However, computer animators who lack an understanding of traditional methods are poorly prepared no matter how many software programs they have mastered.

To that end, what follows is an international history of the medium—a chronicle of the many attempts to bring pictures to life. It tells about the beginnings of animation, the arrival of studios, the introduction of characters, styles, and techniques, and the opportunities available to animators in today's merry-go-round of film, television, computer, and Internet creations.

It's all in the mix, like a fruitcake—and like a story.

Here is the story of animation, and of what makes it move.

— H. B.

PART ONE

An Animator's History of Animation

*The man with a new idea is a Crank until
the idea succeeds.* —Mark Twain

CHAPTER 1

The Curtain Rises

The whole field was virgin soil and we had all the joys of explorers in an unknown country. It was wonderful. —Lotte Reiniger

Animation on film began in the fading years of the nineteenth century, when the early motion picture cameras were manual. It must have been obvious to most camera operators that interference with the steady turning of the crank would destroy the flow of natural action and was something to be strictly avoided. And yet an alert few cinematographers realized the creative and humorous possibilities in cranking, stopping, changing something in the scene, then starting up again.

One of these few, James Stuart Blackton, did a quick sketch routine on the vaudeville stage in New York. His act, filmed by the Edison Motion Picture Company, remains today the earliest example of stop-motion sketches. Titled *The Enchanted Drawing*, it bears the notice "copyrighted entry Nov. 17, 1900," and though there is little frame-by-frame animation in it, the simple changes that occur indicate that the idea was waiting in the wings.

Blackton's 1900 experiment in filmed drawings came approximately seventy years after the discovery of an early ani-mation device, the *phenakistoscope*, and eleven years after the introduction of Edison's movie machines, the *kinetograph* and *kinetoscope*. Winsor McCay, thirty years old at the time, was drawing political cartoons for popular American humor magazines, and Max Fleischer, just sixteen, was working as an office boy in the art department of the *Brooklyn Daily Eagle*. That same year, the future animator Ivan Ivano-Vano was born in Moscow. Lotte Reiniger, in Germany, was only a year old. Walt Disney would be born in Chicago in December of the following year. It was twelve years before Jiri Trnka and John Halas would come into the world, the former in Czechoslovakia and the latter in Hungary. It was fourteen years before Norman McLaren's birth in Scotland and John Hubley's in the United States.

But the real story of animation begins before all of this, before photography, before film, before vaudeville, and before comic strips. It begins, like all stories, at the beginning—the very beginning.

Prehistory: Before Gertie

Making pictures which indicate the passage of time has been an assignment for the artist throughout history. —Donald W. Graham

Why do we always point to cave paintings as the beginning of animation? Some historians get red in the face about this. "Cave dwellers were not thinking about motion pictures," they shout. All the table-pounding doesn't alter the fact that since the earliest times artists have sought to depict action through painting and sculpture. When a contemporary cartoonist sketches a blurred, multiple image it is an extension of an idea that began in the Ice Age. There is evidence on the walls of a cave in Altamira, Spain, dating back 30,000 years, that this desire led to a depiction of a wild boar with two sets of legs. Since there are very few such examples, it could also be assumed that the multiple legs were not a representation of blurred movement but a change of mind on the part of the artist in the placement of the running limbs. Artists

do this all the time. The prehistoric artist would have been unable to eliminate the "wrong" set of legs, since there were no erasers then to do the job.

While we may never know the purposes of cave art, conjecture about the changing shapes of early designs— whether on a cave wall, in an Egyptian tomb, on a Greek urn, or in the gestures of Asian shadow puppets—suggests that these depictions were ways of showing motion. Several centuries would pass before improved technology and specific economic and social conditions would allow for the creation of animated films.

Pictures in Motion

The smooth flow of images that we call the "movies" requires a series of drawings or photographs close enough in sequence and shown at a rate sufficient to make them appear to blend. Conflicting, disassociated images of different shape, tone, or location, projected one after the other, do not create this effect, or at least there are no smooth transitions. The illusion of motion occurs when slightly varying pictures replace each other in swift succession, each appearing for about one-sixteenth of a second.

When a torch or candle is swung in an arc, the illusion of a continuous circle of light is formed, though the movement of the light occupies a series of separate positions. This overlapping was further demonstrated in 1826 with the introduction of a toy called the *thaumatrope*, attributed to Dr. William Henry Fitton (1780–1861) and later manufactured by Dr. John Ayrton Paris

Moving light creates the illusion of a continuous line.

and so on, made this toy visually entertaining. This phenomenon of merging imagery prompted further scientific inquiry by such important minds as John Herschel (1792–1871), Michael Faraday (1791–1867), and Peter Mark Roget (1779–1869). After viewing a passing cart through the slats of his blinds, Roget surmised that the vehicle registered on the retina of the eye for longer than it was actually there. He called this occurrence the *persistence of vision*. The unnoticed blinking of our eyelids, to cleanse the eyes, goes on continually with no disruption in what we are seeing. Present-day investigators state that the persistence of vision only explains why we don't see a strong flicker between images and not why they appear to move. One finding suggests that when an image appearing in one place on a screen suddenly disappears and then shows up in a different place on the screen, the brain decides by inference that the object has moved. Other experimenters have discovered that the mind perceives the *correspondence* between similar, displaced shapes. However, one

(1785–1856) in England. It was a disc much like a large coin with dissimilar pictures on each side, which when twirled quickly gave the illusion that the images overlapped.

Lightly humorous combinations, such as a bald man and a wig, a bird and a cage, a sitting cat and a saddled horse,

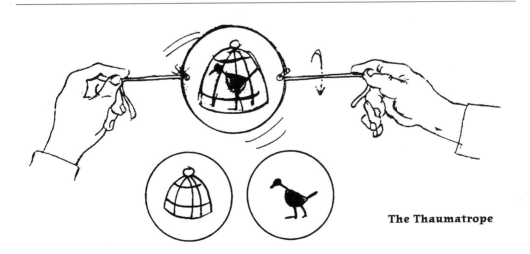

The Thaumatrope

thing remains constant—the steady persistence of scientists who study the viability of the persistence of vision.*

Early Nineteenth-Century Animation

The first animations were created in 1832 using a device developed by Joseph Antoine Ferdinand Plateau (1801–1883) of Brussels and, coincidentally, by professor Ritter von Stampfer (1792–1864) of Vienna. Plateau devised a wheel with slits around its edge. Under each slit was one of a series of closely related designs and when the disc was spun past the eye, facing a mirror, the images appeared to move. The intermittent slits were an important factor—without them the illusion was reduced to a blur. The disc and the repeating illustrations representing close phases of turning wheels, wriggling snakes, or jumping monkeys was called the *phenakistoscope*. Stampfer's similar disc was labeled the *stroboscope* and was spun with the images facing a mirror to achieve the same effect. Thus, with these simple novelties, animation was born.

Plateau, a scientist and former art student, drew the initial actions himself, making him the world's first animator. Other artists were engaged to create sequential designs to accommodate a growing market for the phenakistoscopes, or "fantascopes," as they were also called. A further application was introduced in Bristol, England, in 1834

The Zoetrope

in the form of the *zoetrope*, designed by William George Horner (1786–1837). The zoetrope, or "wheel of life," did not become popular until it was widely distributed in 1867. It had certain advantages over the earlier slotted discs: it didn't require a mirror to provide the illusion; and its drum shape, with the necessary viewing slits around the top, allowed for the insertion of new paper strips of drawings to stave off boredom.

The phenakistoscope and zoetrope artists, painters, and illustrators were anonymous animators, a condition that would continue into early motion picture making. Film historian David Robinson identified some of these artists and, aside from Plateau, his list includes Thomas Talbot Bury (1811–1877), Thomas Mann Baynes (1794–1854), and the famed Victorian illustrator George Cruikshank (1792–1878). As in the case of modern animators, these artists had to contend with time limitations and the subtle awareness of how much change was necessary between the moves. Their work was not yet dominated by the demands of a film projector, but they

---

*Studies of perception refer to the movie illusion by various titles: *apparent motion, stroboscopic motion,* or the *phi phenomenon.*

did have to match their drawn movements to the number of slits that could fit on a small surface. These openings numbered between ten and twenty, and actions were selected that would meld smoothly within those parameters. The illusion remained a simple novelty that played itself out, in mere seconds, for an audience of one or two people at a time. Longer subjects for larger audiences were still to come and would evolve from another device that had been known for centuries.

Light and Lenses

The *camera obscura* was a darkened room with a tiny hole in one wall through which sunrays passed, casting an image onto the opposite wall. This effect was noted by the Greek philosopher Aristotle (384–322 B.C.) and was later incorporated by medieval astronomers to chart the eclipse of the sun. Renaissance artists—Leonardo da Vinci (1452–1519) for one—were aware of the camera obscura and used it in making accurate perspective drawings.

By the 1600s, experiments with the properties of lenses led to the introduction of a projection instrument whose design was attributed to a Jesuit priest, Athanasius Kircher (1602–1680). Kircher made drawings on translucent material, placed a lamp behind the drawings and a lens in front, and cast the drawings' shadows on a wall. He called this ancestor of the present day slide projector *magia catoptrica*, or "magic lantern."

The magic lantern was soon established as a source of amusement and awe, and well into the next century

traveling entrepreneurs took them around to towns and villages. For a small sum, they enthralled the locals with quivering, projected images. Magic lantern showmen strove to simulate movement by projecting long strips of glass or rotating discs bearing phases of an action. By the mid-nineteenth century, it was common practice to view slide programs that produced colorful and humorous effects through the manipulation of a handle or a crank.

The use of slides combined with attempts to tell stories with simulated motion reached its zenith with the introduction of Emile Reynaud's *théatre optique* in Paris in 1892. About ten years earlier, Reynaud (1844–1917) had replaced the viewing slits of the zoetrope with rectangular mirrors that faced the drawings and revolved as the drum was spun. He dubbed his invention the *praxinoscope*, expanding it into an elaborate theater attraction via mirrors and lenses and a belt of painted transparencies. Accompanied by appropriate sounds, the projecting praxinoscope was a forerunner of what would one day become screen animation. Reynaud entertained a record number of people with his *théatre optique* until the close of the century, when moving pictures arrived. Reynaud's enthusiasm waned, he became discouraged and so depressed that he reportedly dumped all of his apparatuses into the Seine.

Photography Enters the Picture

Developments in lens technology prodded the desire to capture permanently views formed by a camera obscura. A chemical means was sought after, and it was found that surfaces coated with a solution of silver chloride were affected by light after exceedingly long exposure. Experiments with this process carried out by Thomas Wedgewood (1771–1805) and Sir Humphrey Davy (1778–1829) in England, and by Joseph Nicephore Niepce (1765–1833) in France, resulted in the first photographic images. Niepce had made successful images as early as 1816 and developed an early form of photoengraving. In 1829 he formed a partnership with Louis Jacques Mande Daguerre (1787–1851), who had been carrying out his own experiments. Daguerre, a Parisian scenic artist, was known for a theatrical novelty called the *diorama*, which featured large painted views of cities and landscapes and was dramatized further by atmospheric lighting effects. Unfortunately, soon after joining his ideas with Daguerre, Nicephore Niepce died and his name fell into relative obscurity, while his partner's became synonymous with the process that was presented to the world in 1839 as the *daguerreotype*. This revolutionary discovery was essentially a glass plate coated with a light-sensitive emulsion, which when exposed for several minutes produced a positive image.

The same year photography was introduced in France, an independent technique was demonstrated in England. Called the *calotype*, it developed out of the extensive experiments of William Henry Fox Talbot (1800–1877) using nitrate of silver. Talbot's discovery resulted in a paper negative from which any number of positive prints could be made. After great success, the daguerreotype eventually gave way to the newer, more versatile calotype.

Motion pictures were not yet possible, as photography of living subjects depended on long exposures and tortuous body clamps to keep people still. It wasn't long, however, before posed photographs were used to symbolize lifelike motion. Initially, some photographers projected sequenced lantern slides of melodramatic scenes to attract audiences. This led, in turn, to posed action phases, which, when dropped into a zoetrope or projected by an altered magic lantern, advanced the transparencies intermittently. Such a machine was fashioned in 1875 by John Arthur Roebuck Rudge.

Muybridge's Galloping Horse

In 1872, Eadweard James Muybridge (1830–1904) began photographing animals in motion using a battery of still cameras. The shutters were attached to stretched strings which were tripped by the subjects as they ran past. The initial trials missed important phases of actions, but by 1880, with twelve cameras equipped with electrically tripped shutters, more movements were captured. Some of the photos were specially aligned and projected through a *zoopraxiscope*, a combination magic lantern and revolving phenakistoscope disc. The importance of the Muybridge shots was that they were continuous, changing views of beings in actual motion and not posed stills.

Prior to Muybridge's experiments,

artists had portrayed horses in positions that were romanticized rather than true to life. After their publication, the photographs had a profound and immediate effect on the rendering of animal motion in artistic works. These clearly delineated actions are still viable and serve as reference for animators.

Muybridge's work came to the attention of the Parisian physiologist Etienne Jules Marey (1830–1904), who had been making drawings and studies of animal motion. Because Muybridge created his pictures by exposing plates in many cameras at once (an expense absorbed by his benefactor, Leland Stanford, a millionaire horse breeder), each view was recorded at a slightly different angle. Marey sought a single camera that would be less costly and cumbersome, but which would record all phases of a movement from a single viewpoint.

In 1882, Marey devised a gunstock camera that took a series of exposures on a revolving plate through a solitary lens, a design similar to an instrument developed by the astronomer, P.J.C. Janssen (1824–1907), to take pictures of the transit of Venus in 1876. Marey was able to get the necessary intermittent motion by means of a Maltese cross gear, obtaining twelve exposures in one second. He began recording the movements of birds in flight, and by 1888 he had developed a new camera design that could take successive pictures on a moving roll of celluloid film.

The Flexible Strip

Once pictures of natural action became possible through photography, inventors pursued their search for a camera with a built-in mechanism for recording motion. No one nation or individual can take full credit for creating motion pictures; the inspiration emerged from many sources and from the work of experimenters and tinkerers in several countries. All of the experiments, however, did share a debt to spinning animation toys, the numerous uses of the magic lantern, and the pioneering work of Muybridge and Marey.

It was Muybridge who approached Thomas Edison (1847–1931) in February of 1888 with a proposal to combine the zoopraxiscope with the phonograph. Although the Edison cylinders were incapable of being heard in large meeting halls, due to inadequate sound amplification at that time, the suggestion was enough to plant the thought in Edison's mind. It culminated in Edison's early research that in 1893 produced the basic elements of motion pictures. The first true movie is traditionally credited to Thomas Edison and his invention of the *kinetoscope* viewing machine in West Orange, New Jersey. Little attention is given to what came with it—the camera that recorded the motion. Edison called this camera the *kinetograph*. It was a very large apparatus that pulled the film through horizontally, like today's videotape machines, and like other Edison contrivances, it was controlled by an enormous electric motor. The mechanism was actually developed through the dedicated work of Edison's assistant, William Kennedy Laurie Dickson (1860–1935). This young Englishman, only twenty-one when he came to Edison's lab in 1881, supervised the experiments

The Road to the Motion Picture

Movies are possible because of the combined use of: ● Sequential images; □ Perforated, flexible strips; ○ Lenses; ◗ Shutters; ▲ Detents

Lenses Camera Obscura. Images formed by light passing through a pinhole was noted in ancient times. Focusing lenses were introduced in the seventeenth century. Shown is a reflex model, circa 1838. ○

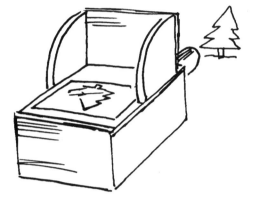

Magic lantern, 1600s. A typical mid-nineteenth-century model. ○

Zoetrope, 1865. Interchangeable strips of pictures. ● ◗

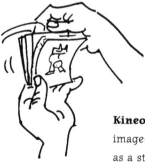

Kineograph, 1860s. Flipping of image-bearing cards. The thumb acts as a stop-and-go mechanism. ▲ ●

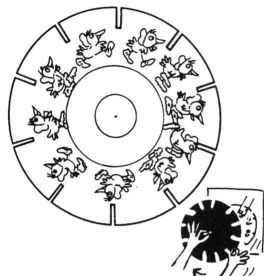

Drawn sequential images and shutters the phenakistoscope, 1839.
Pictures, seen individually through slots, are viewed by mirror reflection. ●◗

Photography: Muybridge, 1870s.
The recording of nature with a series of cameras. ◗● ○

Photography: Marey, 1882.
Natural action recorded on a single negative. ◗● ○

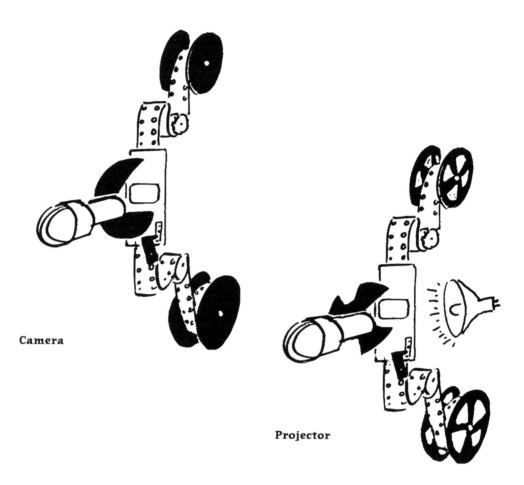

Camera

Projector

The illusion of moving pictures is possible through a combination of: perforated flexible film, a camera with sprocketed gears synchronized with an intermittent claw mechanism and a shutter.

- The claw engages the perforations and pulls the filmstrip down one frame.
- The single frame is stationary for a brief part of a second, with the shutter open to let light pass.
- As the claw reengages with the film and pulls it down, the shutter closes, cutting off the light.
- As the new frame comes into position, the claw retracts and the shutter opens, and the cycle continues. Without this stop-and-go action, the result would be merely a blur. ◗ ☐ ● ○ ▲

Perforated flexible strips and sprockets:

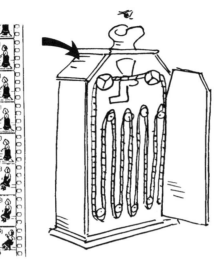

Edison's kinetoscope, 1894. Photographed action viewed by one person at a time.
○ ● ▲ ◗ □

Eastman nitro-cellulose film, 1889.

Lumière's cinematographe, 1895. A portable camera and projector combination, for screening for large audiences. ○ ● ▲ ◗ □

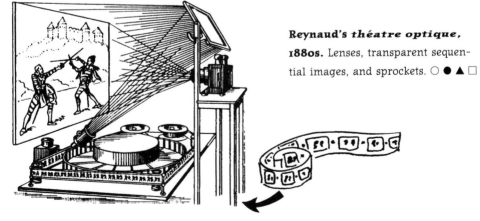

Reynaud's *théâtre optique*, 1880s. Lenses, transparent sequential images, and sprockets. ○ ● ▲ □

that led to the kinetograph's construction. The kinetograph contained an intermittent mechanism that passed a strip of celluloid film behind a lens. A series of sprocket wheels meshed with orderly rows of holes punched along the film's edges.

Edison actually expressed little interest in moving pictures, but as the efforts of others began to show promise, he pressed Dickson to forge ahead. The results culminated in 1889, with the invention of the kinetoscope viewing machine.

By 1895 entrepreneurs, sensing opportunity in the Edison machines, established storefront "kinetoscope parlors." The first of these was installed at 1155 Broadway in New York City, where an amazed public flocked to peek at tiny moving images of featured vaudeville performers. Brief rolls of film emanated in a steady stream from the "Black Maria," Edison's specially constructed shooting stage. Various subjects were attempted, including a dramatization of *The Execution of Mary Queen of Scots*, filmed by Dickson's successor, Alfred Clark, using a man to portray the queen. It became the first film to purposely create an effect by starting, stopping, and restarting the camera. The actors positioned themselves to depict the beheading. The axe was raised, the camera stopped, the person playing the unfortunate monarch was removed, a dummy positioned where he had been, and the filming resumed. The head that rolled wasn't real but to viewers, caught up in the portrayal, it must have been exceedingly convincing. This first recorded use of *stop-motion*, in this case to heighten

reality, became a key technique used by others in the creation of fantasy and animation.

Vive la Cinematographe

On February 13, 1895, the Lumière brothers Louis (1864–1948) and Auguste (1862–1954) of Paris received a patent for their *cinematographe*. This was a portable camera that also served as a projector, not a peephole device like Edison's. These embellishments meant that films could easily be made in any location, and the results shown not to one viewer at a time, but to large audiences at a single sitting. It also put to an end the reliance on limited, brief strips of film and repetitious cycles of action. It was the invention of the projector that opened the path to longer and more complex motion pictures.

In a short time an Edison projector appeared, manufactured for him by the inventors Charles Francis Jenkins (1867–1934) and Thomas Armat (1866–1948). Called the *vitascope*, it debuted at Koster and Bials Music Hall on New York's West Thirty-fourth Street. Magicians and stage illusionists realized the advantages of the new device immediately. Among these were George Melies in Paris and Albert Smith in New York. These conjurers, persistent in their search for anything that might enhance their staged illusions, incorporated magic lanterns, mirrors, chalk talks, and lighting effects to entertain vaudeville audiences. It was as natural for them to latch onto the new projection apparatus as it was for them to pluck coins out of thin air.

Before the decade was out, Melies

and Smith and Smith's partner James Stuart Blackton had employed the trick of substitution in their films. Melies used it to create surreal fantasies and Blackton to recreate his "lightning sketch" stage performance.

The Early 1900s: For Only a Nickel

The Sears Roebuck catalog for the year 1900 is perfectly up to date. Included among its thousands of implements for farm and home are the latest 35mm film projectors. The commercial possibilities of the new medium were at a point where, through the mail, a moving picture machine could be purchased as offhandedly as a shotgun, rake, or suit of long underwear.

As movies grew in popularity, little thought was given to imparting life to drawings. The appeal of early films lay in their recreation of everyday events: people strolling in a park, a train approaching a station, or a horse-drawn fire engine racing through town. This concentration on the commonplace shifted with the realization that entertainers could be enticed to appear before a camera. The twirling jugglers, whirling dancers, and muscle-bound athletes who paraded their talents for the "flicks" would, unknowingly, become the flesh-and-blood models for the cartoon characters that followed. As with live-action film, animation began not as an art but as a business. The entrepreneurs who hustled crowds at the penny arcades, opened storefront nickelodeons, or set up screens at vaudeville houses, were not artists but practical types who

saw an opportunity for making money. The producers who supplied the reels were equally motivated by the comforting clink of coins and in the process they became showmen.

George Melies: Magician on the Moon

Georges Melies (1861–1938) began making short, highly imaginative films in Paris in 1898. A former stage magician, he adapted his knowledge of theatrical illusions to the screen, and over the next fourteen years churned out hundreds of inventive subjects incorporating stop-action, multiple exposures, and fantastic imagery. Although he was an artist before he learned magic, Melies apparently did not use frame-by-frame animation. However, it was through his prodigious imagination that fantasy stories and special-effects productions found a niche in motion pictures.

The often repeated story that Melies stumbled upon the trick of stop-motion while photographing scenes of a Paris street undoubtedly has some truth in it. As it is told, the camera jammed, he readjusted it, and then resumed shooting. The resulting footage revealed a horse-drawn vehicle popping off suddenly and being replaced by a different conveyance. Melies, intrigued, realized that effects that would have been cumbersome or impossible on the stage could now be created by the simple turn of a camera handle.

James Stuart Blackton

In New York, James Stuart Blackton (1875–1941) and his partner Albert Edward Smith were similarly adapting their talents to the new medium. They, too, had observed strange occurrences due to the starting and stopping of the camera when viewing film shot outdoors. Objects in the background moved haphazardly or came and went unexpectedly. In fact, most special effects are the results of using "wrong" methods—those things one is warned not to do, but when used creatively catch the eye. Overexposures become magical glows; film run through a camera twice creates ghostly images; a jiggled camera produces interesting blurs; the scratching of the film's surface creates abstract designs, and so on.

Blackton was primarily a cartoonist who, armed with chalk, crayon, and a ready wit, entertained vaudeville audiences. Through the trick of stop-motion, he leaped from one career to another. In 1900 the Edison cameras filmed Blackton's act. The film, *The Enchanted Drawing,* shows the artist making a series of humorous sketches and includes the substitution of a drawn wine bottle for a real one. On closer view, a frowning cartoon face has been replaced with a beaming smile. Though this was not yet continuous motion, it was a step in the right direction.

Then, in 1906, Blackton made a film that is now considered the first to purposely employ drawn animation. Titled *Humorous Phases of Funny Faces,* the film uses frame-by-frame shooting technique to make blackboard drawings come

Blackton's *Humorous Phases of Funny Faces* (vitagraph), 1906.

alive. There is no story, just a series of brief actions in which an eye blinks, smoke curls from a cigar, and a clown is animated by drawings and cutout arms and legs. Smith and Blackton saw the entertainment value in these interrupted shootings, and adapted the trick to turn an old stage act into the 1907 film, *The Haunted Hotel.* Here, household objects take on a life of their own as they move across the screen and rearrange themselves.

Blackton's third effort, also in 1907 and titled *Lightning Sketches,* was a chalk-talk subject and contained less animation than the 1906 film. *Lightning Sketches* reveals the prevalence and seeming acceptance of racial stereotypes as a source of popular humor. Today, what seems like an obvious lack of sensitivity was a staple of vaudeville comedians. Blackton's metamorphosis of the words "coon" and "Cohen" into caricatures of a black man and a Jewish man likely fell within the bounds of acceptability for most audiences at the time.

Blackton and Smith had earlier become film producers in 1898, when they founded the Vitagraph Corporation of America. By 1909 this Brooklyn-based studio was flourishing, and the increasing complexities of live film production forced Blackton to forego his trick work. Blackton's early experiments in animation inspired others and galvanized interest for further exploration. The others included Segundo de Chomon (1871–1929) in Spain and Walter R. Booth (18??–1971) in England. Around 1906 Chomon used black backgrounds for stop-motion photography of live actors. Among his many films was a version of *The Haunted Hotel*, called *El Hotel Electrico*, released in 1908.

Booth was also an experienced stage magician. No doubt he saw Blackton's work, and since lightning sketches were part of his bag of tricks, he incorporated the theme into the 1907 *Comedy Cartoons*. Booth had applied stop-motion in an earlier film, *The Hand of the Artist* (1906), and produced another in the "haunted" genre, *The Haunted Bedroom*. This last subject, repeated so often by these pioneers, indicates that it was an audience pleaser because of its "magical" properties, and a reflection of a time when mechanization, automobiles, airplanes, and the movies themselves evoked the promise of magic.

Two elements persisted in early drawn animated films. One was the ever-present cartoonist's hand as initiator of the story. The hand, together with the pen clutched in its fingers (usually a cutout of a still photo), drew upon recognizable situations for a laugh—eating, sleeping,

nightmares, bathing, baldness, etc. This device persisted in animated shorts into the late 1920s.

The second factor was the imitation or even direct stealing of others' themes and ideas. Any gag or character that gained audience approval found its way into subsequent productions. This happened as a matter of course with the earliest animations, and it continues even today. The seeds of originality have always been sown by someone else's brainstorm.

Emile Cohl: The First Cartoon Story

Emile Cohl (Emile Courtet, 1857–1938), a French caricaturist, began animating in 1908, and though he picked up on Blackton's lead he was the first to create a complete animated cartoon. Cohl's graphic art reflected the intricate, detailed, cross-hatching typical of nineteenth-century illustration, but Cohl was also interested in humor portrayed sequentially. Around the late 1890s, these depictions began showing up regularly in his work. He may simply have been mirroring what was shown in Paris cinemas of the day, but unknowingly he was forging the path toward animation. Cohl, already in his forties, came to film when he was hired by the Gaumont Company to create scripts for live comedy reels. Surrounded by moviemaking equipment, he attempted the filming of animated drawings.

To create his initial production,

Emile Cohl's *Fantoche*, 1908.

Fantasmagorie (1908), Cohl altered his style by simplifying his designs. The resulting characters are shown as child-like, unadorned, white outlines on a black background, an obvious tip of the hat to Blackton's chalkboard technique. To achieve this he drew the figures with black ink on white paper and had the film printed as a negative. It is entirely animated, except when Cohl's hand is shown briefly adjusting a cutout of a clown character, reminiscent of a similar figure in Blackton's *Humorous Phases of Funny Faces*. However, Cohl's film is a decided improvement in animation technique.

While Blackton's figures are stiff and restrained, Cohl's characters are fluidly active and the movements more convincing. In *Fantasmagorie* he introduces whimsical and imaginative metamorphoses for scene changes. These qualities place Emile Cohl at a key juncture between the aping of stage trickery and the exploration of animation as a medium in its own right.

Having spent his professional life as a newspaper and magazine illustrator, at the age of forty-five Cohl suddenly dedicated himself to film and animation.

Winsor McCay: Genius of the Funny Pages

While Cohl was getting further engrossed in the medium, Winsor McCay (1867–1934), a New York newspaper artist, was just discovering it. Self-taught, his career had begun inauspiciously sketching patrons at a Detroit dime museum, a circus-like funhouse and vaudeville affair. An indefatigable worker and a master storyteller with an extraordinary grasp of perspective and scale, McCay advanced to drawing comic pages for the *New York Herald*. His most ambitious subject, *Little Nemo in Slumberland*, began in 1905 and was a tour de force of pictorial invention. Just as Emile Cohl found his strength in making sequential illustrations, McCay found his calling in these active, changing frames. These detailed phases spilled from his pen as easily as fantastic dreamworlds tumbled from his mind. An earlier series, *Dream of the Rarebit Fiend*, incorporated humorous episodes in its lampooning of dyspeptic dreamers, and made it to the screen as a live-action trick film by Edison's innovative director, Edwin S. Porter (1869–1941).

Winsor McCay's talents were equally at home in vaudeville and, like Blackton, he strode the boards as a chalk-talk headliner. This could easily have brought him in contact with the animated subjects of Blackton and Cohl and sparked his interest in animated drawings. His

Winsor McCay, circa early 1930s.
(Collecton of John Canemaker.)

own explanation was that the simple flipbooks his son brought home had triggered his desire to bring drawings to life. Considering his established interest in sequential drawing, the small printed pads of animated pictures could very well have been the important catalyst.

McCay based his initial stab at the new medium on his *Little Nemo* comic and included supporting characters from the strip. Like Blackton, McCay initially saw the medium as an adjunct to his vaudeville routine, but unlike Cohl, he decided not to alter his realistic style to accommodate the enormous labor entailed in animation. McCay's output eventually totaled ten shorts, completed between 1911 and 1921, each reflecting his prodigious talents as a draftsman.

In some cases the humor in McCay's films was stronger than in his comic pages, which, with their reliance on dream content, tended to be more fabulous than funny. Two of McCay's productions, *Gertie* (1914) and the *Sinking of the Lusitania* (1918), reflect a dichotomy in approach. In *Gertie*, McCay, with instinctive animation timing, brings life to a dinosaur with humor and personality. *Gertie*'s purpose is to entertain. When screened today, the film still gets laughs decades after its debut. The *Sinking of the Lusitania* is different in style and content and like nothing seen before or since. Made as a document of the attack on a defenseless civilian liner by a German U-boat, it is decidedly intended to incite emotions, and uses animation as both newsreel and a wartime propaganda statement. The animation has an eerie, decorative quality, especially in the portrayal of the sinking ship: silhouetted passengers leap from its sides while smoke from the stacks twists in tortured configurations. Its propagandizing tone and its depiction of the innocents who sunk to the depths is still visually powerful, even though it was revealed much later that the Lusitania's hold was laden with munitions for use by British troops.

McCay's *Gertie the Trained Dinosaur* (Box Office Attractions), © 1914.

CHAPTER 2

The Studios Are Born

I didn't have anyone but myself at first . . . After I got going for a few months I took this place on Twenty-sixth Street and that developed into quite a place. —John Randolph Bray

Until 1913, animation was a side-line occupation, but just before the start of World War I, studios formed to churn out cartoons on a regular basis. The work of Cohl and McCay had been created intermittently while they were engaged in related fields. Cohl's arrangement with his distributors included live-action productions, and McCay was in constant demand as an illustrator and entertainer. As far as McCay was concerned, animation was an artform to be nourished and coddled. He never considered it an assembly-line task, but rather a higher calling, well worth the untold hours of personal time and money spent perfecting the medium.

Two entrepreneurial newspaper cartoonists, Raoul Barre (1874–1932) and John Randolph Bray (1879–1978), saw other possibilities in animation. Hoping for success through a steady flow of cartoon reels to theaters, they organized individual operations, Barre in 1913 and Bray a year later. Before a steady stream of shorts could emanate from these New York studios, certain technical problems had to be solved.

The Peg System

The first hurdle was to maintain accurate positioning of the drawings as they were being sketched and again when they were shot. The lack of a system of registry produced annoying jumps on the screen. To avoid this, various strategies were attempted. McCay borrowed an idea from newspaper-plate makers, placing small crosshairs on the corners of each paper sheet. The drawings, sketched on translucent rice paper, were fastened to cards cut precisely along each edge. These were held at one corner by a matching angle on the board in front of the camera. Another approach was to print cross marks onto the papers and then press them over upright pins set into the drawing table. This was a method introduced by the Bray Studio and required delicate maneuvering to avoid being stabbed. A safer, more efficient registry method was sought. It was Raoul Barre, producer of *The Grouch Chaser* series, who hit upon the idea of replacing the crosshairs and pins with two small pegs that matched punched holes in the drawing paper.

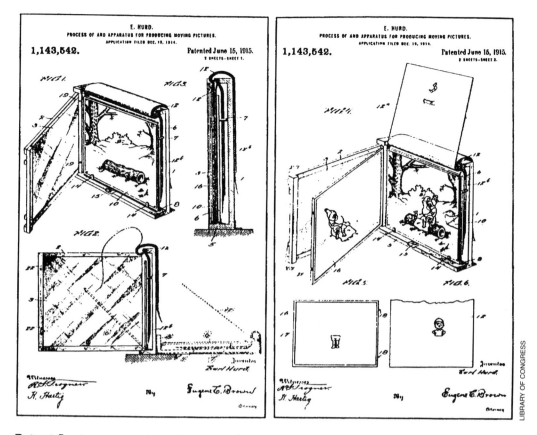

Patent for transparent overlays awarded Earl Hurd, 1915 (detail). (Library of Congress)

Cels

A second concern was the inclusion of backgrounds for the animated characters. Cohl and McCay initially avoided backgrounds, or traced the scenery onto each character drawing. In the case of Gertie the dinosaur the tracings numbered in the thousands and resulted in quivering landscapes. One solution was to cut out the figures and then manipulate them over the background. Cutouts, though used creatively by Cohl and numerous others, did not satisfy the New York animators, who sought the control of subtleties unattainable with jointed figures.

Bray's initial solution was to run off copies of the background on a press and then trace the character outlines onto them. Wherever a part of the background showed through the character, it was scratched out. The search continued for a see-through material, and this led to tracing paper. It was Earl Hurd who finally employed celluloid, the very substance that ran through cameras bearing the light-sensitive emulsion. At first the backgrounds were drawn on the celluloid sheets (cels) and placed over the animation. Soon, for more flexibility, the characters were traced onto the cels, opening the way for detailed backgrounds and for experiments with tonal rendering.

The Slash System. Characters inked on paper placed under a cutout paper overlay "background." (New York Public Library)

instance, championed a method he called the "slash system." Backgrounds, on white paper, were designed with a high horizon line and a great deal of free "playing" area. Each paper bearing the characters, with pegholes intact, was trimmed around the figures and laid over the background. Stark, high-contrast release prints obliterated shadows formed at the edges of the cut paper.

Paul Terry began as a cartoonist and photographer for newspapers, but turned to animation after attending an

Paul Terry (1887–1971) stated that he discovered cels, just as Barre introduced pegs, but it was Bray and Hurd who saw the benefits of owning the rights to these discoveries and made the effort to take out patents. Bray, in an obvious attempt to cover all bases, included most of the known facets of animation in his application. Eventually, a merger of patents led to the formation of the Bray-Hurd Process Company, which licensed the procedure to all other animation studios. Royalties for the use of the technique were collected until the early 1930s, and throughout that period opening titles of cartoons credited the Bray-Hurd Process Company. Today, pegs and cels are universally and freely used.

The Slash System

Cels were expensive for some studios, so in the days of black-and-white filming, there were ways to bypass their use. Knowledge of basic photography was of great aid to the pioneers. Raoul Barre, for

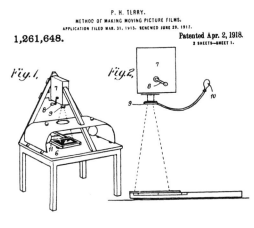

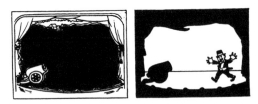

Paul Terry's patented matting technique for combining animated drawings with a background. 1918 U.S. Patent 1,261,648 (detail). New York Public Library.

inspiring lecture by Winsor McCay. When Terry made his initial cartoon, *Little Herman* (1915), he brought his experience to bear and combined the background and the animation by using matting and double exposures, a process for which he received a patent.

It was Bray who put animation production on a factory basis. Other units turning out work with the help of a handful of assistants may have envisioned their efforts as the product of happy-go-lucky artistic cooperation, but Bray's organization was strictly business. His contracts with major distributors demanded weekly releases of short cartoons, and to maintain these agreements, Bray hired a coterie of bright young men. They devised the plots, thought up the gags, and solved all of the problems of design and animation. A small group of lower-salaried artists inked the drawings and did the shooting.

Bray's key character at the start was Colonel Heeza Liar, a woodenly animated takeoff of President Theodore Roosevelt, whose frequent African hunting expeditions became grist for Heeza Liar's exorbitant fantasy exploits. Earl Hurd animated the tribulations of Bobby Bumps, a character who reflected the typical theme found in comic strips of a boy and a dog in small-town America. Additional cartoons were developed by Bray's hired hands to fulfill the assembly-line commitment. Among these were artists who would eventually become producers in their own right, such as Max (1883–1972) and Dave Fleischer (1894–1979), Walter Lantz (1900–1990), and the aforementioned Paul Terry.

The Rotoscope

The Fleischers had spent a year making their first trial animation, which ran about a minute and a half. Seeking a means of hastening the process, they filmed live-action sequences and then traced single-frame projections of it. This saved time in animation, but also added a welcome smoothness to the movements. The projection-tracing device was christened the *rotoscope* and was awarded a patent in 1917. It became the working method by which they introduced Koko the Clown. Brother Dave, cavorting in a clown suit, acted as Koko's model. The hallmark and great appeal of the Koko series was the combining of the characters with photographic backgrounds, a technique that was managed by placing a shot of a static scene under character cels.

Soon after the United States' entry into the war in 1917, Bray convinced the government that animation could speed the training of unseasoned recruits. Max Fleischer, who was still with Bray, was dispatched to Fort Sill, Oklahoma, to do military instructional films. Paul Terry served as an animator of army medical films in Washington, D.C., and eventually Max's brother Dave went into the service. With both Fleischers away, Koko would be shelved until 1919.

Between 1915 and 1918, cartoon production expanded. Bray supplied weekly cartoons through Pathe, and publisher William Randolph Hearst had his syndicated comic features translated into theatrical cartoons. With Gregory La Cava as studio manager, Hearst's International Film Service mined the convivial world of Krazy Kat, Bringing Up Father, Jerry on the Job, and Silk Hat Harry.

Meanwhile, in Europe

While studios were forming in the United States, animators in Europe were opening similar enterprises and meeting with varying degrees of success. Animation's key expansion years of 1914 to 1918 coincided with the bitter and destructive world conflict. Europe's animators were also turning out their share of training films, but American studios, not caught up in the conflict, continued exhibiting their cartoon shorts in the world market. By the 1920s, films featuring popular stars like Chaplin, Fairbanks, and Pickford were being shown worldwide and were accompanied by the freewheeling adventures of Bobby Bumps, Mutt and Jeff, Farmer Alfalfa, and Koko the Clown.

An early maker of commercial films was Julius Pinshewer (1883–1961). Born in Hohensalza, Germany, Pinshewer became interested in animated shorts in 1910. He is credited with opening the field to other Europeans who, unable to gain a foothold in a field already dominated by the New York studios, turned instead to advertising and promotional films for theater screening. Cels, expensive and hard to obtain, were not considered a first choice by European animators, who derived their techniques from approaches used by Emile Cohl and from traditional European illustration.

The lightning sketch format, possibly inspired by Blackton, was used in Britain by Walter R. Booth and the book

Victor Bergdahl's *Kapten Grogg*, circa 1916 (Svenska Bio).

illustrator Lancelot Speed (1860–1931), as well as in the blackboard and chalk work of Norway's Sverre Halvorsen. Other animators in France, Germany, and Sweden produced their own experiments. For the most part they used pen and ink on paper or jointed cutouts. In 1915 the Swedish illustrator Victor Bergdahl (1878–1939) produced three films comprised of short, humorous episodes before launching a series of Kapten Grogg cartoons. Bergdahl's precisely drawn figures owed much thematically to Bray's Heeza Liar, but his popularity in many countries would be credited to his creator's acidulous humor. Bergdahl, at that time, was the most prolific of the artists who did animation in Sweden. He was active until 1922 with Kapten Grogg, completing thirteen shorts. Bergdahl then turned to publicity and instructional films. Emil Aberg, a contemporary, finished only three productions before abandoning animation altogether.

Argentina and the First Feature-Length Animation

In 1916, a seventy-minute satirical animated film was produced in Argentina. Titled *El Apostol,* it dealt with the political policies of the then newly elected President Irogoyen. The film's animator, Quirino Christiani (1896–1984), had come as a child to Argentina from Italy. His first animation was made with cutouts and filmed outdoors in direct sunlight. Created for inclusion in early newsreels, it was produced by another Italian immigrant, Frederico Valle. Christiani and Valle collaborated on the world's first feature animation, using cutouts and based on characters designed by Diogenes Taborda. *El Apostol* celebrated its opening at the Select Theater in Buenos Aires on November 9, 1917. Prints of the film were destroyed in a studio fire years later. A second feature, *Sin Dejar Rastros,* was released in 1918, but was confiscated by a government agency.

Puppets

The success of these trick productions opened a path for the animation of puppets. Arthur Melbourne Cooper (1874–1961), in England, had made a stop-action promotional film, *Matches Appeal,* as early as 1899, and from 1904 on he made various children's subjects using toys and dolls. Similarly, in Chicago, in 1917, Howard S. Moss produced the Mo-Toy comedies with dolls and puppets. Clay was an obvious choice for some, and according to Michael Frierson was used in the United States before World

War I by Helena Smith Dayton and Willie Hopkins. Also in this period, Willis O'Brien (1886–1962) made films for Edison that utilized naturalistic puppets to create long-dead creatures. Titles such as *The Dinosaur and The Missing Link* and *Prehistoric Poultry* attest to his attraction to true-to-life effects, a genre that he would bring to full flower in *King Kong* (1933) and *The Mighty Joe Young* (1949).

The one animator during these years who had as strong a grasp on the technicalities of puppet production as O'Brien did on developing their entertainment value was the Polish-born Ladislas Starevitch (1882–1965). His career would include operating studios in Russia, Lithuania, and France. He turned an interest in the social life of insects into animated subjects employing beetles, grasshoppers, frogs, and other

Publicity drawing for the *Aesop Fables* series (1920s).

animals, achieving humor and great depth of feeling and personality. Two notable releases were *The Grasshopper and The Ant* (1911) and *The Cameraman's Revenge* (1912).

By 1919, animation was equally accepted in theaters as entertainment and advertising. The tentative experiments of the preceding two decades had primed the audiences, but the leading form of humor was still the short comedy reels featuring live clowns like Chaplin, Arbuckle, and Keaton. In the next decade the flesh-and-blood actors would face strong competition from an unusual array of drawn cats and mice.

The 1920s: Invasion of the Clown Masks

Animation during the 1920s was largely the product of New York studios that clustered in and around the Broadway theatrical district. Some ranged farther uptown or into the outlying boroughs of the Bronx and Queens, and though live-action production shifted to the sun-washed streets of Hollywood, animators in this decade continued to arrive at their work by subway. Cartoons also emanated from Chicago or Kansas City, but New York was where the distributors were. It was the center.

During this period at least six studios worked on various series. The late animator George Rufle, in recounting how he got into the field, described how miniscule the business was prior to 1920. Around 1917, unaware of the existence of animation studios and intent on landing a job with a major newspaper, young Rufle tucked his comic strip samples

under his arm, boarded an outbound train in his Pennsylvania hometown, and headed for New York. He found no openings. But one staff artist pointed him toward a company a few blocks away that was doing a new thing—movie cartoons.

Rufle toured what was then the animation business in the Broadway area. His first stop was the Bray Studio. No openings there for a newcomer. Then he went up to Paul Terry's place; no help needed there either. Finally, he came to Max Fleischer's office, and though Fleischer expressed the same lack of need for new help, he showed sincere interest in the young man's samples, took his address, and indicated that he would be in touch. Rufle returned to Pennsylvania. A year later, Max Fleischer, true to his promise, offered Rufle a job.

Studio Techniques

The rigs for shooting animation consisted of a four-posted framework that held the heavy 35mm camera, centered over a table. A handle, with a belt extending up to the camera crank, was in easy reach of the operator. Each turn of the handle exposed one frame of film. The camera remained stationary and the effect of objects coming forward or receding was accomplished with animated drawings. These limitations were an advantage, since the appeal of the films was not their photographic effects but the simplicity of their design.

Cartoons of the period have a specific look. The characters, their bodies inked heavily in black, are offset by

Otto Messmer, creator of Felix the Cat, shown here in 1977. (2004 © Felix the Cat Production, Inc. Collection of John Canemaker.)

went to see the advertised full-length film with the live stars; the short could easily be dispensed with. Luckily, the cartoonists soon learned that appealing animated characters could generate strong audience loyalty.

The Rise of Felix the Cat

Fleischer's Koko the Clown, Terry's Farmer Alfalfa, and Barre and Bower's Mutt and Jeff were amusing, but the hands-down number-one audience pleaser was Felix the Cat, produced by Pat Sullivan. Felix was the preeminent animated character of the decade and he won worldwide acclaim between 1919 and 1930. The irrepressible Felix, revealed through clever animation, captivated his audience. Felix could think and solve problems. He'd remove his tail and twist it into the shape of a telescope or a canoe paddle, and he could seize the question marks that formed over his head and turn them into skis. These were strictly Felix gags, but much of his persona was derived from the actions of Charlie Chaplin (1889–1977). This was no accident, as Sullivan had, in 1916, produced a series of cartoons based on Chaplin as the tramp. Felix, like Chaplin, made audiences laugh, and also like Chaplin, he had a distinct personality that made them care about what happened to him.

Felix was the product of the combined strong points of two very dissimilar people. Pat Sullivan (1886–1932), sometime prizefighter and newspaper cartoonist, arrived in New York as a penniless émigré from Australia. Shortly after he became involved in animation

masklike white visages—graphic billboards for facial expression. They move through landscapes adrift in a sea of white: a simple horizon, a hint of a faraway rooftop, a tree and a fence comprising the stage on which they perform. The shorts borrowed heavily from comic strips, employing similar compositional arrangements and occasional speech balloons, which, when dropped into a scene to be read, caused all action to cease. These stylistic necessities owed their existence to low production costs and sped-up work schedules. The distributors expected one reel a week from the small studios, and the black-and-white silent cartoon, part of the theater fare, was, as Paul Terry would stress, "unable to command a price." It was like an appetizer before the main course: the feature. People production, he hired Otto Messmer (1892–1983). Though younger than Sullivan, and shy and self-deprecating to a fault, Messmer was a funnier and more facile cartoonist. In fact, it was Messmer, on assignment for Sullivan, who created Felix the Cat. The initial cartoon was to be a one-shot called *Feline Follies*. It was well received and more were commissioned, forcing the studio to expand. Messmer outlined the stories, directed the widening group of animators, and even went to the bank for the payroll. The crowds that came to see the cartoons and bought the toys that spun out of its popularity were never aware that it was the unassuming Messmer that deserved the credit, although he was recognized in the field as the man behind Felix. Sullivan, on the other hand, prospered and became the model "famous cartoon producer," boarding oceanliners, giving interviews, and getting his picture in the paper.

During the 1920s, Felix's popularity was such that he was frequently imitated by other studios. Paul Terry's *Aesop Fables* featured a cat named Henry that resembled Felix, and Disney's *Alice in Cartoonland* shorts had a look-alike called Julius. Moviegoers more than likely took the many Felix images to be the product of a single studio, but to a more discriminating eye, the original Felix, created with Messmer's emphasis on personality, was consistently the best.

Walt Disney: From Heartland to Hollywood

Walt Disney was one of the few producers who did not choose New York as his

Lotte Reiniger, *The Adventures of Prince Achmed* (1926). (Primrose Pictures Productions, Ltd. Courtesy of Cecile Starr.)

base. Born in Chicago in 1901, he spent his early childhood years on a farm in Marceline, Missouri, a fact that many biographers emphasize to explain the profusion of animal characters in Disney films. The young Disney learned to empathize with farm life, but animals as stand-ins for people were fairly well established in cartoons before Disney went into production. His fledgling Kansas City studio opened when he was nineteen, and his first major effort, made for a local theater and titled *Newman's Laugh-O-Grams,* included shots of a very young Walt Disney, sans mustache, swiftly sketching and bringing to life local Kansas City scenes. Like many young artists who take up animation, Disney's earliest films dealt with contemporary and socially oriented subjects.

Disney realized that what was immediately acceptable to audiences were stories, and he plunged ahead on a series of retellings of "Puss in Boots," "The Bremen Town Musicians," "Little Red Riding Hood," and other fairytales. In these shorts he established a pattern that held through all of his subsequent productions: the mixture of fantasy with modern American sensibilities. The Laugh-O-Gram Studio faltered when its New York distributor failed, leaving Disney and his small crew of dedicated artists without funds to cover the costs of what they had done. The series had to be scrapped. Among these talented newcomers were Ub Iwerks, Rudolph Ising, Carmen Maxwell, Fred Harman, and his brother Hugh Harman, all of whom would eventually have successful careers in cartooning and animation.

In 1923, Disney packed his few possessions and moved to Los Angeles. Why did he go to Hollywood and not New York, where the business was in full bloom? Having gone bankrupt, he was anxious to try a new way of earning a living. While in Kansas City the animators had supplemented their earnings by shooting live-action subjects, including a short film that combined the antics of a real little girl with cartoon characters. This short, *Alice's Wonderland*, had been sent to another New York distributor, and before an answer came, Disney was off to Hollywood to become a director of live-action films.

But the movie studios already had a full staff of directors and they had little interest in an unknown from Kansas City. Meanwhile, the Alice film had caught the interest of Margaret J. Winkler in New York. Winkler was responsible for the release of Koko the Clown and Felix the Cat and appreciated the novelty of a real child set against a background of cartoons. To produce the *Alice Comedies*, basically a twist on Max Fleischer's *Out of the Inkwell* in which cartoons appeared in real locales, Disney

and his older brother Roy borrowed $500 from an uncle and formed Disney Brothers Studio. Eventually, the series was labeled *Alice in Cartoonland* and a total of fifty-six were animated. To accomplish the effect, the girl (there were four little Alices—Virginia Davis, Margie Gay, Dawn O'Day, and Lois Hardwick) was filmed against a solid white backdrop and the animated characters, drawn on white paper, were shot on a separate strip of film. The white areas of both films, showing as dense black in the negatives, were combined onto a new strip. To avoid problems in overlapping live and cartoon elements, Alice's moves were usually very restricted. The shorts were interesting but repetitious and could not dislodge Felix as king. In an effort to devise a character that would have sharper appeal, Disney developed Oswald the Lucky Rabbit. Oswald supplanted the Alice films and was in production from 1927 to 1928.

Serious Animation

During the decade, there were interesting attempts at informative productions. In 1923, Max Fleischer completed two productions on serious scientific subjects. The first was a four-thousand-foot, part-live, part-animation treatise entitled *The Einstein Theory of Relativity*, and the second, with similar intent to enlighten the average moviegoer, was *Darwin's Theory of Evolution*. These efforts coincided with the Bray Studio's entry into the education field with the marketing of the Bray-Co projector, designed for classroom use.

Around the World

As interest continued in the United States, animation production found fertile soil in other parts of the globe. In 1922 Sergei Tagatz, a Pole, introduced animation in the Croatian city of Zagreb. In London Dudley Buxton, Anson Dyer, and Joe Noble developed various cartoon series, while in Sweden, Victor Bergdahl applied animation to informational films. Japan's Oten Shimokawa, Jun-Ichi Kouchi, and Settaro Kitayama initiated production in that country, and during the 1920s their pioneering groundwork moved forward through the efforts of Sanae Yamamoto, Yasuji Murata, and Kenso Masaoka.

In Barcelona, Ramon Miret (1892–1975) and Ramon Serra experimented by filming animation drawings taped to a large wooden disc. Each turn of the circle brought another drawing into position for shooting. Using an old German camera, they followed this systematic approach to do theatrical commercials. Their work caught the attention of a representative of the Hollywood producer William Fox, who encouraged them, causing Miret to come to New York to offer the idea to the large American cartoon studios. The year was 1929, and though some producers expressed interest, the established production methods and the stock market crash canceled any future plans. Ramon Miret abandoned animation, but stayed in New York, opening a titling service for live-action features.

Animators Mieczyslan, Szczuk, Frankiszek, and Stefan Themersans introduced tentative efforts in Poland,

Lotte Reiniger creates her 1926 silhouette feature film, *The Adventures of Prince Achmed*, while her husband Carl Koch adjusts the camera and animators Walter Ruttmann and Berthold Bartosch assist her. Courtesy of Cecile Starr.

and notable animation in Germany was produced by the commercial filmmaker Julius Pinschewer and the silhouette artist Lotte Reiniger (1899–1981). The latter was among the first women in the field, and starting in 1919 developed a silhouette fantasy world of her own. By 1923, she had animated six shorts. Then, with her cameraman husband Carl Koch, she embarked on *The Adventures of Prince Achmed*, a feature-length animated film. This subject, made between 1923 and 1926, and running slightly longer than one hour, consisted entirely of articulated silhouette figures and was filmed on a multiplane camera stand. To accomplish this enormous task, Reiniger enlisted the assistance of the creative young talents Walter Ruttmann (1887–1941) and Berthold Bartosch (1893–1968). These two were among a growing group of European painters and designers who perceived animation as more than cartoons or entertainment for children. Instead, they saw it as a serious artistic medium that could take its place among painting, sculpture, music, and poetry.

The ferment following the introduction of abstract, cubist, and futurist works paved the way for bold exploration in all of the arts. The shape of change was reflected in posters, architecture, music, kinetic sculptures, and new approaches to film. In Russia the director Sergei M. Eisenstein developed a theory of montagethe editing of shots to obtain various emotional responses. In painting, beginning in 1911, Marcel Duchamp and Giacomo Balla painted overlapping imagery to express motion. During the 1920s, the graphic artists Viking Eggling (1880–1925), Hans Richter (1888–1976), and Oskar Fischinger (1900–1967) joined Ruttman and Bartosch in focusing on animation for studies of

rhythm and tempo. Their efforts, accompanied by live musicians, revealed a harmony between painting and music that foreshadowed the arrival of sound films. These experimental works would not always find a popular audience, but producers of commercial films borrowed unabashedly when the need arose for interesting effects.

#

CHAPTER 3

Sound and music opened an entire new field for animated cartoons. They became in demand again in theaters. —Walter Lantz

Silent movies were never truly silent. There was always some musical accompaniment, a piano, an organ, or, in large theaters, a full-scale orchestra. When Edison had set his workers the task of creating moving pictures, he did so in order to complement his phonograph. He wanted to "do for the eyes what had already been done for the ears." In 1889, while Edison was away, his assistant William K. Laurie Dickson was filmed at the laboratory, his voice synchonized to the picture, asking Edison his opinion of the new device, the kinetophone. On his return, Edison viewed the results and was especially pleased when the filmed Dickson tipped his hat and counted to ten to show the accuracy of the synchronization. The original hook-up of sound to the kinetoscope viewer was never totally successful. The amplification was weak and the thick flexible rubber ear tubes, like earphones for a giant walkman, were cumbersome.

When the first sound films were finally shown in theaters, the problem of inadequate volume remained.

Recorded sound could only be heard by means of a large phonograph horn, and these thin scratchy sounds could not be cast to the ears of two hundred or so theater patrons. Even if sufficient amplification had been possible, there were difficulties in synchronizing sound and image. Edison cylinders, and the discs that replaced them, were separate from the film and mechanical connections between phonograph and projector were undependable. The playback needles skipped and the recordings themselves were prone to scratches, breakage, warping, and being misplaced before a screening. Soon after the introduction of movies, serious thought was given to photographing the sound directly onto the film itself.

Optical Sound Recording

Early attempts at making a photographic record of sounds are attributed to Alexander Graham Bell (1847–1922), who in 1880 patented a method of transmitting speech over a beam of modulated light. He employed a light-sensitive selenium cell to perceive sound fluctuations, an important concept that would reappear in later approaches to sound-on-film systems. Two years earlier, Professor E. W. Blake had captured an image on a moving photographic plate, and Charles Fitts filed for a U.S. patent in 1880 for a method of recording and reproducing photographic sound-trackings. Several inventors contributed to the arrival of synchronous film sound. Ernst Ruhmer in Berlin, Frenchman Eugene Augustine Lauste, a former employee of Edison's, and Professor J. T. Tykociner of Illinois are a few of the many who achieved varying success in the early 1900s.

In 1907, Lee de Forest patented the Audion tube, making electronic amplification possible, and in 1919 he presented a workable photographic sound-on-film system, called Phonofilm. Development continued throughout the 1920s and many sound films, mainly one-reelers with musical themes, were shown in theaters. Max Fleischer made a few Song Cartunes with the Phonofilm system. The first, *My Old Kentucky Home* (1924), reveals that synchronization in cartoons was shaky and a problem that had to be addressed.

The final curtain for silent movies has always been attributed to the arrival of the Warner Bros.' 1927 feature *The Jazz Singer*, a myth that developed out of vigorous press agentry. In the showbiz world of movies, producers intent on attracting audiences would gloss over the facts through opportunistic publicity campaigns.* Yet, why didn't successful

---

*The practice persists with home video releases. Disney's *Snow White and the Seven Dwarfs* is advertised as "the first animated feature."

Hollywood studios snap up the novelty of sound, which had been around for eight years before *The Jazz Singer?*

One answer lies in the popularity of silent films. The not-too-perfect sounds on the musical shorts could not compete with the practiced pantomime of the great silent stars. An important practical factor was that movies without voices were playing everywhere in the world and easily translated explanatory titles were less expensive than rerecording actors' spoken lines. Also, screen actors were not all golden voiced, a reality that would have made audiences wince. Meanwhile, the pit musicians had become proficient at accenting the action on the large screen and saw that their jobs would dry up once "canned" music took over.

Sound projection required additional expense in equipment and in theater acoustics, both factors unnecessary in the operation of a silent movie house. To become involved with sound-on-film, producers were forced to pay handsomely to those that held the important patents on the various systems. In time these reasonings would be seen as shortsighted.

The Warner brothers, as aware of the risks as any of their competitors, were on the brink of bankruptcy, and the addition of synchronized sound was sought as a solution to their financial headaches. They took on the challenge in 1926, a time when sound over the air-radio was growing in popularity. Instead of going with sound-on-film, they decided on a disc system and produced *Don Juan*, featuring John Barrymore. It was ballyhooed as new and innovative, but was essentially a silent movie with recorded musical accompaniment. The following year Al Jolson starred in *The Jazz Singer*. This, too, was basically a silent production with just three segments synchronized mechanically to a phonograph.

The ensuing sensation caused by the film could be stated very simply: Jolson *spoke*. Al Jolson was one of those unique entertainers who could charm and enthuse an audience by sheer talent and personal ebullience. In *The Jazz Singer* he speaks to his film mother in a warm, playful manner. The audiences, accustomed to the usual musical accompaniment, were not prepared for the power of everyday speech. The response to the naturalness of the conversation was so strong that the sound movies that followed were labeled "talkies."

Early cartoon music was synchronized by screening the animated sequences during the recording session. Small round holes were punched on the film next to each frame and acted as a metronome guide to establish the rhythm visually for the musicians.

Disney and Mickey

It was 1927 and Jolson was changing the course of the movies. Unbeknownst to anyone, least of all Walt Disney, who was on his way to New York to discuss upgrading the Oswald shorts with his distributor, another important movie event was about to happen. By now, Margaret Winkler had married Charles Mintz, who assumed much of her business responsibilities, and he had other plans for Oswald and the cartoonist from Kansas City. Mintz revealed an item of small print that proved that Disney, whose studio had created the character, did not own the rights to it. He was willing to make a deal calling for continued production, but at a reduced price. Mintz would, in effect, be the producer and Disney would be on his payroll. The younger man bristled at this and gave up Oswald. Now, walking down Broadway minus a star, a series, and a foreseeable future, Disney was determined to turn this upset into good fortune.

The story of what happened on the train ride back to Hollywood is by now familiar to pretty much everyone. Disney, accompanied by his wife Lillian, spent the three-day travel time making sketches of various characters, finally deciding to use a mouse as his new cartoon star. Disney named him Mortimer, in the tradition of pretentious names like Felix and Oswald. Mrs. Disney thought otherwise and suggested the more proletarian "Mickey."

Walt and Lillian may have been Mickey's natural mother and father, but back at the studio, Mickey's final look was arrived at through additional shaping by his godfather, Ub Iwerks (1901–1971). The early Mickey was frisky, frenetic, and frolicsome, unlike the solid middle-class citizen he would become a few years later. He started life as a skinny-limbed character with ears that faced the same way no matter how he turned. He sported a pair of shorts much like little boys' clothing of the period, with buttons for attaching to a matching shirt, which kept the boys who wore them from looking rumpled.

Mickey was the result of a mixture of influences. The basic pattern for comic mice was set in George Herriman's *Krazy Kat* comic strip featuring the brick-throwing mouse, Ignatz. With little change, Paul Terry injected the style into his *Aesop Fables* shorts and Ignatz look-alikes continually appeared opposite Felix the Cat. The Disney artists applied the style liberally in the *Alice Comedies*, but all of those mice played supporting roles. It was time for a mouse to strike out on his own as a featured player.

But Mickey was never a mouse, he was always thought of as a person, with strong, individual traits. Disney was equally influenced by Chaplin's antics and Buster Keaton's acrobatic comedy, as was Otto Messmer. *Steamboat Willie*, the title of Mickey's 1928 debut film, was a take-off on Keaton's *Steamboat Bill, Jr.* of the same year.

It took a very special event in 1927 to get Mickey off the ground. Charles Lindbergh, piloting a small plane, flew alone from New York to Paris. It wasn't the first flight across the Atlantic, but Lindbergh's was a daring, nonstop solo hop that captured the imagination of millions. It expanded interest in aviation, and Disney, hoping to get the best advantage for his new leading man, took hold of this topical event and cast Mickey Mouse as a barnyard Lindbergh. Animated by Ub Iwerks and called *Plane Crazy,* it also introduced Mickey's longtime girlfriend, Minnie Mouse. The distributors showed little interest and a second short, *Gallopin' Gaucho*, also got no response. The people in power explained to the young producer that nobody had ever heard of Mickey Mouse.

The months went by and the studio was into the third short, *Steamboat Willie,* when Disney decided to do it as a sound film. In the flurry of excitement after *The Jazz Singer*, sound systems were at a premium. Disney located the necessary recording apparatus in New York, and after several tries and considerable personal expense, Mickey was synchronized with music and comic sounds.

Though sound cartoons had been attempted earlier, Mickey's actions charmed audiences through imaginatively synchronized effects and musical strains. Mickey, as had Chaplin, Felix, and Lindbergh, entered the pantheon of fame.

The 1930s: From Spaghetti Limbs to Reality

With the arrival of the 1930s, the studios went through a renaissance, several of them moving from New York to Hollywood. In 1932 Pat Sullivan died at the age of forty-eight, and the Felix the Cat

Max Fleischer shows his affection for his studio's 1930s Betty Boop.
© **Fleischer Studios, Inc.**

artists' capabilities, and introduced new characters: Donald Duck, Pluto, and Goofy. Mostly it was Disney's meticulous regard for story, sound effects, music, and color that was difficult to match.

Color in Cartoons

In 1932, the Technicolor Company announced its greatly improved three-strip process. Since the earliest movies, the desire to add color had provoked many different attempts. Winsor McCay's *Little Nemo* was hand-colored, a practice begun in the late 1890s. In 1901 the Lee and Turner Company constructed a projector that showed three frames simultaneously. The machine had an unusual triple lens and a spinning wheel of red, green, and blue filters. During shooting, these colors registered as shades of gray on black-and-white film stock, but when projected through the spinning filters, the gray frames were transformed into color images. Another process, *kinemacolor*, introduced by Charles Urban in 1910, had a very short but popular run. A special projector was needed here also to handle alternating frames and a spinning disc of red and green filters. After four years of modicum success, with screenings in several countries, the system was abandoned. These mechanical means suffered from a loss of sharpness due to inconsistent overlapping of the images. Typical of this problem were scenes of horses with two tails—one red, the other green.

studio closed. Ironically, it was about the time that NBC engineers, attempting to improve the image of early television broadcasts, chose a black-and-white Felix the Cat doll to focus their cameras on.

Sullivan had steadfastly refused to put color or sound into the popular series. Max Fleischer, on the other hand, was anxious to try new things and introduced Betty Boop, the first truly popular female cartoon character. Betty sang and danced, wholeheartedly embracing the sound era. The decade, however, belonged to Disney.

Disney sought to raise the standards of the medium and to gain greater acceptance for cartoons. Whatever he attempted his competitors tried to imitate with varying success, but Disney always managed to forge ahead of them. He instituted studio classes to expand his

Following those efforts came color films that were chemically formulated. J. R. Bray used the Brewster Color process in 1920 for *The Debut of Thomas Cat*.

This film had an emulsion on both sides and was prone to scratches. The Technicolor Company was having similar problems with its own two-color process. The organization, founded by Herbert T. Kalmus, had made its first color production in 1917. Technicolor initially employed a double component projector that ran red and green tinted films side-by-side. In 1920, this was changed to the cementing of the two filmstrips together. Technicolor's preeminence depended on saturated colors, and by 1927 they were obtaining improved results by shooting two black-and-white film rolls, simultaneously, through filters. The negatives were then transferred to *matrices*, or filmstrips with slightly raised images, to which dyes of complimentary colors were applied. Color prints were created by pressing the matrice against clear film stock. By the early 1930s, Technicolor was able to introduce a three-strip process that reproduced all of the colors of the visible spectrum.

Instead of flocking to use the improved process, producers sat tight. They had already forgotten their initial rejections to synchronized sound. Color, they thought, was too distracting and expensive.

With Mickey Mouse's rise in popularity, Disney saw an opportunity to further experiment with the medium. A separate series of one-shot cartoons, the *Silly Symphonies,* had been alternating on the studio's production line since the release of *The Skeleton Dance* in 1929. Where the concern in the Mickey Mouse shorts was with personality and gags, the *Silly Symphonies* were structured around fanciful situations set to music

and were perfect subjects for color experimentation. The 1932 Silly Symphony *Flowers and Trees* became the first three-color Technicolor cartoon and received the first Oscar awarded for best cartoon. Other producers followed Disney into color in varying degrees, but they were forced to use competitive color systems because Disney had obtained a three-year exclusive agreement with Technicolor.

In the 1930s, color cartoons enjoyed a special place in the public mind. Sandwiched between black-and-white features, newsreels, and adventure serials, they became an anticipated delight. One 1933 *Silly Symphony* that took full advantage of the amalgam of color and music was *The Three Little Pigs*. It became the most popular cartoon short of its time and its theme song, *Who's Afraid of the Big Bad Wolf?*, was the first hit tune from an animated film. It stands as a landmark in defining personality through animation and it was said that New York animators timed their lunch hours to coincide with its repeated appearances at a Broadway theater.

Mickey Mouse's short pants, which were red in the national release of *The Band Concert* (1935), belied their color in a brief color film made three years earlier for the 1932 Academy Award presentations, in which his pants were green. In the theaters Mickey's full-screen visage prefaced each Disney cartoon, and was a promise to Depression audiences of colorful, cheerful respite from grim reality. Public fascination with Mickey Mouse opened opportunities for the studio to ally its product with toys, cereals, clothing, and games. This expanded

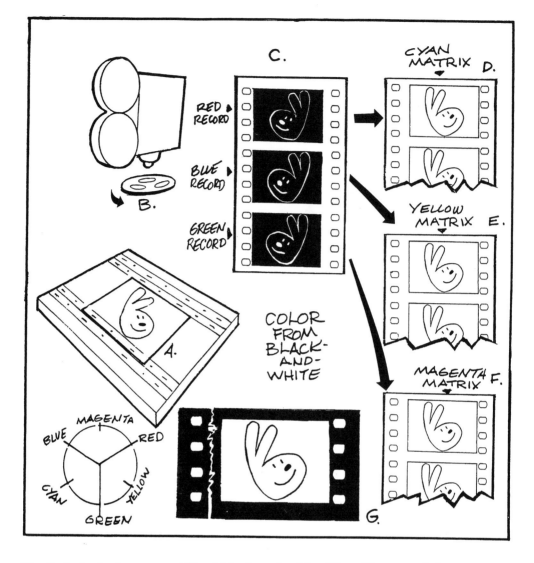

The Technicolor© process utilized black-and-white film, filters, and dye imbibition printing. For color cartoons, art **(A)** is shot with rotating red, green, and blue filters **(B)** making three black-and-white negative frames **(C)** for each individual frame. Positive, relief matrices are made from each series of these frames. The resulting three filmstrips are each coated with a complementary dye: **(D)** cyan for red, **(E)** yellow for blue, and **(F)** magenta for green. These are then printed to form a single full-color strip.

profits for Mickey's creators, as well as many struggling manufacturers, and established a system of licensing, which has since grown to enormous proportions. The Disney studio is credited with glorifying animation during these years, but it was not the only one with cartoons on the nation's movie screens.

The Studios

Cartoons prevailed as an attraction because the major live-action studios that released them also owned many of the theaters where they were shown. This put a limit on the total number of cartoon studios, which hovered around seven or eight, including Disney's. Disney had had a number of distributors, from Columbia Pictures to United Artists and then to RKO. Fleischer's studio entered into sound production with Paramount as distributor of Koko the Clown and Bimbo, an anthropomorphic dog. Koko and Bimbo made way for Betty Boop and soon they disappeared from the screen. Betty introduced Popeye, and within a few years she too faded. Popeye, a favorite newspaper feature, was licensed from King Features Syndicate, but through Fleischer's animators, he achieved a powerful presence that the comic pages only hinted at. In 1935 the spinach-eating sailor was voted more popular than Mickey Mouse.

Paul Terry established a longstanding relationship with Twentieth Century Fox. The characters from Terrytoons, Gandy Goose, Dinky Duck, Puddy the Pup, and Kiko the Kangaroo were lesser known, but filled the bill when a cartoon was required. Leon Schlesinger, a former executive of a titling and effects company, formed a studio with two Disney alumni, Hugh Harman and Rudolph Ising, and produced shorts for distribution by Warner Bros. Harman and Ising had attracted Schlesinger's interest with a character aptly named for the new sound cartoons, Bosko the Talk-Ink Kid. At first Schlesinger's ani-

Animation pioneer Paul Terry gave life to Aesop's *Fables* in the 1920s. (Courtesy of Pat Terry Leahy.)

In the 1930s Paul Terry vacated frantic Broadway for quieter New Rochelle, just north of New York. The studio occupied three floors, including the penthouse with a view of Long Island Sound. (Collection of the author.)

mators tried to match Disney, but they eventually hit their stride in a zaniness that satirized Disney and opened new avenues of humor. Characters such as Bugs Bunny, Elmer Fudd, Daffy Duck, and Porky Pig were under the direction of "Friz" Freleng (1906–1995), Chuck Jones (1912–2002), Bob Clampett (1913–1984), and Robert McKimson (1911–1974), and developed a following all their own.

In 1930 Ub Iwerks, Disney's right-hand man, left to create Flip the Frog and Willie Whopper cartoons with release through MGM. Expectations were high that with Iwerks's fund of knowledge and his role in designing Mickey Mouse, the cartoons would gain the popularity of the Disney characters. The hope was never realized and in 1934 MGM switched its release to the team of Harman and Ising, who by now had parted with Schlesinger. The result was a series of lush, elaborately produced color shorts, but no amount of elaborate visuals could support their standardized characters and generally weak story-lines. In 1937, MGM set up its own unit, installing Fred Quimby as producer. Quimby enticed various talents from studios in Hollywood and New York. One of these was Warner's Tex Avery, who bestowed his broad humor and a wild energy to MGM's cartoons. Avery's influence inspired the creation of Tom and Jerry, MGM's longest lasting series, which, under the direction of Bill Hannah and Joe Barbera, won seven Academy Awards.

After he had appropriated Oswald the Rabbit from Walt Disney, Charles Mintz learned from Oswald's distributor, Universal Pictures, that they actually held the rights to the character. Universal then turned the series over to veteran animator Walter Lantz, establishing what would become a highly successful alliance. In the late 1930s, the arrangement was altered, enabling Lantz to operate his studio independently, while Universal continued distribution. Andy Panda and Woody Woodpecker were introduced during this period. Lantz's productions, by necessity, were made with tightly controlled budgets—no MGM or Disney extravagances here. Yet his cartoons, especially the Woody Woodpecker series, were popular. These were often drawn by the industry's top animators, acquired by Lantz after they were laid off at other studios.

Charles Mintz became the operator of Screen Gems, managing its output until 1940, with distribution through Columbia Pictures. Krazy Kat and Scrappy cartoons emanated from this studio throughout the 1930s, along with a series of *Color Rhapsodies* in imitation of Disney's *Silly Symphonies*. At various times each studio had a series based on animation set to music. The names chosen to identify these color cartoons, as with the Columbia releases, parodied the *Silly Symphony* title. MGM made *Happy Harmonies*, Fleischer Studios called theirs *Color Classics*, and Lantz's were labeled simply, *Cartunes*. Warner's entire output was divided into two labels, *Merrie Melodies* and *Looney Tunes* and all of Paul Terry's productions were under the studio name of *Terrytoons*.

After leaving MGM, Ub Iwerks animated a group of fairytales for distribution by Celebrity Pictures. The shorts were tagged *Comicolor*, and, though lacking any musical reference, they did emphasize the increased importance of color. The New York–based Van Buren Studio, which existed between 1931 and 1936, had similar feelings and produced the *Rainbow Parade* cartoons. Released through RKO, they were initially shot in two-color Technicolor and finally in the three-color process, after Disney's exclusive use had expired. Iwerks's cartoons were filmed in Cinecolor, a two-color system, as were the first Fleischer color shorts. But by the early 1940s, all of the animation studios were working with the superior three-color Technicolor.

A self-caricature of Lillian Friedman, the Fleischer studio's and the field's first woman animator. © Fleischer Studios, Inc.

Working in the Shops: "Hello, Ma, I Got the Job!"

Animation offered one thing that other forms of cartooning did not: a steady job. During the Depression, artists found that supporting themselves as magazine illustrators, cartoonists, or easel painters had become extremely difficult and many of them gravitated to the animation shops. One Disney hand recalled that he had started out to be a fine artist and soon after arriving in Hollywood was ashamed to send home a snapshot of himself taken in front of a Mickey Mouse storyboard. He didn't wish his family to see how far he had fallen, but then he rose in the ranks and stayed with the studio for twenty years. Others told of going without work for so long that getting into animation seemed heaven-sent.

Animators who came into the field in the 1920s generally had little academic background, and many, like Walt Disney himself, had not finished high school. They were a young crowd, their ages ranging from the teens to the early thirties and their attitude about the new business was casual, with everyone on a first-name basis. Only the few old-timers in their late forties and beyond were respectfully addressed as Mr. or Mrs. For the youths with limited art training, the studios became a specialized school. It helped to have some academic preparation, but to be an animator it took natural talent and a lot of hard work.

That the shops were turning out a product for the entertainment and pleasure of audiences did not ease the day-to-day pressures and anxieties of the artists. Insight into the working lives of animators is detailed in the writings of Shamus Culhane, David Hand, Bill Peet, Jack Kinney, Frank Thomas, and Ollie Johnston. They tell of the demands to which they were subjected under Disney, an uncompromising taskmaster, who doled out criticism more frequently than compliments. Yet his emphasis on quality at all costs to achieve his ends deserved their undying gratitude. Working five-and-a-half days a week and often into the night, these veteran animators recall the grueling hours but also the many positive animation skills learned in the process.

Nepotism was another fact of life in the field. It was not uncommon to find more than one member of a family on a studio's payroll. When the call went out for extra hands someone always seemed to have a sibling handily available. Most entrants started off on the same level, the ink and paint department. At the Disney studio men began as in-betweeners and inking and painting was the exclusive province of women. Terrytoons put all beginners through the various stages of inking and painting. Each stage took time to learn and moving up was predicated on an individual's ability to perform. For someone to ascend the ladder, a slot had to be vacant. This vertical arrangement was universal throughout the studios and there was never a timetable of ascension. For some, it took years to improve their positions, for others a matter of months, as occurred when Disney expanded into features. The top-echelon jobs were held by men, and though some women were animators and designers, it was not easy to overcome prejudice. Those women who did attain the higher-paying positions did so through competence and persistence. During the Depression, starting salaries ranged from $16 to $25 a week. At the opposite end of the scale were directing animators or supervisors, who made between $100 and $300 a

week. At a time when items and services were extremely inexpensive (you could get twenty chocolate bars for a dollar), a $100-a-week animator could eat dinner at fine restaurants every night. Most animators, however, toiled long hours for little compensation.

This set the stage for the formation of cartoonists' unions, which caused the polarization of employer and worker, as well as the higher- and lower-salaried personnel.

The possibility of being fired was real, but at a time of low wages this also meant that many could be employed. Studio payrolls numbered one hundred or more and Disney personnel prior to World War II rose to over one thousand. Though the work was tedious and unre-lenting, it would be incorrect to suggest that there was little time for fun. On the contrary, many old timers remember those days as happy and fun-filled. The bringing together of so many youthful artists of both sexes made for a steady round of laughter and clowning. The rooms where the animators worked were usually cloaked in quiet concentration. But when the tension got unbearable, there would be a sudden burst of song, whistle-tooting, horn-honking, and just as suddenly a return to silence. On Broadway in New York, a sudden flurry of paper airplanes would descend upon unwary passersby. Harmless pranks lightened the workload—such as putting foul-smelling Limburger cheese on the light bulb under a desk or surrepti-tiously attaching paper spurs to some-one's heels as they went out the door.

The most popular source of release at all of the studios came in a steady flow of cartoon sketches inspired by any subject of the moment. A worker with a car problem or an unusual hat might set off a stream of hilariously drawn responses. Department heads accepted these small breaks in the daily schedule, but the pressure to keep up production was always there. This kept the artists at their desks, since roaming around the studio was frowned upon. Still, couples met, planned parties and picnics at the beach, got married, had babies, and hoped to keep their jobs. Lurking below the surface were pressures and frustrations about salaries, creativity, disagreements with management, lack of amenities, and poor working conditions. Studio employees in east-facing rooms worked in darkness, the lights from the drawing tables falling on engrossed faces, sweaty in August in the years before air conditioning.

The Arrival of Unions: Wishing on a Star

The 1930s saw a sharp increase in the formation of craft unions in the film industry, but animation staffs were the last to organize. A normal workweek consisted of eight hours Monday to Friday and half a day on Saturday. Producers held fast against any demands made by the first labor group to represent animators, the Commercial Artists and Designers Union (CADU) formed in 1936, which was under the leadership of Herb Sorrell. In the throes of the Depression, the studios depended on low wage scales and a ready pool of artists as eager replacements. Workers were in a squeeze between the scarcity of jobs

and their lack of bargaining power. The first to agree to a contract was Fleischer, in 1937, but only after five months of picketing at his studio's Broadway entrance. Some animators staunchly opposed the union, and when Fleischer moved from New York to Miami, CADU's hold wilted in the Florida climate. The Hollywood studios formed the Screen Cartoonists Guild and by 1940 had a signed contract with MGM. Other studios followed in the union ranks, but noticeably absent was the Disney lot.

Music

Music for animation has its roots in the days when live piano accompanied film screenings. The sound of the instruments heightened the action and also served to drown out the sounds of patrons' coughing, talking, and snoring. The choice of appropriate music to enhance the frantic actors was placed in the skilled hands of the piano players themselves. Themes ran from pleasant, joyous music for happy moments to somber, dramatic chords for scenes of mystery and conflict. Some of these pit musicians joined the staffs of cartoon studios in the 1930s and transferred their silent-movie experience to recorded soundtracks.

Over the ensuing years, studios committed themselves to turning out eighteen to thirty cartoons a year, and entrusted the scoring to staff composers. A few of these composers held their positions in one company for many years, giving each studio its own distinctive sound. Carl Stalling began with Disney in 1928 (it was Stalling who is said to have suggested the *Silly*

Symphonies to Disney), but he left to work for Ub Iwerks's new studio. In 1936 he moved to the Leon Schlesinger outfit, where he remained for over twenty years.

Phil Scheib, a former concert violinist and conductor, created a musical flow for Terrytoons that spanned three decades. Sammy Timberg was given credit on many early Max Fleischer shorts, and Winston Sharples, once the composer for the short-lived Van Buren Studio, moved to Fleischer's, staying with the organization after its name changed to Famous Studios. Scott Bradley added his vast expertise to the MGM cartoon unit, and Frank Marsales, Jimmy Dietrich, and Darrell Calker created the rhythmic accompaniment for the cartoon activities of Walter Lantz's characters.

Though many of the melodies derived from familiar public-domain tunes like *Turkey in the Straw* and *Pop Goes the Weasel*, these musical accents gave American theatrical animation a unique sound. Several studios, whose distributors also controlled the rights to the work of contemporary songwriters, had access to new and popular music. This was the case of Fleischer with Paramount, Lantz with Universal, and the cartoon divisions of Warner Bros. and MGM. Jazz and swing rhythms made their way into the cartoons of the 1930s, making it impossible today to listen to the sprightly stylings of the period without mentally connecting them with the animation of that time. Each studio's distinct musical accents became so familiar that late-arriving theater patrons could detect, while still

in the lobby, which producer's cartoon was on the screen. One clue was the apparent size of the orchestras, which varied considerably. Photographs of recording sessions show a full measure of Disney, MGM or Paramount musicians, maybe fifteen or more, while at other studios, especially Terrytoons, the sound emanated from eight or so dedicated players doubling up.

Features: The Fairest of Them All

Disney's concentration on quality in the *Silly Symphonies* brought improvements in story, animation timing, color rendition, animated effects, improved camera tracking, and multiplane photography that gave a suggestion of depth. The driving reason for this emphasis on raising standards centered on an ambitious feature-length production, *Snow White and the Seven Dwarfs*. A prodigious effort, the film was nearly three years in production and exceeded its initially determined cost. Premiering in December 1937 to wide acclaim, it showed industry doubters that a long animated film could attract audiences, and make money.

Snow White and the Seven Dwarfs was the first animated feature in color and sound. Earlier attempts at long productions, such as Christiani's *El Apostol*, first made in 1916 then remade in 1931, and Reiniger's 1926 *The Adventures of Prince Achmed*, were black-and-white and silent with the exception of the 1931 film, which was synchronized to sound.

Snow White's preeminence in film history is not dependent on whether or not it was the first feature animation. It was hailed as a masterpiece, inspiring the reviewer for the *New York Times* to write: "If you miss it, you'll be missing the ten best pictures of 1938." With profits rolling in, Disney built a modern, air-conditioned studio in Burbank. It was the world's largest complex for the purpose of animation.

Disney's move into feature production gave vent to the musical talents of Frank Churchill, Leigh Harline, Larry Morey, and Paul J. Smith. These composers followed the pattern of Broadway musicals and included work songs ("Hi, Ho, Hi, Ho," "Whistle While You Work"), and love ballads ("One Song," "Some Day My Prince Will Come") that expressed the character's thoughts and advanced the story.

Snow White cost $1,488,000 and made $8,538,000 in its initial release. The risks were high, but the success of this film encouraged other producers to consider the possibilities of features. Only Max Fleischer, backed by Paramount, seriously moved into this area. Before *Snow White* was released, the Fleischer's had made a special two-reel Technicolor production, *Popeye the Sailor Meets Sinbad the Sailor* (1936), and planned two more. In 1938 they embarked on their initial feature, an adaptation of a segment of Jonathan Swift's *Gulliver's Travels*. On its release, it delighted audiences, but critically it was compared unfavorably to *Snow White*. One problem, common to both pictures, was that the closer-to-human proportions of prince and princess were more shakily drawn than the little people and animals. Disney sought to eliminate this weakness, pres-

suring his artists to improve their skills so that the studio could master a feature every year.

Next in line was *Pinocchio*, but storyboards were also in the works for *Bambi, Peter Pan, Alice in Wonderland, Cinderella,* and *The Wind in the Willows.* Scheduled for release after *Pinocchio* was the concert feature *Fantasia,* an ambitious un-*Silly Symphony* with animation set to classical music by Bach, Tchaikovsky, Beethoven, Dukas, and Mussorgsky. Interestingly, this approach had been part of independent animators' work years before the start of the Disney production.

Experimental Animators

Alexander Alexeief (1901–1982), a Russian living in Paris, and his American-born wife, Claire Parker (1906–1981), made a version of Modest Moussorgsky's *Night on Bald Mountain,* employing a large board with thousands of tiny sliding pins. With the pins level to the board's surface, the reflected light is totally white. As the pins are pushed out slightly, gray tones are produced, and when they are fully forward the overall shadows are dense black. The effect is that of animated lithographs. This manual technique can be seen as a precursor of electronic imaging, each cast pin shadow akin to electronically created pixels.

In Berlin Oskar Fischinger increasingly turned his attention to combining animated paintings with music using the latest Gasparcolor process. He formulated synthetic sounds by photographing varied shapes into the film's soundtrack area. Fischinger's talents found their way to the Disney studio, where he spent six months designing the abstract continuity for *Fantasia's* opening Bach segment.

Working with little capital, these self-styled producers developed unique technical innovations. In France Berthold Bartosch used a multiplane camera setup to add dimension to his twenty-minute cutout animation *L'Idee* (1932). Len Lye, who moved from New Zealand to England and then to New York, created cameraless animation by painting and scratching abstract shapes directly onto the film itself. These artists kept up their visionary works by making advertising films on the side. Alexeieff, after working a full year on *Night on Bald Mountain* (1934), found scant financial return for his labors, and accepted commercial assignments cheerfully. Years later he would remember that he "charged them a lot of money."

International Animators

The 1930s witnessed the expansion of animation activities in many countries. The Soyuzmultfilm studio was formed in the Soviet Union in 1935. Staffed with over five hundred artists working on puppet, cutout, and cel productions, it would become an important outlet for animation. One early production was a combination live and puppet feature, *The New Gulliver* (1935). In Yugoslavia in the early part of the decade, the German Maar Brothers produced numerous advertising films. In China Disney's *Snow White* was extremely well received, influencing the Wan Brothers to produce China's first feature animation, *Princess Iron Fan,* in 1941.

Advertising production expanded in Norway in the mid-1930s. Several films were produced outside of the country—for local use—by Desider Gross in Prague and the Gaspar Color Company in Berlin; some popular subjects, such as a 1934 tobacco commercial, *Adventure of the Three Goats*, were made in Norway.

The first Polish sound cartoon was produced by the newspaper cartoonist Jan Jrosz and concerned the adventures of a character named Puk. Much of the equipment used was extremely limited, as Wlodzimierz Kowanko discovered in the making of *The Excursion of Mice to Conquer the Cake* (1938).

Some studios had no animation equipment at all, causing artists like the Hungarian born George Pal (1908–1980) to go where cameras were available. Pal worked for the UFA organization in Berlin on a series of very successful stop-motion commercials of marching cigarettes. Between 1934 and 1939, he developed the first important puppet studio in Holland. The commercials made in Eindhoven for Phillips Radio and Horlicks used an innovation employed by Starevitch in the 1920s, replacement puppets, requiring several phases of moving parts of the characters that, as in cel animation, are changed for each frame. In 1939, Pal visited the United States and showed his work to Barney Balaban, president of Paramount Pictures. Balaban was intrigued with Pal's Puppetoons, and in 1939 Pal moved from Holland to Hollywood.

Television: Cartoons in Your Living Room

The earliest mention of made-for-television animation in America is *Willie the Worm*, an eight-minute cartoon that aired on NBC in 1938. Animated by Chad Grothkopf using cels and cutouts, it was seen in the New York area by a handful of people who owned sets with seven-by-ten-inch screens. Occasionally, sponsored animation was included, such as the Botany Mills weather announcements drawn by Otto Messmer and produced by Douglas Leigh. With the country's entrance into the war, however, these home broadcasts ceased.

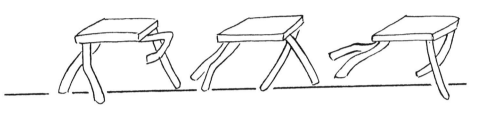

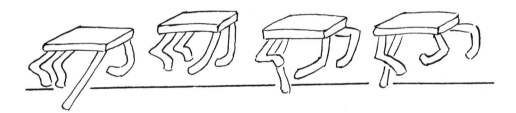

 Cartoonland's Call to Action

The people we were working for were G.I.s. . . . —Frank Thomas,
on animating World War II training films

On May 29, 1941, three hundred Disney artists went on strike. The walkout lasted nine weeks. The grievance was about inadequate salaries, the lack of creative recognition, and exclusion from voicing opinions on company policies. Sped-up schedules imposed at the whim of management were typical. Walt Disney, like many producers, thought he had created a pleasant work environment where problems could be discussed. In truth, the modern, completely weather-controlled studio in Burbank lacked the close comradery of the old cramped quarters, with its daily intermingling of employer and employees. Too many managers stood between the average worker and the headman. Ironically, just before the picket lines went up, the company released the feature *The Reluctant Dragon*, with interspersed cartoon and live segments revealing happy artists making Disney cartoons. Many felt that the dispute was in large part due to the studio's unprecedented growth as it expanded its cartoon horizons.

The new studio had operated at full-tilt to complete two stunning, technically superior productions, *Pinocchio* and *Fantasia*. Both were released in 1940 and both did poorly at the box office. *Fantasia*'s high costs and classical music theme were not what general audiences expected from Disney. The film contained a mixture of exciting animation techniques, but its range of artistic tastes attracted both admirers and detractors. It had a unique stereophonic soundtrack, Fantasound, and was sent out to specially wired theaters where newly installed speakers surrounded the audience years before such sound systems became commonplace.

The strike fell at a crucial time. With war raging in Europe, American films had lost a key market, and *Pinocchio* and *Fantasia* could not recoup their costs. With the studio gripped in the labor dispute, Disney, at the behest of an Inter-American Affairs agency, set off on a goodwill and research tour of Mexico and the countries of South America. This excursion resulted in two film packages, *Saludos Amigos* (1943) and *The Three Caballeros* (1945), in which Donald Duck, now Disney's preeminent star, interacted with Latin American themes. While Disney and a few chosen artists were on this jaunt, the strike was settled and *Dumbo*, the shortest and possibly the most appealing Disney all-cartoon feature, was completed.

By the end of 1941, the United States was also at war. The following four years would attest to changes in animation, its uses, and its graphic style.

The Studios in Wartime

From the day of the attack on Pearl Harbor until the war's end in 1945 animation production in the United States continued unabated. In 1942 two features were released, Disney's *Bambi*, a tender adaptation of the Felix Salten story, and Fleischer's *Mr. Bug Goes to Town*, based on an original script. Short cartoons were still an expected pleasantry in theaters, but they increasingly dealt with the subject of war with morale-boosting enthusiasm. Cartoon heroes gave their all for defense: Superman subdued saboteurs, Donald Duck served in the army, and Popeye in the navy. They peeled mountains of potatoes, fought their sergeants more than the enemy, and camouflaged cannons and planes into invisibility.

Animation served the needs of audiences seeking relaxation, but was cast more and more frequently in the role of teacher, instructing troops and educating defense workers. Immediately after Pearl Harbor, navy personnel occupied the fifty-one-acre Disney facility. Despite a shortage of hands because of the studio strike and the induction of anima-tors into the services, the remaining staff fulfilled the needs of the military. *Bambi* was the last peacetime feature, but the Disney animators produced thousands of feet of government films—more than the studio's total prewar output—detailing aircraft identification, pilot training, and ship navigation.

Disney, enthused by the ideas in Major Victor P. de Seversky's book *Victory Through Air Power*, produced a sixty-five-minute lecture on the effectiveness of long-range bombing. The major expressed his opinions in live action, while fully animated sequences demonstrated them. It was bold for its time, and considering that Disney productions were dependent on revenues from repeated reissues, *Victory Through Air Power* held no such promise of future revenue. Segments of the film have been incorporated in subsequent educational productions picturing aviation history, but until now, *Victory Through Air Power* remains an ambitious subject that has never been revived.

The contact between the nations of the western hemisphere (The Good Neighbor Policy) was enhanced by cheerful views of neighboring peoples and customs in the aforementioned Latin American features *Saludos Amigo* and *The Three Caballeros*. The three heroes of this last title were Jose Carioca, a Brazilian parrot, Panchito, a Mexican rooster, and Donald Duck. The film featured much-publicized scenes of Donald Duck interacting with live performers created by skillful handling of rear projection.

The combining of cartoons and real people had also appealed to dancer Gene Kelly. For a sequence in the MGM feature *Anchors Aweigh* (1945), Kelly approached Disney, even though MGM had its own competent animators. Disney, who might not have wished to accommodate a rival, told Kelly that its technique was not yet up to the job, as evidenced in *The Three Caballeros*, in which the characters and live performers don't move around each other. Kelly went with MGM's own animation team, under the direction of William Hanna and Joseph Barbera. When Gene Kelly appeared in the completed film, he and Jerry the Mouse danced and freely encircled each other by means of precise matte photography.

Each branch of the armed services had its own animation unit. In Culver City the Hal Roach Studio was chosen by the 18th Air Force for the location of its First Motion Picture Unit. Rudolph Ising, now a commissioned major, took charge of animators from Disney, Warner Bros., Lantz, and Fleischer Studios. The location was christened "Fort Roach." In the East, the Army Signal Corps had an expanse of thirteen buildings in Astoria, Queens. The site, called the Army Pictorial Center, had been built in 1919 by Paramount Pictures and contained the largest sound stage on the East Coast. As with the Culver City location, writers, actors, and animators worked clouded in wartime secrecy.

Studios of all sizes were called to action. Suddenly those who were adept at animating technical subjects were in great demand. In 1940 Albert Pagganelli moved into a new Manhattan office to continue animating maps, graphs, and the intricacies of machines for major corporations. Pagganelli had entered the field in 1923, the same year Disney opened his small Hollywood studio. Though the Disney enterprise grew to several buildings, had hundreds on the payroll, and gained worldwide recognition, Paggenelli remained a one-man shop. He did the animation and the airbrush renderings, set titles, and operated camera equipment he had built himself. Dependable and self-sufficient, he would remain in the same office for the next fifty years.

MGM's constant striving for quality in their live features had a positive effect on their shorts department. The seven-minute cartoons were second only to Disney's in excellence of character animation and extravagance of atmospheric effects. In 1939 after years of watching Disney pick up Oscars for best cartoon short, they received their first nomination. It was a cartoon with a serious theme, *Peace on Earth*, directed by Hugh Harman. The studio introduced Tom and Jerry, under the direction of Bill Hanna and Joe Barbera, and collected several more Oscars for this fast-paced series.

Termite Terrace was the inspired name given to the ramshackle structure where the Warner Bros. animators brought Porky Pig and Elmer Fudd to life. The cartoonists uncorked their own unique wisecracking, anarchic, and cheerfully surreal approach to the medium, satirizing Disney films, Hollywood stars, radio programs, and travelogues. Their viewpoint was best expressed through the strong, well-delineated personalities of Daffy Duck and Bugs Bunny. Where a Disney story might be weighted heavily toward affable homespun humor, the goings-on in a Warner Looney Tunes or Merrie Melodies cartoon was wild, wacky, and laced with accelerated action gags.

Bugs Bunny, the carrot-chomping rabbit with the obvious Brooklyn accent, began as an incidental character, but came into full bloom in 1941. That year the Warner directors, Chuck Jones, "Friz" Freleng, Tex Avery, and Bob Clampett each fathered a film starring the rabbit. By 1945, Bugs Bunny had become the most popular cartoon character, surpassing Donald Duck. The humor in the Warner cartoons during the war dealt freely with homefront shortages and rationing. Numerous references to the unavailability of rubber tires, nylon stockings, and sugar would become a puzzle for later generations of kids when these same shorts were screened on television. Bugs's creators also animated the character Private Snafu, a product of the combined minds of Phil Eastman and Theodore Geisel (Dr. Seuss), for the United States Army. Snafu represented the everyman in the service, and in entertainingly informative films blended risqué references and gags about military routine. The animated predicaments amplified the meaning of "Snafu," an acronym for the popular G.I. expression "Situation Normal, All 'Fouled' Up."

The Fleischer Studio changed ownership in 1942 in the aftermath of the release of Mr. Bug Goes to Town. Paramount Pictures had advanced the money for Gulliver's Travels and Mr. Bug, and prodded Fleischer to do an intricate and costly series based on the comic-book sensation, Superman. Now they wanted their investment back. Unable to comply, Max and Dave Fleischer forfeited their company and everything they had produced. The only rights retained were those to Koko the Clown and a shared ownership of Betty Boop with King Features Syndicate. Max went to work for The Jam Handy Organization, a Detroit-based industrial film producer, to create the theatrical short Rudolph the Red-Nosed Reindeer, and Dave went to Columbia Pictures as a producer in their Screen Gems cartoon unit. The Fleischer Studio became a subsidiary of Paramount, and its name changed to Famous Studios. Finally, it was brought back from Miami to West Forty-fifth Street in Manhattan, where it continued to make Popeye, Little Lulu, and Casper the Friendly Ghost shorts. This increase in New York–based animation caused West Coast union organizer Pepe Ruiz to go to New York with the intention of creating an East Coast guild.

The National Film Board of Canada

In 1939, the Montreal-based documentary unit the National Film Board of Canada, in need of an animator, hired the Scotsman Norman McLaren (1914–1987). He had worked for a while at the film studios of the General Post Office in London before coming to New York, where he collaborated on the film Spook Sport with experimental filmmaker Mary Ellen Bute. McLaren had been strongly influenced by the hand-painted films of Len Lye, and with a grant from the Solomon Guggenheim Foundation he set about exploring this technique. His move to the NFBC allowed him to continue his

Nostalgia

Animation is such a comparatively young field that experienced animators could parallel their own careers with that of the growth of the animation medium.

work with cameraless animation, creating *Dots, Loops, Boogie Doodle* and *Stars and Stripes* (all in 1940), which were synchronized to drawn soundtracks. McLaren formed a staff of dedicated artists: Grant Munro, Evelyn Lambert, George Dunning, and Jim McKie. This initial group expanded and grew to become one of the most creative animation organizations in the world.

In War's Shadow

Though fighting in Europe put a stop to most animation activity there, work continued in England and sporadically in countries under German occupation.

John Halas, a Hungarian who had worked with George Pal between 1927 and 1931, teamed with his wife, Joy Batchelor, to do advertising and propaganda films. Starting in 1940, Halas and Batchelor enlivened commercial messages for clients of the J. Walter

Thompson agency in Aldwych, London. Between 1945 and 1948, and in addition to their advertising films, they produced seven *Charlie* cartoons to explain new government programs to millions of people. As their studio grew and achieved prominence, the Halas and Batchelor Studio became the training ground for future animators such as Peter Foldes, who collaborated on the conceptual film *Magic Canvas*. John Halas's experience has enabled him to write several books on animation theory and practice.

Europe After the War

With the end of hostilities the pleasures of animation, color, and fantasy came out of hiding. In Liege, Belgium, production in those repressive years had been brightened by the work of Paul Nagant, Edouard Paepe, Jacques Eggermont, Maurice de Bevere, and Pierre Culliford (Peyo). But animation in postwar Belgium grew more diverse. A short called *Atomic Fantasy*, by Winkler, Colbrandt, and Limbek, was stylistic, while a feature-length puppet film by Claude Misonne, *The Crab with Golden Claws*, was closer to realism in its retelling of an episode of the Herge comic strip, *Tintin*.

Meanwhile, in Czechoslovakia, artists were carving a special niche in animation. In 1944 Hermina Tyrlova made the first Czech puppet film, *Ferda the Ant*. Tyrlova had started animating with drawn characters in 1928 in collaboration with her husband Karel Dodal. With *Ferda the Ant*, she began a long career in puppet work, a technique that fascinated the Czechs and one in which they became masters. Karel Zeman produced *A Christmas Dream* in 1946 with animated toys and live actors. Two years later he crafted an entire production from blown-glass figures and called it *Inspiration*. Jiri Trnka, illustrator and puppet designer, was put in charge of the newly formed Trick Brothers Studio. Here he directed the cel-animated films *Grandpa Planted a Beet*, *The Animals and the Robbers*, and *The Chimney Sweep* before turning his interest to stop-motion puppets. Trnka, a well-rounded artist, established his reputation with two productions, *The Czech Year* and *The Emperor's Nightingale*.

As political tensions grew in Europe, various animators continued their work elsewhere. Several, like Oskar Fischinger, Hans Richter, Alexandre Alexeieff, Claire Parker, and George Pal, came to the United States. While in America, Fischinger pursued his abstract animation experiments and worked briefly with the Hollywood film establishment. At Paramount he created a color-abstract sequence for a musical production, which the film's producers edited out of the final release. Then, at Disney, he did storyboards for *Fantasia*, but the hierarchal studio system conflicted with his strong sense of independence and his personal way of working. Ironically, Fischinger, who had pioneered the synchronization of animation to music, was frustrated at Disney. He designed much of the Bach Tocata and Fugue portion of *Fantasia*, and though he left before the film was completed, his mark was definitely made on the sequence.

In 1944, just before the end of the war in Europe, David Hand signed a five-year agreement with the J. Arthur Rank Organization to create several Disney-style shorts. Hand, the director of Disney's *Snow White and the Seven Dwarfs* and *Bambi*, assembled local talents to fulfill Rank's desire of achieving an expanded British animation industry. The unit in Cookham turned out several films in the *Ginger Nutt* and *Musical Paintbox* series, but the lack of response from world film markets forced a closing of the studio at the end of the contract, and Hand returned to the United States.

Alexeieff and Parker spent the early 1940s living in Connecticut and traveled to Montreal where they did a pinboard film, *En Passant*, for the National Film Board of Canada. Hans Richter hadn't done animation in several years, but he became chairman of the film department of The City College of New York, where he added animation classes to the curriculum.

Hungarian animation owes much to the pioneering efforts of Gyula Macskassy, who produced commercials beginning in 1950, while George Pal, having established puppet production in Holland, sailed for New York in 1939. From there he was soon off to Hollywood, his brief stay in New York resulting in a signed contract for *Puppetoon* shorts, to be released by Paramount. Pal renovated an old garage, brought in skilled artisans to fashion the many stop-motion figures, and began producing shorts. Pal's interest in American jazz and folk themes was revealed in his cartoons of the 1940s. Such films as *Rhythm in the Ranks*, *Dipsy*

Gypsy, and *A Date with Duke*, with a live Duke Ellington, set the pace for the later *Jasper and the Scarecrow* series. These were delightful in design and color, but were singled out as being racially stereotyped. Pal, to show his good intentions, produced *John Henry and the Inky Poo* (1946) as a paean to American black folk heroes, as well as an ode to the country's labor force, which had provided the tools to win the war. Pal also made films of contemporary children's books by Dr. Seuss and of Paul Tripp's *Tubby the Tuba*. In all, he received seven Academy Award nominations and a special prize for the creation of the *Puppetoon* technique.*

Design Takes the Lead

Throughout the decade a quiet revolution in design was taking place. Beginning in the 1930s, magazine and book illustrations revealed an inclination away from realism toward expressive and witty line drawings and colorful graphics. Disney artists who had been exposed to the works of modern art movements were especially enthusiastic about applying what they learned to animation. They were well aware of the forms, shapes, and colors of paintings by Braque, Matisse, and Picasso, and examples of avant-garde animation. One 1934 French production, *Joie de Vivre*, designed by Hector Hoppin and Anthony Gross, had anticipated this approach. Disney films of the 1940s subtly reveal this new direction, and tucked away in

---

*Ladislav Starevitch had incorporated similar methods in his films before Pal.

segments of the features are the crayoned Baby Weems portion of *The Reluctant Dragon*, the wild visuals of the dream sequence from *Dumbo*, various episodes in *The Three Caballeros*, the flat background paintings in *Johnny Appleseed*, and the color styling of *Once Upon a Winter Time*, both from the 1947 *Melody Time*. Key among the designers who affected this new look were Mary Blair, Alice and Martin Provensen, and Aurelius Battaglia. These productions provided an ideal ground for experimentation, but Disney generally clung to the old style, and it was left to a group of his former employees to champion a contemporary look.

UPA and the New Look

United Productions of America, or UPA, began when former Disney animators, some who had been involved in the 1941 strike, took on an assignment from the United Automobile Workers Union. The union commissioned a film to back the election of Franklin Roosevelt for another term as president in 1944. Since direct political themes were avoided in American theaters, Leon Schlesinger at Warner Bros., the first producer approached, turned it down. One of his directors, Chuck Jones, took it to Dave Hilberman and Zack Schwartz, who put it into production in their small studio space. Soon, other colleagues were stopping by and the film *Hell-Bent for Election* was underway. It was an amalgam of styles, part Disney–Warner Bros. and part new stylization that would become a UPA trademark. At first they called their company Industrial Film

and Poster Service, but as other assignments followed, filmstrips and educational reels, the name became United Productions of America. *The Brotherhood of Man*, also through the UAW, and *Flathatting,* a film for the United States Navy, set the style and humor of their work. Stephen Bosustow took on the administrative and business details, and John Hubley, Robert Cannon, and Pete Burness were the directors. Hubley, a former layout and background artist on *Snow White* and *Fantasia,* brought to UPA a painter's talents, an interest in jazz, and a keen intelligence to create films strong in story, design, and music.

Bosustow contracted a theatrical release through Columbia Pictures, which had been having bad luck with its existing animation unit. The first two films, *Robin Hoodlum* and *The Magic Fluke,* starred Columbia's lackluster team the Fox and Crow, but UPA's approach gained them Academy Award nominations in 1948 and 1949. The following year another nomination came for a new, strictly UPA character, the near-sighted Mr. Magoo.

The 1950s: The Triumph of Design and Line

It wasn't apparent at first, but the days of the short cartoon were numbered. In the early 1950s many moviegoers, enchanted with television, avoided theaters. Newsreels were the first to feel the competitive bite from up-to-the-minute televised happenings, and soon cartoons for theaters were cast in a less viable role as on-the-air programming for children included more and more old cartoons. Reels of Felix the Cat, Koko the Clown, Farmer Alfalfa (his name changed to Farmer Gray), Molly Moo Cow, Flip the Frog, and other long-forgotten characters found a new, young audience on television.

Another unsettling factor was the antitrust laws, which required the giant studios to relinquish their ownership of theaters. Production was reduced, causing a reshaping of the entire industry, and as a reply to competition from television, the size of the screen was increased. In an attempt to draw audiences away from their television sets, the studios introduced Cinemascope, Cinerama, Todd A-O, and various other wide-screen formats. The new dimensions took advantage of peripheral vision and brought a sharper sense of reality to theater projections. For a few years there was a spate of three-dimensional film production, the novelty depending on the wearing of special glasses. This proved to be annoying to most audiences and the startling illusion of tomahawks and automobiles coming straight at you could not substitute for interesting, beguiling stories. Disney's *Melody* (1953), Famous Studios's *Popeye, The Ace of Space* (1953), and *Boo Moon* (1954), Lantz's *Hypnotic Hick* (1953), and UPA's *The Tell-Tale Heart* (1953) experimented with 3D shorts before the fad dissipated. But still the studios had to reshape their ideas into wide-screen formats. Disney's *Toot, Whistle, Plunk and Boom,* shot in Cinemascope, won the Oscar for 1953.

One milestone in animation history was based not on screen size but on the artists' approach to graphics. It was the 1951 Oscar winner *Gerald McBoing-Boing,* based on a story by Dr. Seuss. Dr. Seuss's scratchy illustration style was abandoned for more simplified shapes. *Gerald McBoing-Boing* was different from the usual cartoons. Those from Disney, or any other studio, could be compared to a huge Broadway production, with intricate, realistic sets. This UPA short was akin to an off-Broadway basement theater where actors sit on stools in front of a bare wall. The emphasis was on storytelling through design. This UPA short was so well received that adult theater audiences applauded happily at each screening.

Director Robert Cannon used simple imagery to tell the story of a small boy who is ostracized because he speaks in sound effects. The sparsely designed scenes consist of lines and patches of color that eschew unnecessary details. Radio broadcasting is satirized in a sequence, in which the actors clutch their scripts in front of microphones, their bodies motionless, and only their mouths move. In 1950 this depiction of radio actors delivering their lines got a laugh. Not too long after, static bodies with mobile mouths became a mainstay in the production of low-budget television animation. Most UPA productions were fully animated, but designed and planned to avoid excess. UPA kicked off

a wave of limited, stylized animation—and everyone else followed.

Rhythm in the Ranks

During the war years, swing and Latin rhythms infiltrated cartoons. But in the 1950s there was a heavy lean toward contemporary jazz and UPA brought in leading recording artists and composers to create rhythmic sound tracks. The enthusiasm came from the directors, notably John Hubley, who felt strongly about combining modern cartoons with equally modern music. Other animators, Norman McLaren and John Whitney, for example, discovered they could fabricate sounds by drawing directly on the film or by affecting the optical soundtrack mechanically.

Disney and Bunin in Wonderland

The last Mickey Mouse cartoon, *The Simple Things,* was issued in 1952 and the flow of Donald Duck subjects trickled out. The studio re-released classic shorts from earlier years, but its main concentration was on features, live as well as animated. *Alice in Wonderland* (1950) and *Peter Pan* (1952), productions that had been in the works for many years, were at last released.

Alice in Wonderland was in story development as far back as 1939, but was shelved with the coming of war. In the late 1940s interest in the story was renewed, but it was again put on hold, giving impetus to another producer, Lou Bunin, to launch a puppet version of the Lewis Carrol classic. Bunin, who with

Lou Bunin, a sculptor turned puppet animator. (Courtesy of John Canemaker.)

his brother Morey had performed on stage as The Bunin Puppets, was experienced in animation. Among his film credits was the elaborate stop-motion sequence at the beginning of the MGM feature *Ziegfeld Follies* (1946).

An arrangement between Bunin and the British film producer J. Arthur Rank promised a colorful *Alice* that would have a live actress playing against animated puppets, and was to be filmed both in England and France in three-strip Technicolor. Meanwhile, Disney put his *Alice* back into production and took Bunin to court to contest a competing *Alice* in the market. The judge ruled that the property was in the public domain, and anyone could make a film of the book. Bunin won the case, but when he took his negative to Technicolor's British lab, he was unable to have it processed. As a result, the color prints of the Bunin *Alice,* which had to be realized through a non-Technicolor method, suffered

noticeably. Disney's *Alice* was secure in its intricate animation and color, but the reviewers were unmoved by either film.

A Changing Landscape

Disney continually explored new avenues of entertainment, branching out into a wildlife film series and a theme park, Disneyland, which opened in 1955 in Anaheim, California. By 1949, Terrytoons were booked into more theaters than any other cartoon, but Paul Terry realized what was in store. In 1955 he retired, selling his studio and its assets to CBS. Two years later, MGM, without warning, shut down its cartoon unit. By then, George Pal had quit making *Puppetoons* and was pioneering production of live-action special-effects features.

UPA expanded its operation to include commercial studios in New York and London, and embarked on *The Boing-Boing Show,* television's first half-hour color-animated program for children. In 1959 UPA released a feature production, *1001 Arabian Nights,* starring Mr. Magoo, but here too things were changing. After turning the industry on its ear with a new brand of intelligent and beautifully designed animation, things went downhill for UPA. The TV program, though highly acclaimed, died from a lack of sponsor interest. *Terror Faces Magoo,* UPA's final theatrical short, was animated at the New York studio, but a few months later the Manhattan and London offices were closed and Steve Bosustow sold the company to producer Henry G. Saperstein. In subsequent work, the novel UPA design and adult view of animation was jettisoned and the studio's efforts applied to made-for-television animation.

This accent on design was still well established in other areas, such as art for movie titles, and many features were suddenly less interesting than their opening credit sequences. Designer Saul Bass was largely responsible for this emphasis on stylish animation in title sequences for *Man with the Golden Arm*, *Anatomy of a Murder*, *Around the World in Eighty Days*, and *Exodus*.

Storyboards, necessary for theatrical cartoon production, became increasingly important for television programming.

Television Commercials

The most significant thrust in the 1950s was in commercials. To fill the needs of advertisers, animators from the theatrical cartoon studios opened small shops in major centers to bid on ad agency accounts. Not surprisingly, the earliest television spots resembled the look of theatrical cartoons, but their tight budgets turned the agencies toward simplified, stylized art, the kind championed by UPA.

Among the popular themes were the Harry and Bert Piel's beer spots, (beginning at UPA's New York branch before going on to various other studios), Jello's Chinese Baby, and the sweet little old lady, Emily Tipp for Tip Top Bakeries.

John Hubley left UPA long before it changed hands. After a sojourn in feature production (an animated *Finian's Rainbow*) was terminated, he headed for New York where he established Storyboard, Inc., to bring his brand of filmmaking to the world of television commercials. Clients and awards flocked to his small company, but advertising

was not his true interest. By 1958, Hubley, with his wife Faith, began using part of each year to create films that expressed their personal point of view. One short, *Moonbird*, is a charming departure from the run-of-the-mill cartoon. In *Moonbird* the Hubleys avoided traditional cel overlays and painted the characters on black paper for double exposure over lush watercolor backgrounds.

Another novelty was the film's adlib soundtrack of two of the Hubley children acting out the story. The combination of real boys' responses and the novel art style won them the 1959 Academy Award for best cartoon short. Storyboard, Inc. had broken the hold that major studios had on the Oscars. In the years that followed the award went to other small independents and foreign studios as well.

The rise of television and the hot competition for agency assignments gave impetus to the start of many new companies, and in 1952 the International Alliance of Theater and Stage Employees (IATSE) became the representative of Hollywood and New York animators in the theatrical and commercial studios. Though the center for animation had long since moved to Hollywood, studios popped up in Chicago and commercial production expanded in Manhattan to include thirty to forty studios.

Commercials were in black and white, but lack of color, rather than hindering the spots, was one of the creative challenges for directors. The animators, used to being kingpins, stepped aside for young designers who had strengths in graphic stylization and were more concerned about lines and shapes then the intricacies of motion. A friendly enmity became apparent, the animators complaining about character models that showed limited views of the flat, stylized figures and the designers expressing disdain for excessive animation, which they felt distorted their carefully arranged compositions. Since the designers dealt directly with the agencies, they gained the edge, and throughout the period their efforts achieved recognition. The animators, who brought the various styles to life, were pushed further into anonymity.

After CBS acquired Terrytoons, Gene Deitch, a former UPA director of commercials, took creative command and implemented contemporary styles. Deitch surrounded himself with the period's exciting young talents: R. O. Blechman, Jules Feiffer, Ernie Pintoff, Ray Favata, Eli Bauer, Al Kouzel, and Tod Dockstader. At first, the old-timers were irritated by the changes, but some developed pride in being part of the new wave. One film, based on a traditional tale, *The Juggler of Our Lady,* became their most prestigious production. Taken from an illustrated book by R. O. Blechman and narrated skillfully by the venerable actor, Boris Karloff, it presented Blechman's minute line figures enlarged to massive Cinemascope proportions.

The 1950s brought new developments in animation technology. Studios like Terrytoons, which used formidable but ancient equipment, looked toward modernization. CBS upgraded the Terrytoon sound-recording studio and added a state-of-the-art animation camera and an electrostatic copying setup for inking cels. This last was a method similar to one installed at Disney's in an elaborate assembly-line arrangement. Developed by Ub Iwerks, it took the transfer of pencil drawings to cels from the hands of inkers and brought it into the sphere of the Xerox machine. The technique was used initially in the short *Goliath II* and the feature *101 Dalmatians,* but UPA also experimented with the method during the making of *The Boing-Boing* television show.

New cameras, developed shortly after the World War II, were made by John Oxberry to supplant the homegrown equipment that most studios depended on. Oxberry, tall and lanky, laughingly stated that he redesigned the equipment not just for added proficiency but also to eliminate protrusions on the old stands, which were forever bruising his shins. The new equipment brought greater flexibility, camera moves were motorized, and the compound table moved in all directions, and these new capabilities met the burgeoning demand for low-cost television animation. John Oxberry sold his cameras worldwide, and for years the name "Oxberry" remained synonymous with animation.

Improved art materials came along, which altered traditional work habits. Storyboard drawings were always done in pencil, pastel, and crayon, but color-dye markers changed this. A sepia-toned marker, the Flo-master, had appeared years before as a sketching tool, but in the 1950s, Magic Markers, in many subtle shades and tones, became readily available. Another technique long in use was "hot-press" printing of opaque letters onto cels by means of heated type. Studio artists circumvented this method with pressure-sensitive type that sold over the art-store counter. It gave them more control and was easy to apply, making special outside services unnecessary.

Another innovation that took hold during the decade was the use of high-contrast sheet film. Sold under the name Kodalith and originally designed for the lithographic printing trade, it became the material of choice for preparing titles and masks for backlit photography. Videotape recording, spurred on by 3M Corporation, came into use in 1956. There was the usual disinterest in its swift incorporation, since much programming was still expected to be live, but its creative use in editing eventually made tape an industry standard.

If the frugality of television influenced animation in any specific way, it was in the simplification of what went on the screen. To simulate anima-

tion, methods of shooting still photos and illustrations were introduced. One reference came from the *Baby Weems* segment of Disney's 1941 *The Reluctant Dragon*, in which storyboard stills, with mere touches of animation, told a convincing story. Labeled variously *animatics*, *slide motion*, or *filmographs*, the *Baby Weems* approach became an industry staple and depended on the creative use of camera moves and the panning of artwork.

A popular variation on these methods was squeeze motion, essentially a technique by which cutout photographs of people and objects were shifted around on the animation stand. The name originated during the production of a Ford commercial at Abe Liss's New York–based Elektra Films. The spot, with a series of stills of a man squeezing his gangly physique into a compact shape, became the model for numerous others. As a design motif it imparted a subtle humor to advertising and enjoyed almost as much popularity as another 1950s style: the use of nineteenth-century copyright-free line engravings.

Ernest Pintoff, after spells at UPA and Terrytoons, set up his own studio in the late 1950s. A painter and sometime jazz musician, Pintoff had little patience for the tedium of traditional animation. Determined that his films be bold and concise, he instructed his artists "to just whale it out." The resulting spots had a rough appeal, much like the barnyard humor of the early Mickey Mouse or the gritty urban atmosphere of the Fleischer Popeyes. Pintoff produced several personal films, hiring comedy talents from the recently terminated Sid

Caesar television program, to voice his conceptions. The key to the acceptance of such Pintoff shorts as *The Violinist* (1959) and *The Critic* (1963) was in their similarity to the popular, gruff "studio cards" made by small art shops in defiance of the sugary greetings from traditional card companies.

While most Hollywood producers paid scant heed to television, hoping that it might go away, Walt Disney saw it as a medium to advertise his feature productions and his theme park. Starting in 1954, a year before Disneyland opened, a program of the same name featured old and new animation, with Disney as the affable host.

Cartoons made specifically for television had an inauspicious start. The introduction of Jay Ward's and Alex Anderson's *Crusader Rabbit* in 1950 heralded no great technical breakthrough, but was instead a declaration that animation could be truly funny no matter how cramped the budget. Prior to *Crusader*, there were sporadic attempts at placing animation into children's shows, where live puppets or cartoonists doing chalktalks dominated. One example was *Cartoon Tele Tales*, with Jack and Chuck Luchsinger reading stories and illustrating them live on ABC.

Animation for television has always been dominated by program costs, and in the beginning, when advertisers were less convinced of the new medium's viability, the budgets were miniscule. One series, NBC's *Telecomics*, by Dick Moores starting in 1950, used camera moves but avoided actual animation. *Jim and Judy in Teleland*, also created with limited animation, appeared briefly, but it was

Crusader Rabbit, his sidekick Rags the Tiger, and their spoofs of adventure yarns that captured a following. Toward the end of the decade television was ready for new, specially made animation.

The closing of MGM's cartoon division propelled directors Bill Hanna and Joe Barbera into their own business. Finding that commercials were not their meat, they created *Ruff and Reddy*, a series of five-minute episodes that were heirs to the *Crusader Rabbit* format. Other newly made animated television series, each running four or five minutes, were Terrytoons's *Tom Terrific*, by Gene Deitch, Joe Oriolo's revival of *Felix the Cat* in two hundred and sixty color shorts, and Jay Ward's *Rocky and Bullwinkle*. A new era of animation dawned with Hanna and Barbera's launching of the half-hour *Huckleberry Hound Show* in 1958.

This decade after the war was not the wholly tranquil time suggested by increased prosperity and active production. Creativity was hampered by the zealous probes of Senator Joseph McCarthy and his supporters, who had singled out the entertainment industry as a bastion of communist sympathizers. He was eventually denounced, but not before scores of innocent individuals had been accused of injecting propaganda into films and television shows; writers, directors, actors, and even animators lost their jobs or suffered great personal damage. As a result, films of the latter years of the 1950s are soft and lacking in those strengths that were prevalent before fear gripped the artists who made them.

World Animation

In England, Halas and Batchelor continued to do advertising and entertainment films, but in 1954 they released Britain's first feature-length animation, based on the George Orwell satire *Animal Farm*. Backed by Louis de Rochemont, producer of *The March of Time* documentaries, it resembled a Disney film, but its deft depiction of the corrupt abuses of power took it out of the sunny realm of the average cartoon feature. Though its ending is more upbeat than in the book, *Animal Farm* was an adventurous attempt at expanding animation content, and it continues to be shown in schools.* Where film production had been stamped out during the war, and in places where animation had never been, artists were grouping to create commercials or independent work. American animated films, again on the world screens, inspired others, but as appealing as the Disney productions were, their opulence was impossible to match.

It was the stylized, simplified UPA cartoons that showed the way. Their impact was felt very strongly in Zagreb, where *The Big Meeting*, a seventeen-minute cartoon with a modern look, came out in 1949 after two years of concerted effort. Duga Film was Yugoslavia's first but short-lived official animation studio, employing close to a hundred people. It closed after only a year. In 1955, a handful of artists began develop-

Improved working conditions brought animators together after hours

ing their personal animation techniques. Guided by a copy of Preston Blair's book on Hollywood animation technique and by studying cartoon films frame-by-frame, Nikola Kostelac, Vladimir Jutrisa, and Aleksander Marks created advertising shorts. Out of this came original productions that were strong in design and humor, including a version of *Little Red Riding Hood* designed by Boris Kolar. Kolar, still in school, joined with the original three to form the nucleus of the Zagreb Film studio.

By the late 1950s feature productions were underway in Czechoslovakia. Trnka animated sequences of Jaroslav Hasek's novel *The Good Soldier Schweik*, and in 1959 he turned his attention to Shakespeare's *A Midsummer Nights Dream*, an extravagant and beautifully designed

---

*Research indicates that the CIA suggested the production of the film and its sunnier ending. See Frances Stoner Saunders's *Who Paid the Piper? The CIA and the Cultural Cold War*.

Cinemascope puppet production. Karel Zeman completed *An Invention for Destruction*, which combined live actors with special effects and scenery that had the quality of old line engravings. Bretislav Pojar received acclaim for the alcohol-awareness short, *A Drop Too Much*, while Hermina Tyrlova created a series using wool, marbles, a knotted handkerchief, and other simple props.

In France, Julien Pappe opened the first commercial animation studio in Paris; Jean Image produced *The Adventures of Monsieur Pinceau*; Jacques Forget started Cineastes Associates; and Rene Goscinny produced a feature based on the comic-strip hero, Asterix.

Alexandre Alexeieff experimented with a technique he called "illusory solids," a method of using trajectories of light to build images. This effect would be reflected in television program openings and commercials twenty years hence.

In Portugal Vasco Granja created a spate of short films, and Chinese animation continued with the opening of the Shanghai Animation Film Studio, under the direction of Te Wei.

As television use increased, local animators in major centers became the source for advertising spots and children's films. This new appreciation of the homegrown product led to increased production of theatrical features that reflected individual and national themes and tales.

CHAPTER 5

From Bullwinkle to Bart, and Beyond

The day has gone when it is possible to attract . . . audiences with a film which is merely entertaining, amusing, and beautiful. —Osamu Tezuka

Animation went truly international during the 1960s. The rise of film festivals as a place to screen work and meet other animators became increasingly important during this decade. Previously, recognition for animation was hard to come by unless an animator had theatrical distribution. The independent, working in obscurity, looked toward 16mm rentals to schools and universities, but now festival screenings opened new doors for personal films. Events were established in Venice beginning in 1932; Cannes and Locarno in 1946; Edinburgh in 1947; and Melbourne, Tours, Oberhausen, London, San Francisco, Berlin, and Gijon, all dating from the 1950s. These festivals, primarily for live films, would only occasionally recognize animation, but events devoted exclusively to animated films became a reality when various cities set aside funds for international participation.

Festival Frenzy

The largest and longest running animation festival began in 1960 in the French resort town of Annecy. Originating as a section of the Cannes Film Festival the animation festival became the model for similar gatherings in other cities. The growing festival idea created a demand for an organization to keep independent animators apprised of competitions, rules, and awards. To this end, the International Animated Film Association (ASIFA) was formed in 1960, with Norman McLaren as its first president. The organization attracted International animators, became a forum for disseminating information, and offered patronage to animation festivals. The festivals encouraged innovative productions, and as the traditional theatrical shorts faded into oblivion, the films to receive the Academy Award for best animated short went increasingly to independents, and to animators from outside the United States. An Oscar was awarded to the independently produced *Munro* (1960), based on a story by Jules Feiffer, directed by Gene Deitch, and animated by Al Kouzel. The very next year the prize went to the Yugoslav Studio Zagreb Film for *Ersatz*, directed by Dusan

Vukotic. In 1965 Chuck Jones was at MGM and his production of *The Dot and the Line* was awarded an Oscar. By 1968 and 1969, when the Disney studio was cited for *Winnie the Pooh and the Blustery Day* and *It's Tough to Be a Bird*, it was competing heavily with independent animators and studios in Canada, England, Italy, and Czechoslovakia. It was obvious from the Academy nominations that good things were happening in animation around the globe.

Triumph of the Tube

With the success of *Huckleberry Hound* and *Quick Draw McGraw*, Hanna and Barbera increased their staff and experimented with evening shows for the whole family. *The Flintstones* was the successful result. Comic-book superheroes who had been around for years were suddenly discovered by programmers in 1964, and a steady flow of muscle-bound crusaders spread their capes across the screen. But an outpouring of criticism from parent groups and educators expressed disapproval for the exuberant action in these cartoons. The networks modified the content of the shows and emphasized less violent programs. One of these was Jay Ward's *Rocky and His Friends*. Rocky, a flying squirrel, and his companion, Bullwinkle the Moose, were updated versions of Crusader Rabbit and Rags the Tiger, but Rocky and other segments of the show, Aesop and Son, Mr. Peabody and Dudley Do-Right, expanded upon the adventure theme with wacky humor that earned thousands of dedicated fans.

Television commercial production alternated between heavy and sparse periods. The workload often depended on the length of commercials, which formerly averaged one minute but by the 1960s ran half as long. In one-minute live-action spots there was room for animation. The thirty-second announcements meant less plot development and less animation. This second decade of vigorous activity in the commercial field saw the demise of some of the pioneering studios. New contenders eagerly took their place, and by the end of the 1960s another crop of small companies was attracting the agencies. Previously, Madison Avenue had come to the animation companies seeking ideas, but art directors had acquired knowledge of the medium and began to show up with completed storyboards, expecting the studios to follow them closely. Still, there was room for studio creativity. The most inspiring and popular commercial of the late 1960s was the Alka-Seltzer spot, suggested by an agency that showed a cartoon man in conversation with his stomach as he sits opposite it. Redesigned at Elektra Films by R. O. Blechman, it was interpreted in layouts and animation by George Cannata, Jr., and Jack Dazzo.

Cigarette spots were discontinued during this period, and beer commercials dropped their animated approach in favor of live-action renditions. Advertisers, though, continued heavy use of animated commercials of products on children's shows.

Working conditions for animators in the United States revealed the ups and downs of the network schedules and ad agency needs. The pressure to win assignments was rugged, and though many studios prospered, animators were less sure of their frequency of employment. Most of the children's programs were produced in Hollywood in a pattern that had animators working eight frantic months, followed by layover periods that lasted till the next network season. The half-hour shows were being churned out faster than the old theatrical shorts. Where previously a seven-minute cartoon took a few months to complete, the demands for television had the studios pushing out several hours in the course of a few weeks. This resulted in a reliance entirely on formulaic methods lacking in interesting movement and background detail. The limited animation was abetted by an insistent dialogue track that carried the weight of the story. The need for competent low-cost workers raised the issue of using overseas help (the initial series of *Rocky and His Friends* had been animated partially in Mexico City), but the animation unions were still able to keep the work in Los Angeles. The higher salaries were in the smaller studios that made television commercials, though frequent layoffs cut into those paychecks too.

Independent Filmmakers

Isolated animators clung to the belief that animation was more than just depictions of funny animals. Robert Breer, Douglas Crockwell, Harry Smith, Charles and Ray Eames, John Whitney, Stan Brakhage, Mary Ellen Bute, and Dan McLaughlin are just a few of the independents who explored the medium as an art. The career of John Whitney is worth examining. Working with his brother James, Whitney began making experimental films in 1938 with an 8mm camera, then graduated to more elaborate equipment. Much of their earlier efforts relied on homemade pantographs and hardware-store items for the creation of abstract images. Whitney's move to early computers in the 1960s was a natural continuation of his search for challenging techniques.

World Animation Expands

Animators with distinctive styles arose outside the United States: Yoji Kuri in Japan, Raoul Servais in Belgium, Bob Godfrey in England, and Bruno Bozzetto in Italy. A studio was started in Cuba under the direction of Norma Martinez and using Russian equipment. In Belgium the popular character Asterix became the subject of the feature *Asterix the Gaul* (1967), using traditional animation techniques.

Dr. Osamu Tezuka, a former medical student with a penchant for cartooning, joined the large Toei studio in Tokyo to direct animated programs and features. In 1962, he formed his own company, Mushi Productions. Tezuka's early contributions were the television series *Alkazam the Great, Astro Boy*, and the elaborate feature *One Thousand and One Nights*. Ion Popescu-Gopo, Romania's premiere animator inspired the younger artists Sabin Balas, George Sibianu, and Horia Stefanescu with broadly designed productions such as *Homo Sapiens* and *Kiss Me Quick*. In Brazil, Roberto Miller employed conceptual imagery in *Sound Abstract* and *Dance Color*.

In many small countries animation was just a staple of filmmakers' necessary bag of tricks for credit titles, maps, and diagrams, and in travelogues, documentaries, and training films. Such was the case in Israel where animation was embraced by eighteen-year-old Yoram Gross. Gross began his experiments while serving in an army film unit. By the 1960s he was making commercials, public-service spots, and the first Middle Eastern stop-motion feature, *Joseph the Dreamer* (1961), before moving to Australia to produce television series and theatrical features.

When Montreal launched Expo '67, among its many exciting events were special animation screenings and exhibits. It also brought together an array of animation personalities that would never be possible again. Included among the guests were Paul Terry, Bill Tytla, John R. Bray, Ub Iwerks, Dave Fleischer, Walter Lantz, Norman McLaren, Grant Munro, and others. Missing from the event was Walt Disney, who died on December 15, 1966.

To the world, Disney and animation were synonymous, and his passing raised questions about how things would be without him. By his own admission, he had grown weary of animation, and though his studio continued its yearly production of features, his interests for many years had widened to include television, theme parks, and live-action films. The by-products of Disney animation, the licensed character spin-offs, and the Disney name, were still out there pulling customers in. This was as much a result of Walt Disney's insistence on quality as it was of well-orchestrated

Czech director and puppeteer, Jiri Trnka, adjusts a figure for his 1959 version of Shakespeare's *A Midsummer Night's Dream*. (Courtesy of Cecile Starr.)

publicity that hailed his triumphs at every opportunity. Wading against this steady tide of homage to the man who had launched Mickey Mouse, the *Silly Symphonies*, *Snow White*, and *Mary Poppins*, came critic Richard Schickel's 1968 biography *The Disney Version*. Without ignoring Disney's organizational and entrepreneurial gifts, Schickel described him as someone who could not draw Mickey Mouse and who rarely gave credit to the hundreds of his talented artists who actually could. Schickel's summation was that "In the last analyses, Walt Disney's greatest creation was Walt Disney."

Another animator conspicuously missing at Expo '67 was Jiri Trnka, whose film masterpiece *The Hand* (1965) was a commentary on the constant struggle between the personal bent of artists and the expectations of the state. Like Disney, he was an indefatigable worker who sought flawless perfection in his productions, but unlike Disney, who had given up drawing to command others, Trnka was a painter, sculptor, and designer. His children's book illustrations, personal canvasses, and finely crafted puppet films attest to his artistry. Trnka was rarely seen smiling in photographs, but his smile could be found in the content of his films, which were always a tasteful blend of humor and incisive understanding of the human condition. Trnka died on December 30, 1969.

Animation had often taken cues from live-action productions, but the 1968 release of Stanley Kubrick's *2001: A Space Odyssey* employed extravagant special-effects techniques that harked back to the extravagances of *Fantasia* and Fleischer's *Superman* cartoons.* Kubrick's space epic was a far cry from the low-budget science-fiction movies audiences were used to and it caused ripples in commercial production. It incorporated slit-scan techniques that had advertising agencies clamoring for similar streaking and strobing effects in television commercials. "Whoosh-whoosh" was the way one Madison Avenue executive described it. Suddenly every production, live or animated, sprouted glows, sparkles, and animated lights.

Another influential film of the decade was a joint American and British production, *Yellow Submarine*, the second

---

*Kubrick's inspiration was *Universe*, a National Film Board of Canada 1960 special-effects film.

full-length animated feature to be made in England. Produced by King Features and directed by George Dunning, its springboard was the universal popularity of The Beatles. The group contributed only their singing voices to their animated selves (their spoken lines were recreated by skillful voice stylists) and they appeared in a brief live-action scene at the end. The music shared distinction with Heinz Edelman's designs, which reflected romantic, colorful, and imaginative 1960s graphics. *Yellow Submarine*'s psychedelic array of flowered, filigreed images merged with the aura of the posters and paraphernalia of the anti-war protestations and "flower children" of those years.

The Beatles film, with its accent on music and color, fostered imitation among a growing horde of animation students and affected the look of television commercials for several years to come.

The 1970s: Sparkle and Glow

Although a remarkable growth of interest and variety in animation production would be evident during the 1970s, the first few years of the decade saw the closing of many leading commercial studios. One reason for this was the reduced length of TV spots from one minute to thirty seconds. These shorter announcements placed more emphasis on hard-selling, live actors, causing animation companies to take on the complexities of live-action production. The growing weekly payrolls, further burdened by slow payments from agencies, forced studios to reduce staffs or simply to go out of business. Suddenly, animators and other studio employees found that they had to fend for themselves.

Some established their own small shops to produce commercials and to satisfy a growing demand for educational films. Major corporations were caught up in the manufacture of specialized equipment for schools, sending them in search of animators to produce brief, single-purpose reels. These were super-8mm cartridges containing concise information about a facet of a larger subject, used in simple projectors for viewing by individual students. When state budgets for education were sharply reduced, corporate interest faded and the small studios, out of necessity, turned elsewhere for assignments.

A bright star beckoned from the Public Broadcasting System, which was beginning to institute programming for preschoolers. *Sesame Street* and *The Electric Company*, the creations of the Children's Television Workshop, were shows that appeared daily and depended on a wide range of short animated segments. The growing demand for these types of programs provided a welcome boost to established studios as well as to independent animators versed in making concise films on miniscule budgets. These new shops could operate without large staffs and expensive equipment, as the older studios had out of necessity. Times had changed and clients cared little that studios used outside services for animation, ink and paint, and camera work.

Part of the appeal of *Sesame Street* was its simulated "commercials," running

In the 1960s and 1970s, there was a rise of independent animation. Artists, like New York–based Iris Beckerman (shown here preparing cutouts for stop-motion shooting, circa 1971), employed techniques that didn't require large budgets and huge staffs.

a minute or less, which touted the merits of individual numbers and letters. These pitches for the number 4 or the letter *E*, for example, enlightened small children and expanded their knowledge while satirizing the glut of television advertising. Imaginative, humorous, and entertaining, these assignments became bread-and-butter for the small studios. A technique that enjoyed a vogue during this period was the use of markers on cel. Quick to apply and fast to dry, these colors flashed and jittered across the screen for several years before their use subsided.

The overwhelming praise for *Sesame Street* from parents and teachers did not go unnoticed by the commercial networks and soon they were launching full-scale shows with an intermingling of educational spots. One notable series combined bright lyrics and contemporary rhythms in the sprightly "Multiplcation Rock" and "Grammar Rock" episodes, produced by New York studios normally accustomed to animating the praises of soaps and headache remedies.

After an initial burst of enthusiasm much of this programming disappeared, but *Sesame Street* continued to prosper on public television stations. The commercial networks, bowing to the needs of breakfast cereal companies and toy manufacturers, transformed their Saturday morning shows into extensions of advertising messages, drawing out the wrath of groups abhorring these half-hour commercials aimed at kids.

The lingering excitement of the 1968 *Yellow Submarine* to teenagers and young adults prevailed and its bold graphics inspired a new generation of animators. No previous production had sparked so much interest, and the styles portrayed in the Beatles film were implemented in television commercials and Children's Television Workshop programs. Animation had entered into the consciousness of a counterculture that viewed youth as a powerful influence on everything from habits of dress to approaches to communication. The *Yellow Submarine* sparked its college-bound audiences, who were determined now to make their own films. Animation increasingly became their technique of choice and every school or university film department was besieged with applicants intent on learning how to do it. The prevalence of inexpensive but sophisticated super-8mm equipment made filming easier, allowing students of all ages to express themselves with clay, cutouts, or drawings.

This generation saw animation as individualistic, personal, and freewheel-ing. The 1970 re-release of *Fantasia*, advertised with newly created psyche-delic green and magenta posters, attracted college-age audiences, some viewing it through a haze of marijuana smoke, perceiving images that hadn't been imagined by the Disney artists.

In previous decades the isolated experimental animator was all but invisible, but changes in attitudes gave encouragement to young artists who saw a market for their ideas. Will Vinton and Bob Gardiner worked together in Portland, Oregon, and created a short entirely in clay, achieving realistic facial expressions. Called *Closed Mondays* (1974), it earned an Oscar in competition with entries from Disney, Hubley, and the National Film Board of Canada. Gardiner went on to other things, but Vinton formed a studio and became the fore-most commercial clay animator in the United States. Frank and Caroline Mouris found their métier in the won-drous cornucopia of clippings of national magazine advertisements. They produced the 1973 Oscar-winning short *Frank Film*, a maze of beautifully crafted images in a collage animation that topped all others: the intricately con-structed patterns of familiar objects were synchronized to two levels of nar-ration in a highly original and unusual use of the medium.

George Griffin, Jane Aaron, Al Jarnow, David Ehrlich, John Canemaker, Jimmy Picker, and others explored animation outside the world of com-mercial studios.

Disney's new releases, *The Aristocats* (1970) and *Robin Hood* (1973), were skill-fully animated and pleasantly entertaining, but lacked the old spark. The nature of Disney output for many years had been self-assured but safe. The studio's graying animation staff, those who had arrived during the great spurt of the 1930s, were heading for retirement and the hiring of young talent began in earnest. The new animators grew ever more sure of their skills and impatient to take on projects of their own. To quell this impatience, the studio assigned them a two reeler, *The Small One*. Released before Christmas 1978, it tells of a little boy and his donkey who accommodate Mary and Joseph on their journey to Bethlehem. It proved an adequate test of the talents of the eager new group, but it was *The Rescuers* (1977), a feature that combined the work of the last of the old guard with the rising strengths of the younger animators that was Disney's best effort during the decade.

In 1979, thirteen younger members of the Disney staff followed director Don Bluth out of the door in protest against what they considered to be the company's abandonment of the classic techniques of the earlier films. Bluth had been in charge of the younger animators and together in his garage at home they had fashioned a fully animated half hour called *Banjo the Woodpile Cat*. This moonlighting excursion allowed them to incorporate many animated effects that were being bypassed in their work at Disney. *Banjo* proved to investors that Bluth and his team could produce work only previously expected from Disney, and Bluth subsequently formed a studio to produce features.

The studios could not have foreseen a major change in audiences. Though they had always denied that their product was strictly for kids, they steadily avoided subject matter that offended traditional mores. A youthful population, expanding and enmeshed in protest against the establishment, was ripe for different approaches to animation.

A New Kind of Cat

Ralph Bakshi, trained in traditional modes at Terrytoons, had an overriding desire to break out of these constraints. His interest in underground comics suggested that the time was right for animating that genre's prime antihero— *Fritz the Cat* (1971). Fritz came out of the musings of cartoonist Robert Crumb in a coarse style reminiscent of the 1930s Fleischer films, turning crosshatched characters into offbeat caricatures of society. Originally intended as a short, Bakshi and producer Steve Krantz expanded it to feature length.

Production began in New York using the best local animators, but a decision to relocate and complete the work in Los Angeles was provoked by two things: protests by some of the staff against doing sexually explicit material, and Bakshi-Krantz's tight-fisted budget. Made for under a million dollars, *Fritz the Cat* grossed over $5 million and was the first animated feature to be released with an X-rating. Bakshi's success gave him the opportunity to pursue a theme of his own in his second feature, *Heavy Traffic* (1973). In *Traffic*, Bakshi incorporated ideas he had formulated for years growing up in a tough Brooklyn neighborhood. Based in Hollywood, Bakshi retained several of the New York artists he had depended on for *Fritz* and together with a strong coterie of West Coast animators, turned *Heavy Traffic* into an acerbic look at New York's seamy side.

Ralph Bakshi was an alumnus of Terrytoons, but it was as director of Paramount Cartoons, the former Famous Studios, that he came in contact with producer Steve Krantz. Krantz had contracted a series of programs based on Marvel comics heroes, and when Paramount Cartoons closed suddenly, Bakshi and Krantz teamed up. Their working relationship, though instrumental in bringing about two well-received features, was shaky. Eventually, there was a split, and Krantz went on to produce a poorly conceived sequel, *The Nine Lives of Fritz the Cat* (1974), based on Robert Crumb's character, and Ralph Bakshi created several other films with varying degrees of critical and financial success.

Coonskin, a retelling of Joel Chandler Harris's *Br'er Rabbit* stories with contemporary black characters, was withdrawn from theaters after being denounced as a racial slur. Bakshi defended his work, stating emphatically that there was no bias intended. The resentment to *Coonskin** affected the box office fortunes of another production with a Brooklyn accent, *Hey Good Lookin'* (1975/1982). Its poor showing sent Bakshi in search of viable subject matter and he found it in a growing interest in science fiction and sword-and-sorcery material. His subsequent productions, *Wizards* (1977) and

Lord of the Rings (1978), lacked the verve of *Fritz the Cat* and *Heavy Traffic*. *Wizards*, a hodge-podge of design styles, enjoyed some popularity, but it was with *Rings*, a tedious retelling of the Tolkien stories, that Bakshi became enamored with rotoscoping—the tracing of live-action footage to ease the laborious task of animation.

Several key personalities died during this period: Paul Terry in 1971 at the age of eighty-four; Max Fleischer in 1972 at the age of eighty-eight; and John R. Bray at ninety-nine in 1978. George Dunning was only fifty-eight when he died in 1979, leaving partially finished a highly expressive feature-length version of Shakespeare's *The Tempest*.

John Hubley was sixty-two when he succumbed during open-heart surgery in 1977. He had produced several films in the 1970s, sharing the creative work with his wife, Faith. Among these were the shorts *Cockaboody* (1972), and *Voyage to Next* (1974), and two longer television productions, *A Doonesbury Special* (1977), based on the characters from the Gary Trudeau comic strip, and the seventy-two-minute view of the various stages of life, *Everybody Rides the Carousel* (1976), adapted from the writings of Erik Erikson. After Hubley's death, Faith continued to create personal productions that maintained the humanistic qualities that had been the hallmark of her work with her husband. These efforts, interweaving myth, history, and art include *Whither Weather* (1977), *Step By Step* (1978), and *Sky Dance* (1979).

Coonskin was later released as *Streetfight* on home video in the 1990s.

John Hubley, animation's leading impressionist.

Independent Features

Sensing a growing interest in features, new producers acquired the rights to popular subjects. Martin Rosen, an American, turned to animators in London to adapt Richard Adams's best-selling novel, *Watership Down* (1978). Rosen initially engaged John Hubley to direct, but disagreements over stylistic handling led to Rosen's taking on the directorial chores himself. This story of the struggle and survival of a community of rabbits turned out to be a hard-hitting, uncompromising production. The heavily realistic art is balanced by stylized opening and closing scenes suggesting the hand of John Hubley.

One production, which began with great fanfare but turned into a disappointment, was Lester Osterman's *Raggedy Ann and Andy* (1977), based on the popular stories by Johnny Gruelle. It was the first animated feature produced entirely in New York, and though most of the work was done in Manhattan, crews in Hollywood were recruited for additional portions of the picture.

Robustly brought to life by skilled animators under director Richard Williams, the characters carried the weight of sixteen songs, a sprawling plot, and characters that inspired little empathy. A Canadian, Williams operated a studio in London and had been chosen to command the corps of talents because of his stunning mastery of techniques in scores of commercials and animated segments for live features. He had won an Oscar in 1972 for his half-hour rendition of Charles Dicken's *A Christmas Carol*, which depended stylistically on nineteenth-century book illustrations. Williams had a feature of his own, *The Thief and the Cobbler*, which was struggling to be realized. The production was in the works off and on and passed through many hands, including the great lights of Hollywood animation: Grim Natwick, Ken Harris, Art Babbitt, and Shamus Culhane. Williams, ever the perfectionist, saw to it that scenes of intricate design and movement were included, but the production had been grinding on for years, and as the decade closed, it was far from finished.

As tensions lessened in the Middle East, Israeli animators went to study abroad. Among these were Roni Oren, Michael Ron, Turia Kurtz, Thelma Goldman, and David Shalita. Some took jobs in studios overseas, but others returned to create animation for Israeli television, with varying success.

In Italy, Bruno Bozzetto, a producer of shorts, commercial spots, and a couple of features, introduced a satire on Disney's *Fantasia* titled *Allegro Non Troppo* (1977). Cruder than the Disney classic, it nonetheless presented a mixture of clever animation and broadly silly live segments. Its jaunty quality had much in common with Terry Gilliam's earlier collage animation for British television's spoof, *Monty Python's Flying Circus*.

At the National Film Board of Canada, Norman McLaren was beset by continuing health problems and wound down his daily schedule, but not before producing a series of short instructional films, *Animated Movement*. Designed for beginning animators, the shorts were made in collaboration with his long-time colleague Grant Munro. The Film Board took on a group of lively younger filmmakers who brought with them an amazing display of individual styles. Among them were Ishu Patel, Paul Driessen, Co Hoedeman, Jacques Drouin, Derek Lamb, and Caroline Leaf. Many of them incorporated solid storytelling and unusual techniques into their films, but it was Leaf who amazed all with her painstakingly direct under-the-camera method. In her rendition of an Eskimo tale, *The Owl That Married a Goose* (1974), she used delicate sand silhouettes, and her adaptation of Mordecai Richler's short story *The Street* (1976) was painted on glass. In Leaf's films the techniques never outweigh the warmth, humor, and appeal of the story and characters. Encouraged by their own success with animation, the Canadians launched two ambitious international festivals in the capital city of Ottawa in 1976 and 1978.

At the Pannonia Studios in Budapest, feature productions gained importance, and between 1971 and 1980 the studio animated five long films. In Belgium a second foray into early history was made with the well-received feature *Asterix and Cleopatra* (1970), and five years later with *The Twelve Labors of Asterix*.

Animators, already beset by the move away from pure cartoon in the years since the release of the film *2001*, were thrust further into the special-effects genre with the arrival of George Lucas's *Star Wars* (1977). It fostered a wave of interest in realistic effects. Every animated production, from costly features to mundane theater announcements, contained elements that glowed or zapped across the screen. At first, these demands fell on optical printing houses who in turn hired animators to create the effects, but by the end of the decade, these illusions were being created by a tool that softly glowed and hummed, and was growing in acceptance: the computer.

Enter Electrons

By the 1970s, computer technology had advanced to such a degree that not only the manipulation of abstract shapes but primitive figure animation would be touted for commercial purposes. Actually, what appeared to be a sudden explosion in technological achievement was similar to the career of an actor who, after a lifetime of unacclaimed performances, is suddenly hailed as an overnight discovery. Animators, however, were frustrated. There were too few systems and too much difficulty and expense required in using computers. And when animators did have the opportunity, they had to work through a programmer, someone who translated ideas into a code the computer understood. That was the case in 1964 at Bell Labs, when scientist Ken Knowlton undertook image formation and developed the computer language BEFLIX, working in close association with artists Lillian Schwartz, Stan VanderBeek, and others.

The introduction of the Scanimate system, a product of Computer Image Corporation in Colorado, was used by affiliates in Los Angeles and in New York. Scanimate was an analog system that built sequential images by distorting and manipulating the rasters on a cathode ray tube. It was used in commercials and for logos. A further development from Computer Image Corporation was CAESAR, which attempted to create character animation. CAESAR only partially fulfilled expectations and Scanimate faded from use as more sophisticated digital computers proliferated. An important development was ray-tracing, the work of Phillip Mittleman of MAGI Synthevision, whose invention created startlingly realistic shadows and highlights with a digital computer. By the end of the decade, most animation camera stands used in commercial production had their controls adapted to computer commands, making precise intricate special-effects scenes commonplace. In the 1980s, computers would build up a head of steam.

The 1980s: Features to the Fore

This was a time of theatrical and television animation expansion. Flat-cel work dominated, but the use of stop-motion increased surprisingly and an important spurt of computer creations stirred animator interest.

The introduction of IBM's portable units in 1980, following on Apple Computer's lead, brought electronic equipment into the sphere of small companies and individuals. Most animators gave salutary heed to the new technology, but a few, like veteran producer John Halas, saw the arrival of these advanced tools as a necessary evolution in the animation process. Halas, in his role as president of ASIFA-International, was persistent in his cry for acceptance of the inevitable. In an article in a 1981 *Business Screen* magazine, he pointed to the historical beginnings of animation on paper, followed by the advances made possible with cels, and now by the arrival of the next phase, computers. With so many hours of intensive labor necessary in making the simplest animated film, a helpful tool was not to be scorned. To quote Halas: "Human inventiveness and technological developments often occur just at the point of decay in an existing condition or way of doing things." An article in the same issue balanced the attitudes of local New York animators who championed cel animation and waved off any hint of its demise. Cel use expanded considerably throughout the decade, but, ironically, due to the ups and downs of the television-commercial field, most of

those studio owners who extolled cels closed or reformed their studios during this period, and the magazine in which their views were aired changed its name, accommodatingly, to *Computer Pictures*.

Computer imaging combined with video editing made deeper inroads into traditional film methods. Television commercials, formerly sent to stations on tiny 16mm reels, were now on three-quarter-inch videotape for broadcast. It became the industry standard to transfer the original film negative to videotape and then edit and add effects and graphics. This was a major change in production procedure. Once the film was processed it was sent to one place for transfer to one-inch tape, then to another for editing, and to a different location for special effects, the mixing of soundtracks and finally the reduction to three-quarter-inch cassettes for release. Eventually, videotape houses absorbed all of these tasks in one location, making it fashionable for agency personnel to spend an entire day in these windowless confines, overseeing the post-production of a single commercial. They loved this new production power—the video companies catering to them by appointment and seating them in comfortable lounges. Some editing facilities soothed impatient clients by including a full-size billiard table in their cushioned surroundings. If there was one material besides tape that set video suites apart from film studios, it was carpeting. Film editors and animation services were content with clean, polished linoleum on the floors, but in the world of video, not only were the floors completely carpeted, but so were the walls and ceilings. Ensconced on soft couches in darkened, air-conditioned rooms with the soft glow of video screens reflecting off their anxious faces, agency personnel took full advantage of the immediacy of video technology.

Every commercial contains type, logos, and occasional diagrams that had always been routinely assigned to animation studios, but that now fell more and more into the province of electronics. Type no longer had to be handset and reproduced by hot press onto cels, or photographed as a high-contrast Kodalith and then placed under an animation camera. Titles and graphics were now created during the course of editing the spot. Diagrams, sparkles, glows, flips, and wipes, usually days of work in traditional animation, were similarly created by the press of a button. The allure of the new electronics reached a heated pitch when the Disney studio announced its inclusion of computer techniques in its latest feature productions.

Disney's Ups and Downs

By 1981, when Disney released *The Fox and the Hound* after delays due to the sudden departure of key animation personnel two years before, it was actively implementing changes to alter its public perception as a producer of movies for children and gentle adults. *The Fox and the Hound* did not assuage this notion, with its overly cuddly animals and its folksy human characters, but one section of the film was widely praised as gripping and exciting. The climax of the story is one of ferocity and brilliance, where a bear and the key dog character engage in a life-and-death struggle. Animated by Glen Keane, the scene was a reminder of the force the medium was capable of delivering, and hinted at future potent work from this young animator. The studio, intent on putting more of this power into its productions was caught in the situation of maintaining benign family fare at a time when those over twelve were sidestepping Disney for more gritty stuff.

Attracting contemporary audiences became a priority. Since Disney prided itself in being first in the industry, the studio launched an ambitious experiment in computer animation in the 1982 science-fiction feature *Tron*. The effects in *Tron* were exceptional, the studio going outside for much of the technology to create the video-game interiors of the film's theme. Dark and depressing, *Tron's* story lacked a necessary balance of lightness and humor to match its technical innovations.

Improved electronics had altered audience expectations of movie-theater sound so much that in 1983 it was decided to re-record the deteriorating soundtracks of *Fantasia*. Irwin Kostal, who orchestrated for *Mary Poppins* and other Disney films, was chosen as conductor. The sounds, now being picked up by the most magnificent state-of-the-art equipment, were post-recorded for a film whose animators had—forty-three years before—meticulously synchronized thousands of drawings to the pre-recorded Stokowski tracks. This classic production was altered further by the elimination of the on-screen presence of narrator, Deems Taylor, a move which alienated the critics who rejected this repackaging of a classic for a new generation.

Walt Disney's son-in-law, company president Ron Miller, had worked up through the live-action ranks and understood that a new production arm should be established. He created Touchstone Pictures for the development of films with adult subjects to compete with live-action studios. The first release under the new logo was *Splash!* (1984), a live film with humorous episodes inspired by a scantily clad mermaid. It was a hit and somehow, it was hoped, this new outlook would seep into the animation division to recapture the teenage audience. The success of *Splash!* and the cheerful reception of the animated featurette *Mickey's Christmas Carol* (1983), with Mickey Mouse's first screen appearance in thirty years, did not obscure the reality of several recent box-office failures. The Walt Disney organization, it was felt, was in need of new management, and in the freewheeling economic spirit of the time, outsiders eyed the company as an excellent candidate for corporate takeover. After several months of anguished maneuvers during 1984, Ron Miller resigned and Michael D. Eisner, a creative executive formerly with ABC Television and Paramount Pictures, stepped in as president of the company with Frank G. Wells as chief operating officer. Walt Disney's nephew, Roy E. Disney Jr., whose late father had managed the company's business affairs since its beginnings, was put in charge of the animation division. The corporate raiders were vanquished, but at a cost of $325 million. The need to recoup the loss was evident, and in an uncharacteristic move, the studio's prized classic *Pinocchio* was released to the home-video market. It sold extremely well and established a pattern of video distribution for most of the Disney features.

The first animated feature to be released under Disney's new management was *The Black Cauldron.* Several years in production, and costing more money than any previous Disney animation, it was an effort to cash in on the sword-and-sorcery themes popular at the start of production, but which had waned by the film's release in 1985.

By 1986, and with the arrival of *The Great Mouse Detective*, the studio showed signs of getting back on track. The story featured a Sherlock Holmes mouse based on the children's book *Basil of Baker Street*, by Eve Titus. The charming characters and intriguing sense of locale was heightened by an innovative climactic scene inside Big Ben, where cartoon figures meshed with computer animations of clock gears. The combination of the two techniques was accomplished by printing out the computer drawings and then inking them on cels to match the cartoon style.

The Disney studio had survived a possible calamity, and the general public saw it as a viable company. Its films were in evidence at local theaters, Disney had a cable channel, and it produced a new series of animated daytime children's television shows, *The Gummi Bears* and *The Wuzzles*. As ever, thousands of licensed articles displayed the likenesses of the Disney characters, and three theme parks beckoned to tourists in California, Florida, and Japan. The allure of all this fame and money guided other producers in their desires to cash in on these Disney-dominated worlds.

Steven Spielberg earned his reputation with audience pleasers like *Jaws* (1975) and *Raiders of the Lost Ark* (1981), but deep down he admired the success of Walt Disney. Deciding that Don Bluth, after Disney, was the most capable of delivering full character animation, he contracted for two features. Bluth and his crew, now situated in their own studio, had produced a $6.1 million–version of the book *Mrs. Frisby and the Rats of NIMH*. Released in 1982 as *The Secret of*

NIMH, it exhibited fine animation but, due to insufficient advertising and promotion, it failed to excite the public.

Bluth then entered an agreement with a manufacturer of video arcade machines for an extravagant interactive adventure called *The Dragon's Lair* (1983). It employed laser discs, cost a million to make, and created interest, but just as a second subject was being readied, the video-game craze slowed and Bluth was again in search of an outlet. Enter Steven Spielberg with *An American Tale* (1986), about a family of Jewish immigrant mice, and *The Land Before Time* (1988), a dinosaur adventure falling somewhere between *The Rite of Spring* sequence in *Fantasia* and the natural world of *Bambi*.

The realities of everyday life became prominent in animated productions from around the world. The grubby individuality that gave the Fleischer *Popeye* series its appeal was popping up en masse in the sunny world of animated features. *Plague Dogs* (1982), Martin Rosen's tough, unstinting look at animals used for scientific testing, based on the novel by Richard Adams, maintained its sharp focus in the film's detailed, hard-edged backgrounds. *When the Wind Blows* (1987), a rendering of Raymond Briggs's illustrated book produced by Britain's Channel 4 and directed by Jimmy Murakami, received acclaim for its poignant view of the futile efforts suggested for withstanding an atom-bomb blast. In the film drawings of an average, middle-aged couple move with extreme subtlety among sturdy representations of a house and furniture. In a departure from the norm,

Disney's *Oliver and Company* (1988), a contemporary version of *Oliver Twist* with hip New York cats and dogs, included a large Coca Cola ad in the opening Times Square scenes.

The same year, Disney made another unusual shift from its standard approach when the company released *Who Framed Roger Rabbit?* It was shaped as an homage to the cartoon shorts of the 1940s, and in an unusual twist for studios scrupulously protective of their licensed properties, included almost every major cartoon character from that golden age. Made in conjunction with Steven Spielberg's Amblin Entertainment, it had been in consideration for several years, but once in production it became the most ambitious combination of live-action and animation until that time. Many in the field had loathed the flat, pasted look that cartoons acquired when tossed in with real people. All such productions strictly avoided camera movement and shifting angles in the live shots to ease the matching of the two mediums.

Richard Williams and Robert Zemeckis, respectively the film's animation and live-action directors, decided it was time to break with tradition. Zemeckis shot the film just as he would any normal feature and Williams's corps of animators tediously injected the characters into its numerous shifting perspectives. *Roger Rabbit*'s extravagances included shaded and modeled cartoon figures to simulate the live photography, and scenes with intricately rigged props, such as pulling a cushion from underneath a chair to indicate the weight of a sitting character. The film was praised worldwide for its technical perfection, but its lead character was bothersome.

Serious thought had gone into delineating Roger's physical and psychological attributes but he lacked empathy. Though this was Roger Rabbit's first screen appearance, in the story he is a star of many cartoon shorts. The Disney studio, alert to this, created new productions to give him a "past." Within months of the feature's release two shorts with Roger were put into production, *Tummy Trouble* and *Rollercoaster Rabbit*, and again in 1993 with *Trail Mix-up*.

Acclaim for the technical bravura of *Who Framed Roger Rabbit?* went to director Richard Williams, leading to talk of Disney or some other major producer picking up the funding of his feature *The Thief and the Cobbler*, which was still in production.

Not Your Normal Family

The Simpsons arrived inauspiciously in 1989, in edgy spots among the live comic skits of *The Tracey Ullman Show*. Cartoonist Matt Groening invented the daily perturbations of Homer, Marge, Bart, Lisa, and Maggie, and within a few months they became the first animated evening half-hour series since the debut of *The Flintstones* in 1960. *The Simpsons* would become the longest running show of its kind in television history.

Focus on the World

In Japan there seemed to be an endless supply of lavishly produced action adventures filled to the brim with explosive personalities and pyrotechnics. Of this type of story, *AKIRA* (1988), is the most vivid: a wild, two-hour journey through magnificently animated cityscapes and crashing vehicles (motorcycles run amok in this bloody animation extravaganza).

In Britain, attention was focused on an explosion of animation that was richly raucous on one hand and softly moving on the other. The *Snowman*, based on another of Raymond Briggs's books and sponsored by Channel 4, was a lyric masterpiece. Running a half-hour, it included the breathtaking animated views of the characters flying over the countryside and a moving, bittersweet ending. Animation activity soared in everything from commercials to features to ambitiously produced student films. Not only was there a surge in quantity, but also the quality of work, aided by amazingly innovative design, caught the world's attention. The stop-motion efforts from the studio of Aardman Productions were especially interesting. Here, Peter Lord and David Sproxton created *Babylon*, about the overwhelming influence of the world's arms traders.

In Canada Frederick Back animated *Crac* (1981). This ten-minute short about a rocking chair joyfully spanned Canadian history and won an Oscar. Back's next production, *The Man Who Planted Trees* (1988) was even more remarkable. It is a half-hour retelling of a tale by Jean Giono and was made with the aid of one assistant during three years of work. At the Annecy festival, Back received a sustained standing ovation for this account of Elzeard Bouffier, who single-handedly grew a forest in a fierce, barren landscape.

Cuba's animation humorist Juan Padrone created several shorts during the 1980s, including *Filmnutos* (1980) and *Quinoscopio* (1985), the latter based on the magazine cartoons of the Argentine cartoonist Quino. Also notable from Havana's Estudios De Animación, ICAIC, were the works of Modesto García, Mario Rivas, and Mario García-Montes.

In 1989, Disney released its exuberant *The Little Mermaid*. Based on the Hans Christian Andersen fairytale, it is tuneful and colorful, and substitutes a spunky redheaded teenager for the original mermaid who suffered and died for love.

When the Berlin Wall fell in 1989, animators in Europe found themselves without government sponsorship. As studios shifted from state-owned to open-market entities, animators considered this change a mixed blessing. Now free to go their own ways, they turned to commercials and assignments in foreign television. Some became itinerants, traveling to distant cities to pitch in on features.

The 1990s: Ugly Is Beautiful

In the final decade of the century animation was more popular than ever. In the United States, cable television interjected cartoons into every crevice of its broadcast day. Nickelodeon launched three programs for Sunday mornings to counter the mundane tastes of the major networks. Each offering reflected its own form of irreverence. *Doug* was cartoonist Jim Jinkin's view of an Archie-like character minus sexy co-eds and high school frivolities. Instead it detailed the lives of the eccentric inhabitants of a small town, offering a comic view of Jinkin's own boyhood. *Rugrats*, by Klasky Csupo, the original *Simpsons* animator, is a more solidly drawn family group that celebrates the joys of edgy humor from the mouths of babies.

The most popular program, and the one to cause the most commotion, was *Ren & Stimpy*. Created by John Kricfalusi, it retained the loose, manic drive evidenced in his work on Ralph Bakshi's short-lived television remake of *Mighty Mouse* (1987). Wild and chock-full of disgusting bits, it nonetheless enchanted cynical sixteen-year-olds ready to move up from the robotic *Masters of the Universe* to the fluidly gross antics of a strangely configured dog (Stimpy) and cat (Ren). Its wildness aside, the true appeal of the show was that the two characters reflected human qualities, expressing a great need for each other by exhibiting heartrending loss when separated. After two years, Kricfalusi ran afoul of the network and was ousted, and he was not the first creator forced to give up his brainchild to satisfy the front office. *Doug* also fell from grace, a victim of its normalcy in the competition for crassness. But since cartoons never die, *Doug* was acquired by the Disney Company and whipped into a feature, *Doug's First Movie* (1992), and the series has found its way into home-video release. Jinkins then created another show called *PB and J Otter* geared for young children.

MTV, on the other hand, produced its own brand of "gross" cartoons. It selected Mike Judge's *Beavis and Butt-Head*, in which two teenage boys lob snide comments at pretentious music videos. Soon, late-night talk-show hosts, in an effort to stay current, were including the characters' imbecilic laughter in their routines. The Turner Broadcasting Company created a Cartoon Network that airs animation all day long, and most of the films were selected from the company's vast cartoon holdings through its ownership of the Metro-Goldwyn-Mayer and Hanna and Barbera studios. The Cartoon Network has sponsored original and energetic productions such as John R. Dilworth's *Courage the Cowardly Dog* series and Tom Warburton's *Kids Next Door*, and invites other young animators to submit their offbeat ideas.

Features

As smaller companies sought diversity, the larger producers discovered an increasing demand for animated features. The major obstacle was the Walt Disney Company, which in 1991 hit the decade running with the wonderfully scripted *Beauty and the Beast*. Its orchestration won two Oscars and possessed the solid feel of a Broadway musical. It was the first animated feature to be considered seriously as competition against live-action films for the Academy Award for best film. Before the production was completed, the studio uncharacteristically screened it at the prestigious New York Film Festival at Lincoln Center. With scenes of rough storyboard and pencil animation drawings intermingled with fully colored sequences, this glimpse of the bare bones of the art of animation charmed critics.

Several live-action producers scrambled to announce plans for animated features. The comparatively cheaper budgets were seen as favorable alongside the hefty costs of filming real people. The initial enthusiasm wavered when independent productions like *Little Nemo* in 1990, *Fern Gully*, *Bebe's Kids*, and *Cool World* in 1992, and *Once Upon a Forest* in 1993 plunked into theaters and remained for the blink of an eye. All of these went on to home video, where a box-office frog often becomes a prince. This is especially true when children are concerned, since families and kids themselves spend millions buying cassettes for personal collections.

With so many productions formed in the Disney large-studio style, it was refreshing that a wide audience welcomed Bill Plympton's seventy-two-minute *The Tune* (1992), in which he did every drawing. Although others helped in the coloring phases, it was essentially a one-cartoonist movie and received encouraging reviews.

The arrival of Tim Burton's *The Nightmare Before Christmas* (1993) heralded a return to witty and inventive design. In the 1980s, Disney and the studios that had challenged its hold on the feature field had hovered around the classic realism of the 1940s animation. Don Bluth and others believed that features with UPA stylized graphics couldn't hold up for eight reels. Burton's radically clever twist on the Christmas theme played havoc with this notion. Released under Disney's Touchstone banner to keep its scary presence from frightening children, *Nightmare* was geared to capturing the teenagers that flocked to *Yellow Submarine* reissues.

Clay and Substance

In earlier decades British producers looked far and wide to staff their studios; by the 1990s this changed considerably. A vanguard of young artists appeared who attacked the medium with a fresh, no-holds-barred intensity. Raised in the wake of *Yellow Submarine* and schooled in university animation classes, animators like Paul Vester, Joanna Quinn, Candy Guard, Mark Baker, Peter Lord, David Sproxton, and Nick Park created work that expressed personal viewpoints. Park, working with Lord and Sproxton's company, Aardman Animations, employed an adept clay technique combined with naturalistic soundtrack recordings of everyday people. Park's riotously funny short about opinionated zoo animals, *Creature Comforts*, won the Academy Award in 1991. Encouraged, Park began new half-hour cartoons starring Wallace and Gromit, *The Wrong Trousers* and *A Close Shave*. Each were Oscar winners, 1993 and 1995 respectively.

The Century Fades

In the 1920s, Felix the Cat and Koko the Clown defined animation, while for years afterward the outpourings of the Disney studios were considered the final say on the medium. This view, held securely in the popular mind, vies with the truth. As Felix, Mickey, and Bugs romped across the screens of the world, artists in diverse locales explored animation in a more personal manner. Lotte Reiniger, Berthold Bartosch, Len Lye, Norman McLaren, Yoji Kuri, and Jiri Trnka were some of those animators who persevered in redefining the nature of animation. Their experiments were continued by others, some of them resurfacing in the cartoons of Disney and UPA, and in the styles of hundreds of television commercials.

Over the last thirty years the list of creative individuals exploring animation has grown considerably. Young animators are imbuing everything with an enthusiastic, pungent sensibility at the beginning of the twenty-first century. This is evident in work for MTV and Nickelodeon, the variety of independent productions shown at world festivals, the theatrical programs of the International Tournée of Animation, and the omnibus theatrical releases of the offbeat animation of Spike and Mike.

Hours of startling and exquisitely animated adventures continue to pour out of Japanese studios, most notably in the films of Hayao Miyazaki. This director's engrossing work has broken attendance records in Japan and gained a worldwide following with films like *My Neighbor Totoro* (1988), *Kiki's Delivery Service* (1989), *Princess Mononoke* (1997), and *Spirited Away* (2001).

Meanwhile, video subjects produced by New York's Michael Sporn Animation and the Connecticut-based Weston Woods continue to proliferate. In Vancouver an enthusiastic center of animation, Marv Newland's International Rocket Ship created an adaptation of Gary Larson's *The Far Side* for television in 1994, and productions for various children's television series continue in Toronto at the Nelvana studio, as well as at Nickelodeon's New York headquarters.

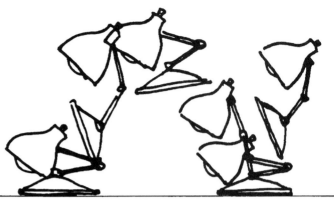

In *Luxo Jr.* John Lassiter brought traditional timing to computer animation.
© Pixar/"Luxo," a trademark of Jac Jacobsen Industries AS. © Association of Computer Machinery, by permission.

In Hollywood, Chuck Jones, in his eighties, spun out an updated Road Runner cartoon for Warner Bros., while Disney's *The Lion King* (1994), *Pochohontas* (1995), and the fully computer-animated *Toy Story* (1995), created with Pixar, dazzled audiences and made gobs of money. A critically acclaimed sequel, *Toy Story 2*, followed in 1999. Live-action producers planned, once again, to back animated features. The competition from Disney has been formidable, with the releases of *The Hunchback of Notre Dame* (1996), *The Legend of Mulan* (1998), *Hercules* (1997), *Tarzan* (1999), and *Fantasia 2000*. Richard Rich's production of *The Swan Princess* (1994) proved that studios other than Disney or Bluth could do competent and entertaining full animation. But no amount of technique could rescue Turner Broadcasting's *The Pagemaster* (1994) from a depressing story and so-so reviews. Stephen Spielberg talked of producing an animated version of the Broadway musical *Cats*, but completed *Balto* (1995) instead, a dog story based on a factual event. Spielberg, with the newly formed Dreamworks, SKG, with former Disney production chief Jeffrey Katzenberg and record tycoon David Geffen, then announced several ani-

mated features. Their initial choice, *Prince of Egypt* (1998), abandoned the usual fairytale for the Bible. In 1999, Warner Bros. released the superb *Iron Giant*. Not to be outdone, MTV presented a feature *Beavis and Butthead Do America* (1996). And (oh yes) Richard Williams's *The Thief and the Cobbler* was finally released in August 1995, its title changed to the regrettable *Arabian Knight*. Reviewer's praised its jewel-like design and noted that though it had gone into production thirty years before *Aladdin* it was ironically overshadowed by the Disney film.

Cross-Dissolve to the 2000s

The new century is digital. It is normal now to tote miniaturized everything: cell phones, cameras, computers, CD and DVD players, video cameras, and TVs. Our eyes, however, are big for 3D computer animation. The success of the two Disney/Pixar *Toy Story* films inspired Dreamworks to acquire Pacific Data Images to produce 3D features. They beat Disney by a bug's whisker in 2000 with *Antz*, as Disney was readying *A Bug's Life* for theaters. These contemporary insects reflect the times, especially *Antz*, with its affinity for the whining humor of Woody Allen, the voice of the film's hero. Some big 3D hits were to follow: Dreamworks's remarkable *Shrek*, a humorous twist on fairytales, was countered by Disney's warm take on childhood fears with *Monsters, Inc.*, and Blue Sky Studios's *Ice Age.*

Computers now play a giant role in all movies, for special effects in live films and as helpmates in creating 2D animation. Producers have not completely forsaken traditional animation. There is a growing consensus that there will be room for all techniques. Recent films like *Atlantis: The Lost Empire* (2001), *Lilo and Stitch*, and *Treasure Planet* from Disney, Dreamworks's *Spirit: Stallion of the Cimarron*, Bill Plympton's *Mutant Aliens*, Klasky-Csupo's *Rugrats* and *The Wild Thornberry's*, all released in 2002, exhibited the pleasures of drawn animation mixed with computer embellishments. Suddenly, things changed when rising costs and box-office competition lead studios to begin layoffs of animation personnel, and Twentieth-Century Fox shuttered its Don Bluth animation unit. Animated television commercials became scarcer and though animation was still produced around the globe, the boom that began in 1988 seemed to be over. Yet in 2001 the members of the Academy of Motion Picture Arts and Sciences came to the landmark decision that with the prevalence of so many first-rate animated features it was time to award an Oscar to the year's best. The winner was Dreamworks's *Shrek*. The following year the Oscar went to Hayao Miyazaki for his masterful *Spirited Away*.

***The Tune*, a feature animated by Bill Plympton.** © Bill Plympton.

Recognition for animated features was years coming and, ironically, it came at a moment when more and more live-action films were aping animation, flying sword-wielding actors about the screen, or casting live actors in comic roles that could have been more readily played by Daffy Duck.

And So . . .

For a century animation shared the stage with good times, bad times, wars, depressions, economic swings, censorship, and new technologies. Then came the tragedy of September 11, 2001, and soon it felt like all of these things could happen at once. But, such dark thoughts lose their nightmarish power when brought into the light, like the light of a brilliant screen that is charged with color, movement, and joyful sounds. An illusion? Perhaps, but listen—listen carefully: you can hear the laughter.

1920s

1900s

1940s

1930s

1950

1950s

1960s

1970s

1980s

1990s

PART TWO

The Story Takes Shape

Imagination is the beginning of creation.
—George Bernard Shaw

CHAPTER 6

Drawing: The Bare Bones

*Make figures with such action as may be sufficient to show what
the figure has in mind.* —Leonardo da Vinci

Try to reduce everything you see to the utmost simplicity. —Robert Henri

From the storyboard stage through the design of characters and throughout production, drawing is essential in animation. Through conceptual sketches, intricate ideas are simplified and a production is given its style. Drawing involves a balance between flat design and solid shapes. An example of this dichotomy is a closed door, suggested by a simple outline, but when it opens in animation it moves in space and follows the rules of perspective. Daily drawing practice is necessary for handling the shifting forms and shapes that are the province of animation. The following are five important aspects of drawing that animators must understand:

1. Gesture
2. Weight and balance
3. Solidity
4. Proportion
5. Silhouetting

There is no definitive order that brings these five principles into play. In drawing a figure it is a good policy to start with the gesture, but it is also wise to consider the silhouette or design, the solidity of form, the displacement of weight, and whether an object or a figure is in balance. Each aspect presents itself as the drawing proceeds.

Gesture

The posture and movement of figures is determined by gesture. All things— people and animals, as well as bottles, chairs, trees, typewriters, hats, and umbrellas—exhibit a stance. Observe the model or object before putting lines on paper, not for details, but for the overall sweep, the thrust of the action. Develop a feel for the inherent movement in things and allow your hand to draw the lines as if you were in a trance. These sketches are for practice, merely to gain

PUSH

PULL

Balance and Gesture

When drawing from life or from memory, concentrate on the way figures stand and bend.
Try to capture the thrust of the action simply and directly.

efficiency. Making this exercise a daily habit will free you from conventional thinking and help you to visualize shape and direction. Shamus Culhane discusses this type of drawing at great length in his book *Animation: From Script to Screen*.

Weight, Balance, and Gravity

The second "invisible" element is the affect of gravity. Suggesting where the greatest concentration of weight occurs adds solidity to drawings and believability to animation. All figures and objects have a center of mass, and all figures, unless they are falling, are always in balance. A figure is balanced when it stands squarely on both feet or shifts its weight from one foot to the other. When the inside ankle of one leg is in direct line with the breastbone, the figure is in balance. With the weight on one foot the center of mass shifts very slightly, but as the figure leaps into the air the center is entirely displaced. Four-legged animals shift their weight to any one of their legs to maintain balance. No matter how crudely sketched, figures look convincing if the line of action and the balance points are well established.

Draw objects and figures to show the effects of gravity, which pulls everything downward.

Solidity

With gesture and balance suggested, the relationship between forms must be dealt with. Draw as if you were modeling shapes with clay. Observe a figure, a tree, an automobile, and notice how one shape overlaps or locks into another. A dinosaur, a person, or a spaceship are similar in that they are each comprised of interlocking and overlapping forms. Apply the clay-shaping approach to the

Gravity works against the body, requiring effort to overcome it.

drawing of anatomical forms to understand how bones and muscles affect the movements of people and animals.

Proportions

Drawing from life is a form of measuring with eye and hand. When observing people, compare the length of the head or the hand to determine the sizes of other parts of the figure. A normal figure is seven-and-a-half heads tall, idealized bodies are eight heads, while classic or heroic figures are eight and a half to nine heads tall. In cartooned or stylized figures exaggerated forms usually emphasize one shape over another, as when a head is designed to be much larger than the body. The distortion of the shapes does not preclude balanced design or satisfying patterns.

Silhouetting

Establish obvious silhouettes of shapes for quick recognition on the screen. Draw actions so definitively that they can't be mistaken for any other. Hang a sheet in a doorway and position a strong light a few feet to one side. Between the light and the sheet, place various articles so that their silhouettes are

Clarity of action depends on strong silhouetting.

Solidity and Weight

Draw as if you were modeling with clay.

Carry a sketchbook at all times and put down what you see in everyday situations.

visible from the opposite side. Study these forms and draw what you see. Watch the changing silhouette of a moving hand and draw it as an extension of the line of action of the arm.

The Sketchbook: Observation

Observation and patience are the keys to drawing. The secret is to carry a small sketchpad at all times and use it at every opportunity to draw what you see. Sketch actual appearances before you idealize them. If a cushion has a rip in it, draw the rip. If someone's jacket is too tight, draw the bad fit. Make quick studies—gesture sketches—of people in action on the street, at the post office, park, concerts, beach, or on the bus. The more you draw, the more you will develop a sense of which details to include and which ones to ignore.

Arrange a group of household items on a table and sit in front of them with a pad and a few soft pencils (2B to 4B). Before you draw any lines, notice that each object occupies its own space on the tabletop and that it blocks parts of other objects. Draw a frame on the page and look at the objects through a similar-shaped cutout. Note the distances between the arrangement of shapes and the edge of the viewing frame. Sketch the outlines of the shapes lightly, noting which shapes are taller, how far the edge of one shape is to another, and so on. Rearrange the objects and make more drawings.

Look for the interlocking of masses and sketch the *form*. Be aware of shadows and gradations of light on surfaces. In this way you develop an appreciation for solidity and grow less concerned with producing rigid, unyielding lines and fussy details. With very soft pencils or chalks, smudge in tones with your finger. You'll get interesting results (and a messy finger).

Roughs serve to pin down quick observations before they are forgotten. Notice how people move, walk, run, bend, lift, and carry. The body is capable of vigorous actions and is more flexible than most people realize. Sketch someone preparing to sit and observe the surprisingly extreme bending that takes place in simply getting in and out of a chair.

Discover the effects of wind on swaying trees, plants, and swirling dry leaves. Observe chimney smoke as it rises, the changing shapes of clouds, rain glancing off a shingled roof and then splashing on pavement. Draw animals at the zoo as well as pets in your home.

Once filled, date and store your pads, or discard the bad stuff and place the things worth keeping in folders or attach them to larger sheets. Everything saved has a future use. Sketches made years before become models for new characters while doodles and notes, long forgotten, surface as plans for fresh productions.

Variety

The wonder of the world is its infinite variety of living things. There are thousands of different kinds of leaves, flowers, animals, and insects. Of the millions of people in the world, no two are alike, and the variety of things that people make is staggering. There are hundreds of styles of chairs, houses, and conveyances, and a clutter of just "things." Simple props are subtle clues to setting a locale. A small grocery store differs from a huge supermarket and a high-class restaurant contrasts with a fast-food outlet. As an exercise, consider the thousands of designs of doors, for example, and how each expresses a different type of house, office, or shop and the types of people that use them.

Negative and Positive Space

Positive space refers to a shape and its relation to the important negative area around it.

Start by drawing shapes, not details. It may take several sketches to find the best arrangement for a shape and its surrounding area.

When you are satisfied, add the details.

Memory Drawing

Memory drawing forces you to observe. Think of activities you've witnessed during the day and sketch what you recall. After a day of sketching at the zoo, try to draw the animals again at home from memory. If you can't visualize the form of a lion's face, take another look at the lion and draw it with a sharper eye toward that which you had trouble remembering.

Negative and Positive Space

The areas shapes occupy are known as "positive space," and the areas that surround them are called "negative space." The shapes that negative spaces take in a storyboard or scene layout are important to the overall design, often more so than the shapes themselves.

A Drawing Routine

The ability to represent figures and objects with a few simple strokes is a

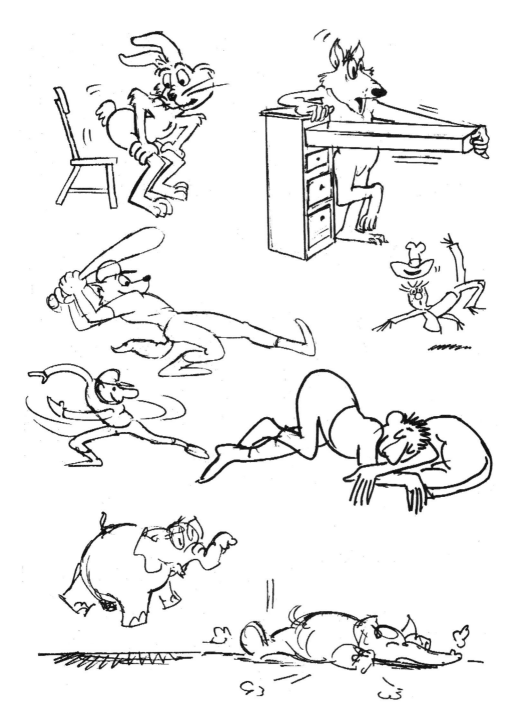

Emphasis and Exaggeration

Explore ways to stretch and expand on actions. You don't have to look far for subjects. Just sitting in a chair or taking a nap offers examples for creating exaggerated movement. When these and other actions are distorted further they become humorous.

valuable asset. To do this requires the conditioning of eye and hand through daily practice. Ideally, one to three hours set aside each day is necessary, but even if you can only spare twenty minutes you will notice marked improvement. Try to draw freely and avoid strain. Be patient: you will encounter good days and bad days as you progress through stages of success and frustration. Draw what you observe, but also draw what appeals to your imagination.

Give yourself daily tasks. One day draw people sitting in as many poses as possible; follow that with a day of children playing or people climbing. The next day draw only animals. Try offbeat situations like placing a giraffe in a living room or a bear on a bicycle. Don't settle for the first sketch, make several attempts to discover the best pose or composition.

Perspective

To accurately represent the three-dimensional world, it is necessary to understand perspective and foreshortening. A moving cup and saucer turn from one flat, stylized shape to another, and to draw the changing shapes requires that all of the in-between drawings obey the rules of perspective. You will note in the accompanying illustration how the

shape of the top of the cup and the saucer changes from a circle to an oval.

All things occupy their own space. If you look at items from a normal eye level arranged on a tabletop, the standing objects are either behind or in front

Shapes above eye level curve upward, while shapes below eye level curve downward.

A Model Chart

of something else. Only when you observe the same setup from overhead do they appear as separate and spaced apart.

Your eye level determines the horizon line and affects the invisible lines that run to the vanishing point. To get an idea of how this works, obtain an 8½ x 11 sheet of clear acrylic, or glass if you prefer, and stand it perpendicular to

the ground, at eye level, to represent the picture plane. Then peer at a scene or object through the glass and draw what you see directly onto the clear surface. When you try to indicate a three-dimensional picture on a two-dimensional surface you are in effect plotting it the same way as when you are using this makeshift picture plane.

Design

The exploration into design that constituted much of the 1950s UPA studio work and the subsequent explosion of varied approaches in commercials has too often been replaced with representations of uninspired reality and imitations of live action. Advances in computer graphics have expanded this concept, but what has been forgotten is that animation is an *exaggerated impression of the real world.* What is needed is the imagination and individuality that is locked in your personal view of things, and is just waiting to be drawn. Get your ideas down in your sketchbook; it's the best method for finding your own direction.

One more word about drawing.

Much animation is created under pressure to meet deadlines, and a solid background in drawing carries most animators through such times. Computers are helpful but you must know what it is you want to do with them. Before computers, Mary Ellen Bute made experimental films incorporating electronic devices. When she ran into difficulties with the equipment she filled in the necessary movements by drawing them. "Sometimes you've got to do that," she would say matter-of-factly.

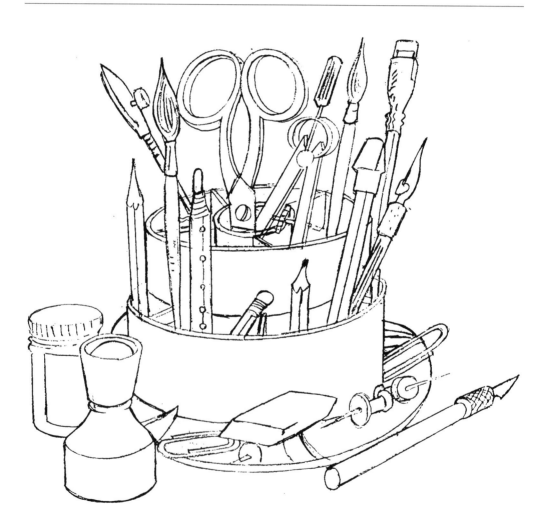

CHAPTER 7

Character Creation

The author's object in this work was to place before the reader a constant succession of characters and incidents; to paint them in as vivid colors as he could command; and to render them at the same time lifelike and amusing.

—Charles Dickens, preface to *The Pickwick Papers* (1837)

Characters are not what they look like, but the way they move.

—Chuck Jones

A major New York banking company once considered starring Bugs Bunny in a demonstration video. Why had they chosen the Warner Bros. wise-cracking, street-smart rabbit to represent their staid organization? They had checked the list of popular cartoon characters and found that Mr. Magoo was too crusty, Mickey Mouse too childish, Donald Duck too excitable, Daffy Duck too wacky, Bart Simpson too immature, and Popeye too gruff. With Bugs they knew they had a strong, individualistic, self-assured personality. They felt he possessed a critical attitude that cast him as totally honest and that customers would accept any information he offered. The planned video was never made, but the decision on the part of a sober banking institution to give center stage to a cartoon rabbit illustrates how strongly established the viability of cartoon characters is in the public mind.

Characters are essential to animation. They create interest and generate action, and without them there are no events, calamities, humor, tension, or suspense—in short—*there is no story.*

When designing characters, give them sufficient differences in physical attributes and attitudes to separate them from each other without veering from the graphic style of the production. Each should have an instantly identifiable and uniquely distinctive personality. Design each character for ease of animation and eliminate details that become tedious and time-consuming to draw, such as excess lines for hair, wrinkles, buttons, or patterns on clothing.

Personality

Popular characters are based on everyday people to give them strong recognizable human traits. They represent familiar types. Bugs Bunny is on top of everything, Daffy Duck is hyperneurotic, Bullwinkle is dense but loyal, Betty Boop is independent and creative,

and Ren and Stimpy are a zany but devoted pair.

Animated characters are full of spirit, but it is beyond them to ever attain the depths of personality that live actors bring to a role. Your animated actors are limited in the shades of emotion that they can show, but you can imbue them each with at least one strong recognizable characteristic.

When you are creating a personality, imagine the character in a frustrating situation and envision how he or she would react. For instance, imagine a window that's difficult to open. How would Donald Duck solve the problem? He might get angry, lose his temper, and smash it. Bugs Bunny, being the shrewd operator that he is, would convince someone else to open it for him. Mr. Magoo might not realize that he is looking through a window but think it is a television set and attempt to change the channel.

Think of the people around you. Think of yourself. All of us share the same strengths and weaknesses in our personalities. We all have similar emotions, needs, and desires in varying degrees. Each of us can be generous or stingy, relaxed or anxious, imaginative or dull, cheerful or sad, silly or serious, humble or pompous, downright practical or hopelessly idealistic. Television sitcoms are an excellent source for studying established character types. Here the performers have done the necessary groundwork and have gone through the detailed thought processes and rehearsals to develop the portrayals. While their examples are fine for study, keep in mind that these characterizations are someone else's creation and shouldn't be plagiarized. Stealing another artist's conception is not professional, but you can learn from them and adapt what they do in your own original way.

A drawing of a character can suggest a voice and a voice can create a mental image of what a character looks like. Either way, use experienced performers to record various voices and listen to them over and over again. Sketch the stance and posture that fits the sounds and inflections. You might have to tape several versions before you connect with the right one.

Characters in animation become more rounded by the addition of a secondary trait or a specific physical condition. Superman has the power to do everything. He flies, he sees through walls, he has unusual amounts of strength, and we know that he will always succeed. So why then are we still interested in Superman stories when we know he can overcome any obstacle and a good outcome is ensured? He has even been killed and brought back to life. His flaws have been introduced, such as his weakness in the presence of kryptonite, which attempt to deflect his strengths. And there is one mitigating factor that is always present: his everyday guise as Clark Kent.

As the mild-mannered reporter, he purposely acts ineffectual, hampered; also, he cannot reveal his true identity. As Kent, Superman becomes like us— ordinary. Essentially all of us are Clark Kents, and we relate to Superman's helpless state when his red-and-blue costume is concealed beneath a business suit and his actual strength is held in check. Superman reflects our problems in attempting to control the world around us, but it is the Clark Kent part of him, the part that we are innately familiar with, that establishes him as a sympathetic character and keeps the stories going.

Heroic figures, like Superman, Spiderman, and Wonder Woman become more believable if they are given softening traits along with their muscles. Add a drop of compassion to their natures. Show them liking children or puppies and allow them to reveal themselves as embarrassed, eccentric, anxious, fearful, softhearted, or gentle to evoke empathy from viewers. Humor also adds credibility and warmth to a stiff and wooden personality. Suggest concern for catching colds, going out without an umbrella, or losing the house keys. Superheroes, as well as green-skinned aliens from distant planets and stock villains, require the addition of humanizing qualities, weaknesses, and soft spots to make them believable.

Daffy Duck's personality makes him sympathetic to audiences, despite his offbeat behavior. Empathy grows from his helplessness and confusion whenever Bugs Bunny gets the best of him in their frequent contests. Most of us have at some time been taken advantage of by someone who is shrewder. While Goofy may have a low I.Q., he is another example of a character who tries to surmount his limitations but is continually frustrated by everyday occurrences. Donald Duck is a prime example of a sympathetic character who exhibits many human faults; he looses his composure, can be stingy, doesn't accept criticism, and likes practical jokes as long as they are at someone else's expense. He does have a good side, but it is those attitudes that we recognize as weaknesses that make him an interesting character. Where do animators find inspiration for these personalities? Well, there's always the mirror.

Animal Characters

Even before Aesop, animals were used as caricatures of human weaknesses because they could deflect emphasis from individuals. The animation of characters with animal like-nesses is so commonplace that it is easy to forget that Mickey Mouse, Donald Duck, and Goofy are not really animals. They never deal with mouse, duck, or dog-related gags. Their attitudes are strictly human. Bugs Bunny, conversely, chomps carrots and lives in a hole in the ground, but he also is less a hare than a human.

Almost every animal has become a cartoon character, but the choice generally falls to those that are most familiar and acceptable, such as small, furry mammals. This accounts for the prevalence of mice in cartoons, even though in real life many people abhor them. Snakes and insects have appeared in cartoon roles but they have yet to be popular.

Give a Character a Handicap

Vulnerability is an important trait and a slight physical handicap makes a character more human. Taste and astute handling are necessary here so as not to offend. Mr. Magoo is a good example of turning nearsightedness into a positive feature. The humor and warmth in the farfetched stories about him and his optimistic mumblings tell us that this is a satiric view of our own distorted perceptions and not a put-down of people with poor eyesight. He's Don Quixote in a homburg.

Yet a physical trait can take a sinis-ter turn in characters like Richard II, Long John Silver, or Frankenstein's mon-ster. The challenge, always, is to come up with a solution that relates to the story and that doesn't make light of human suffering. A mummy that walks the halls of a museum at night because he has insomnia—that's O.K. A cartoon giraffe that can't reach the topmost branches to feed because he has a knot in his neck—that's all right too.

Character History

Create imaginary histories for your characters. Along with names, give them birth dates, families, schools, friends, and important life events. Here is a middle-aged elephant named Baggzby. He's about sixty-five and still hasn't met the girl of his dreams. He was an only child and was very precocious, learning to trumpet, with his trunk of course, at the age of six. He attended the best musical schools for pachyderms and for a while played in the all-jungle orchestra. One day he developed a cold in his trunk and from then on he never sounded the same. As a result of this misfortune he had to take up another line of work. He became a stomper for an airline. Some airlines use elephants to stomp on people's onboard luggage for a better fit under the seats in the coach section. One day Baggzby met a young lady elephant, the star of an international circus. It seems that she was traveling first class . . . and so on.

Chaplin

It is no secret that Charlie Chaplin, in his characterization of the Tramp, has been a powerful influence on animation. Otto Messmer, the creator of Felix the Cat, pointed to Chaplin as the chief inspiration for Felix's personality. Messmer started out in the field in 1916 animating short reels of Chaplin, an early example of character licensing. The experience resounded in 1919 when Felix made his debut reflecting the humor and poignancy of the Tramp. Felix, similarly, was generally homeless, in search of a meal and prepared to take on any chore to earn a day's wages.

Walt Disney was also very aware of Chaplin's persona, and he injected it into Mickey Mouse's skinny arms and legs. One cartoon, *The Klondike Kid* (1932), is a direct reference to the Chaplin feature, *The Gold Rush* (1925). Chuck Jones also made a close study of Chaplin finding ways to insinuate aspects of his pantomimic techniques into the actions of Bugs Bunny. Jones has stated that

there was nothing they, the Warner Bros. cartoon group, ever did that wasn't preceded by something in Chaplin or Buster Keaton. Whenever cartoon characters attempt an air of sophistication they are aping Chaplin. The tramp, attired in castoff clothes, acts assuredly and with aplomb. His gloves may be lacking their tips but he dons them like a man of means heading for an evening at the opera. The hat may be too small but he wears it jauntily and tips it respectfully to all. The jacket may fit too snugly but it is properly buttoned and belies the baggy pants and the oversize shoes.

Chaplin displayed a profound understanding of comic structure. Whenever his films became contemplative, pensive, or overly sentimental, he released the tension with humor. If he was enamored of a young woman and gazed adoringly at her, his reverie was destroyed by a well-timed splash of cold water or a sudden knock on the head from a falling flowerpot. In this way the audience discovered Chaplin's serious side, but before this could cause distress, relief arrived through laughter.

As a character's personality takes shape and matching attitudes fall into place, an artistic style also forms.

Design Styles

Character shapes and outlines go through phases. At one moment they are appealing and easy to take, and at another time they are grotesque and disturbing. There are many reasons for this. Styles are affected by what is in vogue, by the individual approaches of various artists, and by the limits of technique. Animated films have had to contend with all of these, but mostly the medium has been inhibited by its production-line nature. The reality of using so many drawings, so many creative hands, just to get it done, demands that the designs be easy to replicate.

The proportions of a character hint at his or her personality. Soft, round shapes define the lovable character; large, broad shapes indicate an overbearing and aggressive personality; scratchy, crotchety outlines define

someone who is nervous or eccentric. Maintaining scale is necessary in establishing characters, as in juxtaposing a giant with a broad expanse of chest and a small head with a child with a large head and a small body. Characters are also defined by their actions. The villain in Trnka's *Song of the Prairie* acts in subtle ways, as when, having tipped his hat, his arms and hands fall to his sides in a snakelike manner.

The horizontal film frame seems to work best with shapes that are squat, like Felix the Cat and Mickey Mouse. Thin, lanky characters have always been thought to create problems in layout and lack the advantage of dumpy figures, whose large heads, eyes, and mouths fill the frame so neatly. In a full-figure shot the tall and narrow designs of the Peppermen from the *Yellow Submarine*, or Jack Skellington in *The Nightmare Before Christmas*, leave a great deal of space around them, requiring astute placement in the film frame.

Research

Make notes on the character designs in new and old cartoons but don't be influenced strictly by animation styles; investigate what has come before in the excellent works of the world's graphic artists. Study and collect the variety of styles of illustrators of children's books and posters; check library picture files for illustrations from past decades. There are many surprises and a wealth of character ideas in cartoons and illustrations created over the past two hundred years.

Inanimate Things

Bringing inanimate objects to life is a strength of animation. Familiar objects are explored for their unique personalities. A pickle jar, a much-used coffee pot, or an old jalopy spring into action with idiosyncratic traits. The jar is boisterous, the pot is cantankerous, and the car complains of an aching axle.

Try this. Design objects without eyes and limbs. Express the peculiarities of each item through the movement of its basic form.

Character Design

When I design characters, I start with a symbolic body posture and search out the poses that indicate a character's personality.

I must decide if the character is shy, aggressive, puzzled, snobbish, ghoulish, fawning, domineering, depressed, acquisitive, and so on.

Eventually characters take on a life of their own and reveal who they are.

Expression

Once I'm satisfied with a particular body pose, I concentrate on the head and face, especially the eyes.

Hands and Feet

I then experiment with the hands and feet to find those appropriate for the character.

Costume Styles

Finally, I research costume styles to make the character distinctive, to visually set it apart from established characters, as well as to fit the needs of the story.

CHAPTER 8

Storytelling with Animation

You cannot make a good animated picture without a good story. —Grim Natwick

A story is a sequence of events that involves characters. —John Kricfalusi

A production starts with an idea, but no matter how intriguing the idea is, it is only a jumping-off point. To interest an audience, an idea must be expanded into a series of events that are brought to a satisfying fulfillment.

Since animation is a pictorial art, the story might as well be worked out in visual form by sketching a series of panels—a *storyboard*. Plot and scenes are grappled with and subdued in the process, and a continuity is set in motion as the individual panels are rearranged, redrawn, or discarded. A storyboard's prime purpose is to guide the animator, but it is also an excellent method for presenting a story to anyone who has difficulty visualizing a written script. The storyboard phase should not be avoided; it is time well spent. The weaknesses in a story do not go away but haunt you forever. Simply put, the success of any production is built on the strength of the storyboard.

Storyboards have been compared to comic strips because they are comprised of a series of pictures, but there the comparison ends. A comic strip is an end in itself, while a storyboard is the means to an end. A comic strip is entertaining in itself, the characters voicing their thoughts in overhead balloons, allowing the reader to absorb the ideas, chuckle, and then move on to other parts of the newspaper. A storyboard has a different purpose. It is a tool, a *plan* for a film. Since only what is shown on the screen is defined in the panels of a storyboard, there are no word balloons or lettered descriptions

BREAD, JAM—

SPOON—

SPONGE !

A comic strip is an end in itself.

A storyboard is a tool for making a film.

Woman: "Bread, jam---"
Medium shot of woman bringing in bread and jam to man.

Woman: "Spoon---"
Close-up of woman accidentally flicking jam out of frame.

Woman: "Sponge!"
Medium shot of woman sponging jam off of man's tie.

---

unless they are an intentional part of the screen image. All of the explanatory stuff about who is saying what to whom, the sound effects, and music goes underneath the pictures. When the production is finished, the storyboard is filed or unceremoniously thrown out.

As important as they have become, storyboards have not always been an integral part of animation. In the silent days, a theme for a cartoon was conceived in discussions between the animators and a supervisor before the film was begun. With nothing more than a few ideas, say, on the subject of ice-skating, the artists concocted a series of gags about winter and frozen ponds. This scant preplanning set the story, which was then fleshed out as the animation was being drawn.

There must have been an occasional request for more explicit information, but silent films could make up for inconsistencies with descriptive titles.

If a character appeared in one scene riding a galloping horse and then in the next a hopping kangaroo, the two conflicting images could be interspersed with the statement, "He wanted to get a *jump* on him!" When movies found their voice, such casual attention to plot gave way to precise synchronization of the picture with music and dialogue. It was then that storyboards became a necessity.

At the Walt Disney studio in the late 1920s, such intricate planning took hold through Webb Smith, who saw the practicality in sketching the situations and gags. Soon, the drawings found their way to panels of cork board, measuring four feet by eight feet, to be shunted from room to room, stacked one on another, or conveniently hung on the walls. These were appropriately referred to as "storyboards." Over the years, they were imitated, with variations, by every other studio.

Producers of commercials found it more convenient to print paper pads of storyboard panels that could be used anywhere. Today it is such an important aspect of preproduction that every television commercial or Hollywood special-effects scene is storyboarded.

Storyboards in Use

In the world of commercials, storyboards start at the advertising agency and are plotted by art directors and copywriters. They go through several hands before reaching the animation studio, where they are again readjusted before going into production. Storyboard creation in theatrical studios is also the product of several minds operating in conference. One or two writers take the theme as far as they can, making as many sketches as they think necessary. They then gather with additional storyboard artists, gag writers, the director, and possibly a couple of animators to iron out the rough spots. A group could become discouraged, tossing around disparaging, counterproductive comments. Chuck Jones and his Warner Bros. cohorts avoided this possibility by using a method described in his book, *Chuck Amuck*. Jones preferred a "Yes Session," where only positive suggestions were allowed. This is an excellent rule to follow since a "no" mentality stalls the meeting and cuts off the flow of ideas.

Getting Started

Begin sketching a storyboard as a series of doodles on inexpensive paper. Establish your own panel size and make

Xerox copies of it. Preprinted pads of translucent paper are available at art stores for ease in tracing and are perforated along their edges. The standard panel size reflects the four to three ratio of the traditional movie and video screen, except if you are planning a wide-screen production. In that case the ratio of the panels could vary between five-and-a-half to three or seven to three, depending on the system being used. Until the day when television goes wide-screen, stick to the four-to-three ratio.

Draw storyboards with whatever is handy—anything that makes a mark. Use pencil, ballpoint pens, color markers—it doesn't matter what you prefer, because at this stage it is best to free associate and to get the ideas down fast. How many panels are needed for productions of varying lengths? As the work progresses you will find that you are using about twelve to fifteen panels for a thirty-second commercial; 150 or so for a seven-minute cartoon; about five hundred for a twenty-two minute television program; and three to four times that for a feature running an hour and a half. In actual practice there are many more preliminary sketches made than go into the final storyboard.

Getting Ideas

The conference technique, mentioned earlier, illustrates how one idea generates another, something that occurs even when you are working alone. It's a lot like writing a letter. As soon as the initial sentence is out of the way the rest follows quickly, one thought reminds you of a different experience trailing into another incident, until you have a letter that contains more information than you originally had in mind. Storyboards, as are all creative endeavors, are dependent on this gush of inspiration.

One way to take advantage of this is to list items as they occur to you, filling a sheet of paper with associative thoughts. Put down anything that comes to mind and eventually you'll find the thread that develops into a continuity. Sketch these impressions as they present themselves—get them down any way you can; don't bother erasing, just cross out things you don't want; add written notes and whatever symbols that make sense to you. The result will resemble King Tut's tomb after the grave robbers left, but at least you will have gotten started. Once you have nailed down the overall concept, you have a base for revising, reshaping, and polishing the final story.

Carry a small notebook at all times, so that anything worth recording won't go astray. It is a ready file for your imagination, a repository for thoughts that strike suddenly regarding plots, gags, or solutions to technical problems. Jotting down your thoughts should become a habit when biding time on the bus or in the dentist's waiting room.

All ideas for stories are valid, whether they come from personal experience, an overheard conversation, something you've read, or a notion off the top of your head. The next step is to create interest through continuity and story structure.

Storyboards: Visual Continuity

Concentrate on a series of joined screen units. Total effect overrides sequential elements.
—Sergei Eisenstein

All things are beautiful if you've got them in the right order. —John Grierson

Audience perception of action and scenes depends on continuity. Action occurs in *scenes*, which in animation is any artwork or *setup* placed before the camera. Running time for scenes depends on the tempo of the action.

The planning of continuity in an animation storyboard serves the same purpose as editing in a live-action production, where the cutting and rearranging of shots takes place after days of filming. This reverse situation is an advantage only if all-important details are put in at the storyboard stage and not left to whim or chance after animation has begun. Unresolved story problems have an annoying habit of not going away.

You may be brimming with ideas and may have, as suggested earlier, put them down quickly so as not to lose them, but now they must be arranged and joined in a seamless union from beginning to end. No matter how unusual or fantastic the characters or plot, there should be no confusion about what is happening.

Unexplained changes in a scene or leapfrogging from one situation to another affects the smooth flow of a story. The attempt to create surprise or suspense should not be an excuse to confuse or frustrate an audience with a jumble of poorly linked scenes. Continuity must be preserved.

Continuity begins when a storyboard is drawn. As soon as you start to sketch a series of panels, a flow of action develops. To maintain this flow, scenes and incidents that you like very much, but which disrupt the course of the story, must be cast out.

Transitions

To maintain continuity there are several ways to go from scene to scene. In animation the terms for these transitions are the same as in live-action filming. This include *cuts, fades, dissolves, trucks, zooms,* and *pans.*

■ *Cuts*

A *cut* is the quickest way to go from scene to scene. One scene ends and on the very next frame another scene begins. If the two scenes are to be in the same locale, but shown from a different angle, then all of the details appearing in the initial scene, and still present in the new view, must be identical. This includes the attitude, style, shape, and colors of characters, props, and backgrounds. With the correct information retained in the new scene, the inference is that the action taking place is a continuation of the previous action.

Obvious? Sure, but in animation everything is fabricated, and in the course of creating the enormous amount of necessary artwork accidental variations in character proportions, color patterns, and connecting action between shots appear as glaring errors.

Each story reflects a specific mood, which is maintained by the comparative length of scenes. This serves equally for commercials and music videos made with numerous, seemingly disjointed cuts that build excitement and tension in the space of a few seconds. Here the technique is used primarily to arrest the viewer's attention before they have time to press the remote switch.

  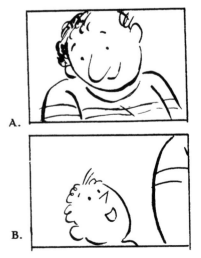

A.   B.   A.

B.

Continuity in Cutting

ABOVE: The direction that elements are facing in a long-shot must be preserved when cutting to a close-up.

RIGHT: The angle of view between characters should be maintained.

■ *Fades and Dissolves*

There are other methods of going from one shot to another. A *fade-in* starts in total black and gradually brings the image up to full exposure. The reverse of this is a *fade-out*, which begins in full exposure and gradually becomes completely black. By overlapping a fade-out with a fade-in, a *cross-dissolve* is created. Since it is a gradual change, lacking the directness of a cut, a cross-dissolve is used to show a passage of time between the shots. Fades and cross-dissolves are also employed to create the illusion of objects or titles appearing or disappearing.

Two other transitional techniques, the *wipe* and the *metamorphosis* change, are done through animation. Wipes take many shapes and are used to indicate one scene breaking away to reveal another. In metamorphosis the elements of a scene evolve into the patterns of the next. Both of these effects, though traditionally filmed with an animation camera, are also done through *optical printing*, *video editing*, or with a *computer*.

■ *Variety*

Variety in continuity is obtained through changes in views of the visual image. In layouts these are referred to as *field changes*, but when indicating them on a storyboard or in a script, the terminology of live-action production applies.

The designations are arbitrary but are easily explained by using a shot of a standing character. A view of the full-figure constitutes a *long shot* (L.S.), from the waist up it is termed a *medium shot* (M.S.), and a view where only the character's head fills the screen is called a

close-up (C.U.). Showing the subject very small on the screen, as if from a distance, is called an *extreme long shot* (E.L.S.), while a tight close-up of the character's face or eyeball are examples of *extreme close-ups* (E.C.U.).

There are no hard and fast rules for using these views in a scene, but there is a basic approach that experience has proven to create effective continuity. An extreme longshot establishes where the action takes place, followed by a long shot to indicate the focal point of the scene, in this case a single character. Then go to a medium shot of the torso or a close-up of the face to see exactly who it is, and then to a close-up or extreme close-up of his eyes for further emphasis. These changes in shots not only indicate direction, but establish mood as well. Cuts are direct and intensify the action, while slow dissolves make the change of shot seem leisurely and languid.

■ *Zooms and Trucks*

Zoom and *truck* are different terms for indicating moves toward or away from a portion of the screen. A truck gets its name from the live-action practice of

The Reveal

A camera shift reveals surprise elements that affect the story.

LEFT: The climber arrives majestically at the summit.

RIGHT: A similar camera move presents an alternate reason for the climber's frantic actions.

putting a camera on wheels to physically move it through a scene. An animation camera physically moves up or down to create field changes, but a zoom is a reference to lenses that create the same effect by adjusting their optical components without a change of camera position.

■ The Reveal

A *reveal* is a simple transition through which various situations are created. A typical gag sequence shows a medium shot of a character scrambling up the face of a mountain, but then a quick truck to a long shot reveals that he is being pursued by a huge lumbering bear. In contrast, a sense of grandeur is suggested by showing the same climber again in a medium shot but this time arriving at the summit. Followed by a slow truck out, the reveal shows the full majesty of the scenery and the boldness of his accomplishment.

■ Pans

Like the zoom and the truck, a *panoramic (pan)* shot helps build continuity and establishes direction and mood. A pan is made by sliding the artwork under the camera, in contrast to live-action where it is the camera that performs the move.

A *slow pan* describes a leisurely view and emphasizes the expanse, bulk, height, and depth of a scene. A very *fast pan* (called a *zip* or *swish pan*) indicates swift travel to another location.

■ Title Pan

When lines of type are panned in to the center of the screen it is important to

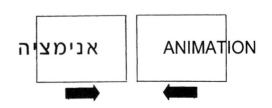

use a direction that is easily read. For languages that read from left to right, the words should pan from right to left. Reverse the direction for languages that read from right to left.

Costumes and Props

Costume details reinforce time and place, but consistency is important to give the audience clues about what is intended. If all of the characters in a film are dressed as ancient Egyptians, then a historical locale is suggested. If a scene is shown in which characters are wearing contemporary clothing surrounded by modern props and then a character enters wearing medieval armor, viewers will make the assumption that this guy is (1) someone on the way to a costume ball, (2) a time traveler, or (3) in the wrong picture.

Color

Color also enhances continuity and should be indicated in a storyboard with this in mind. Any object or character, such as a red hat or a green horse, that recurs throughout a sequence or at strategic points in a film becomes a connecting device linking actions. Colors that change represent shifts of mood or humor, like a character turning blue from the cold.

Sound

Music, voice, and effects create continuities of their own and though they are not chosen until after completion of the storyboard, suggestions for sounds are indicated on the board where necessary. Many directors will admit that the soundtrack is equally important to the visuals, and in some cases more so. A single narrative voice running through a production ties disconnected sequences together. Similarly, a sound effect or a musical signature accents screen action while repetition of a melody, in various moods, acts as a connecting motif. Off-screen sounds are used to tell a story of their own and to eliminate unnecessary animation.

Working from a Prepared Script

Productions made for clients and sponsors start out as typed pages. When creating a storyboard from a completed script, you will need research materials to fill in details on the subject. If the script is for advertisers, then they should supply you with pertinent information, technical specifications, photos, or diagrams to aid in making the visuals.

Scripts generally require editing. Be alert for statements that destroy continuity and narrative flow. Here is a typical example:

> Bart is working with handtools, and he's using the handle of a screwdriver in place of a hammer, to hit a nail. This is wrong.

Why describe what is being shown? The narration should amplify the meaning of what the character is doing, such as:

Using the wrong tool in place of the one intended for the job is bad practice.

On screen it is easier to reveal events chronologically, rather than to go back and forth as can be done with the written word in a book or pamphlet. An example is this statement, which suggests that something that once existed has disappeared:

> The hill was bleak now that the stately mansion had crumbled to the ground.

The sequence is easier to comprehend if the mansion is shown before the vacant, bleak hill. Start with the mansion in full splendor and then, through a dissolve, reveal the contrasting appearance of the empty hill.

The following is from the opening lines of Rudyard Kipling's *Jungle Book*:

> It was seven o'clock of a very warm evening in the Seeonee Hills when Father Wolf woke. . . , scratched himself, yawned, and spread out his paws one after the other to get rid of the sleepy feeling in their tips.

This opening tells us where the action is taking place and the time of day, and introduces a key character in the action to follow. No words need be changed here, but they are so vivid that they can be dropped and the animation remain faithful to the original without the benefit of narration.

This storyboard illustrates how continuity and plot are developed. A story begins by establishing a locale (panel 2). Characters are introduced (panels 3, 6, 9, and 14) each with a defining personality trait.

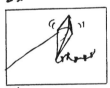

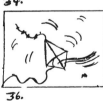

A man with a bike is introduced
(panel 14). Interest and tension are
established between him and the woman.
(panels 16, 17, and 20).

**The kite is introduced and the action
expands our involvement with the key
character.**

**The kite plunges beyond the
woman's reach.** This establishes
the central problem, or *conflict*.

The woman devises a course of action
(panel 50) **and executes it** (panel 52). She
appears to be succeeding (panel 54) but
stumbles (panel 55). This increases tension.

The locale shifts to events taking place just under the tree with the kite (panel 65). Previously established characters are reintroduced (panels 67 and 68). The action then cuts back to the heroine (panel 70). This adds to the suspense.

The woman's predicament gets worse (panel 73). The man with the bicycle re-appears (panel 78).

The heroine explains her problem (panel 88) **and the story approaches its climax.**

Through the combined efforts of the guests, the kite is retrieved, resolving the conflict.

106.

107.

108.

109.

110.

111.

112.

113.

114.

115.

116.

117.

THE END

Tension between the woman and the man is resolved (panel 106). The other characters, their purpose in the story fulfilled, go their separate ways. Essentially the story is over, except for a final touch (panels 113 to 117).

Storyboards: Structure

A good sketch (story) is, well, someone in trouble. It's tragedy dressed up so we can laugh at it. —Sid Caesar

. . . maybe animation ought to be yanked out of art schools and put into drama schools. . . . There are far too many artistic considerations and not enough dramatic or story-structure considerations. —Bob Godfrey

Continuity is about the smooth flow of visuals. Structure deals with cause and effect in the development of a story. It is the plotting of sequences, the framework that establishes the time and place of the action. It includes the conflict, crisis, climax, and, finally, a resolution that brings the events to an end. Many animated productions seemingly avoid the demands of structure. Yet the gags of Tom and Jerry, the sales pitch in commercials, and the whirling images of experimental videos benefit from the precise positioning of scenes.

The strength of a production depends on the use of characters and incidents. In animation the characters and incidents are any possible, or impossible, thing that acquires uniqueness from a little turn of thought, style, design, or expressive action. Intuition is more important in creating storyboards than a tedious list of guidelines, but no storyboard should be considered finished without checking its structure.

Conflict

It is not enough that a tale be of a magic kingdom where people fly and flowers sing; there has to be something to make it go as a story. The characters must confront adversity, conflict, a disturbance, or a predicament. These trials must be so important to the characters that the events gain the audience's concern. The main thrust of a story can usually be expressed in one or two sentences. Here are examples of simple plotlines from familiar animated productions:

1. A coyote in his efforts to catch a swift roadrunner is consistently defeated by his own incompetence.
2. A wooden puppet, naive and immature, hopes to become a real boy, but is confronted by a series of trials.
3. A compact, spinach-eating sailor duels with an overbearing opponent in competition for the woman he loves.

Once the premise is set, the forming and shaping of the plot begins. Interrelated ideas are sketched, arranged, and rearranged until the scenes fall into a logical pattern, each event advancing the plot. It has always been said that anything can happen in an animated film. Actually, it is in real life that oddities occur. (Flip through any daily newspaper for proof.) Animation is not reality, but a reflection of reality through the use of the imagination. Characters and situations need to be believable and plausible, within the confines of their world, no matter how distorted or abstract the action.

Conflict and the Key Scene

As the characters are introduced, so is the conflict. This occurs in a sequence that emphasizes the focus of the story. It is the action from which everything else in the film evolves. In *Boop-Beep* (1983), set in a small fishing village where events occur between the intermittent beam of the local lighthouse, each of the principle characters is introduced doing something typical of his or her personality. These traits take on meaning as the characters' motives intertwine. Their actions reach a climax and finally a resolution that satisfies the substance of the story.

In *Dumbo*, the key moment occurs when the stork delivers the baby elephant to the expectant mother and it is discovered that he has unusually large ears. The other elephants deride him for being different, but his mother caresses him lovingly, establishing empathy for Dumbo and disdain for all those who see him as ridiculous. Once this information is solidly in place, the audience's sympathy for the baby elephant is heightened before the body of the story unfolds.

Character Interaction

Through the interaction of characters, *conflict* and *confrontation* occur. This becomes the substance of the story, the overriding theme. How the characters are affected by the conflict or incidents and their reactions becomes the driving force and the bulk of the story.

Stories are about characters who actively move forward. They have goals, ideals, and desires. It's important to state early in the story what these desires are. Let it be known what they yearn for. This sets their personalities and reinforces the conflict. Wile E. Coyote wants to catch the Roadrunner. Pinocchio hopes to become a real boy. Popeye wants Olive Oyl. Snow White wishes for her prince. And Dumbo seeks approval and his mother's release from shackles.

Simplify the Cast

Avoid unnecessary characters. Individuals that overlap in function should be eliminated. One authority figure stands for all authority figures so that an army sergeant represents a father, a mother, a teacher, or a police officer. Similarly, one irate citizen serves as a representative of thousands of irate citizens and one extraterrestrial suggests an entire planet of similar beings.

Believability

Believability and reality are not the same thing. Our everyday experience is real. When we accidentally cut a finger we feel the pain. A character, drawn in ink, implies cartoon pain, but we must be made to understand the character's discomfort. We know that he is not real, but his reactions are necessary in making the story believable and the reactions must be consistent with the nature of the story. If in a zany cartoon a character is flattened by a steamroller and then walks off accordion fashion, this is acceptable because it is in agreement with the overall wacky style of such a production. In a film in which the ani-

mation is more restrained, the characters reflect a closer approximation of actual people, and being run over by a steamroller could be considered life threatening, the flattening, and resulting accordion effect, would be inconsistent and destroy the film's believability.

Story Structure

A story that holds our attention has a beginning, middle, and end. Animators' concern for this basic structure should take precedence over glossy technique and jazzy screen effects. It is this underpinning that supports everything else in the production.

■ Beginnings

The opening scenes are where story points are established. The locale is shown and the timeframe set. A view of a farmhouse, a row of skyscrapers, the tower of a castle or an extreme close-up of an eye are all indications of specific places. Costumes and props serve to indicate historical periods, while snow on the ground, a field of flowers, a starry sky, or the pages of a calendar indicate seasons or times of day. Many of these, worked over since the early days of filmmaking, are considered corny in live-action productions, but in animation they are graphic and still effective.

■ Prologue

Some films begin with a prologue that shows what has occurred before the events to be seen. The prologue is also used to establish the story's major themes. Fairytales are likely to begin with explanations of how a character was put under a magic spell, or a cartoon might be introduced showing a character engaged in an activity that pertains to the main story that will follow. After the prologue, other characters and any new locales must also be established.

■ Foreshadowing

An action that occurs at the beginning of a story is many times a hint of a recurring event. If a character avoids taking a shortcut across a field because there is an angry bull grazing there, this image will resound during the climax of the story when he accidentally dashes across the same field. The initial danger of the bull, having been planted in the viewer's mind and then forgotten, is suddenly recalled with all of its evident peril when the bull and the field are shown the second time. Insinuating this seemingly unrelated event at the beginning of the film and then reintroducing it when it is least expected can enhance tension, excitement, or humor.

■ The Middle

A plot develops as one event leads to another. As actions follow in sequence, the intensity increases until a turning point or climax is reached. If the events are insufficiently motivated, then concern for the characters is undermined and audiences fail to develop empathy with them.

As each episode is revealed, it should cause concern in the viewer for the plight of the characters and create suspense about what will happen next. Scenes that do not hook up or do not relate to the overall action destroy the flow of the plot, making it disjointed and confused. The action in the 1940s' *Tom and Jerry* shorts, and in the later *Roadrunner and Coyote* films, develops out of a simple premise from which a series of gag situations follows. The shorts retain a unity in style and locale. The events never deviate from their established structure. When this becomes formula—each episode a mirror of the last—audience interest wanes.

■ Climax

The climax represents a crucial moment for the characters and is the pinnacle of tension in the plot. The preceding scenes have been building to this moment and it is during the climactic scene that the conflict reaches its peak. The climax in *Dumbo*, for example, occurs when he actually flies. In *Beauty and the Beast* the crucial moment occurs when Belle realizes her love for the Beast. The climax must be visual and not merely a thought in a character's mind. In *Pinocchio* the climax, following the escape from the whale's belly, shows Pinocchio lying face down in water and apparently dead. In the climactic scene in *Mr. Bug Goes to Town*, Hoppity and the bug colony arrive at the top of the skyscraper and fail to find the promised penthouse garden. As the hero or heroine's plight is brought into focus, the path is opened to a resolution. Dumbo's flying capability restores the circus community's trust in him as well as the release of his mother from leg irons. Pinocchio's selfless act of rescue is rewarded by new life as a real boy, and Belle's love brings about the freeing of the Beast from the magic spell. With the climax secure, the story can move toward a conclusion.

■ *Endings*

The conclusion of any story, whether happy, sad, expected, or unexpected, must satisfy the demands of the plot. Endings have their own logic. The final scenes of a story fit the events established earlier. If the story of Hamlet is being told, the ending will be tragic. If you are animating a spoof of Shakespeare's play, the ending will be full of humorous surprises. Dreamy endings may be satisfying in fairytales where everybody lives happily ever after, but while a storyboard about a character who runs off to a tropic isle for a vacation and enjoys it so much that she decides never to return may satisfy the filmmaker, such an ending is a cop out. Even in a cartoon, a vacation represents a short reprise from everyday toil. Characters should learn something at the end, or find a solution to what was suggested earlier. It is more believable to have the character resist returning but finally come home, wiser and better equipped to accept responsibility.

When a story concludes with the principle character going off into some fantasyland where there is no work, care, or woe, it must first be established that the character has been deprived of the good things in life and is deserving of paradise. Hans Christian Andersen's *The Little Match Girl* is an example of this, ending with the death of the child main character and her ascent to heaven.

Funny endings, to be effective, require previously established information.

Something established at the start of a story must be resolved by the end. In this example a girl's desire for a doll can be concluded in various ways: **(A)** receiving the doll; **(B)** giving the doll to someone else; or **(C)** deciding that she no longer needs the doll.

If a heroic knight has won the hand of a princess and he takes her home to his castle and the drawbridge caves under them as they cross the threshold, the gag gains emphasis only if it has been established earlier that the castle is run-down. Or, if at the opening of the same story the knight absent-mindedly forgets to turn off the water in his bathtub, this bit of information is recalled, at the end, when the couple arrive at the castle to find the furniture floating near the ceiling.

If your character dies at the end, you will have to establish this possibility earlier through the mood of the story or through indications in the character's nature. If the individual has committed terrible crimes, the death will be accepted as retribution. If it is a sympathetic character, then you should prepare the audience for this tragic eventuality and give the viewer something to hang on to, as in Frederick Back's *The Man Who Planted Trees*, in which the character's thoughts and deeds remain in memory after he is gone.

If you have trouble deciding on an ending, review the storyboard several times; the clues to the final scenes are there. Just as two plus two equals four, the characters and events that you have created will add up to the ending. Finally, except for a short finishing touch—an epilogue, additional gag, or visual accent—the story is over, *fini*, "the end." Anything more is unnecessary and extraneous.

■ A Final Touch

A final note about endings. There are usually two of them in any story. One is the windup of the crucial point of the plot. The second is a topper that indicates that life goes on. For instance, in the film *Gerald McBoing-Boing* the small hero, annoying to others because of his proclivity for making strange noises, uses his talent to succeed as a radio performer. His achievement is given reinforcement by an additional scene showing him in a chauffeured limousine passing a crowd of adoring fans. In many cartoons the topper is merely a reaction by one of the characters, like a frustrated roll of the eyes that says "here we go again," an embarrassed smile that indicates, "I was only kidding," or the throwing up of hands in an "Oh, Lord!" gesture.

Snow White and the Seven Dwarfs ends when Prince Charming awakens Snow White and lifts her from her glass coffin. All details of plot have been resolved, but a scene of the two lovers going off to the shining castle in the sky, followed by a shot of a closing book, frames the end of the film. In *Boop-Beep*, the plot winds down when a miser and an old woman discover that they've taken home the wrong sacks. The woman has the miser's gold and the old skinflint has just a fish. The "final touch" ending that puts a cap on this has him marrying her, essentially for *his* money.

Narration

Some stories work best with a narrator *filling in* important points of the action. As indicated earlier, narration that explains what is already being shown on the screen is unnecessary and boring. Let the animation advance the plot.

It is redundant to show a character

pouring a pot of tea, while a narrator states, "Harvey poured himself some tea." Much better to lead into an action with, "Harvey had a lot of things on his mind," giving the audience information that is not visually evident and then accenting it with animation of Harvey absent-mindedly pouring hot water into his shoe.

Comic narration, though hilarious in print, should not be depended on to carry the weight of a picture. Since pantomime expresses so much more, spoken humor is best used for establishing character. An example is to imagine a tennis match described by separate narrators reflecting different attitudes, such as gruff, sleepy, stuffy, or maniacal.

In other instances a narrative line enhances the visuals and adds something to the story that pictures cannot do by themselves. This includes the most famous line of all, "Once upon a time." Whether spoken or shown as a title, it carries sufficient weight to guarantee that it will be a necessary part of animation scripting forever. Other examples are simply clever tag lines that bring a story to a pleasant close. One such example is Dr. Seuss's comment at the end of *The Five Hundred Hats of Bartholomew Cubbins*: "Nobody knew why it had happened. It just happened to happen and wasn't very likely to happen again." Or the last line in *Madeline* by Ludwig Bemelmans: "And she turned out the light and closed the door and that's all there is, there isn't any more."

Narration creates a sense of a third person distancing the viewer from the interplay of characters. An inspired narrator can reduce this gap by creating the right note of warmth, authority, or suspense, but audiences get closer to the events through characters who speak their own lines.

Dialogue

Animation dialogue is most effective when it is sparse. Avoid long speeches and eliminate lengthy, explanatory sentences. Keep all dialogue concise and see that the words reflect the personalities of the individual characters. To do this, it is not necessary to depend on regional accents but statements that reveal uniqueness. There's the rough and tough cowboy who remarks, "I wear a five-gallon hat because a ten-gallon hat gives me headaches." Or the witch who explains, "Can't go riding tonight, 'cause I just washed my broom and I can't do a thing with it."

Cut the dialogue mercilessly. Don't fall in love with clever nuances that distract from the story. When possible, avoid stating important information in single-word exclamations that go by so fast they are lost or muffled. Instead of just "Turn!" try "Let's turn," "Please turn," or "Turn, turn, turn!"

In answer to a direct question, a character needn't respond verbally. Let the answer be shown in a facial or bodily expression. Keeping speech at a minimum gives a production an international quality; it can be shown anywhere on the globe. Years of television dialogue have distorted the fact that animation is primarily a visual medium. The feature *Bambi* contained only eighty-three lines of dialogue, and the star of *Dumbo* didn't speak at all.

A Different Mood

Stories stir the soup of conflict and turmoil, but other moods are worth building a fire under. There are subtle experiences, normally expressed by poetry, which create their own specific problems in the melding of sound and picture.

When animation and orchestrations are brought together, as in *Fantasia* or in a music video, are the pictures illustrating the music or are the rhythms accenting the visuals? Music without benefit of pictures feeds the listener's imagination, but when an artist's vision is interposed, the animation must improve the total effect to insure that adding visuals to Mozart or Madonna is worth the effort. Animation is not about showing pretty pictures; it's about telling stories with movement. The ideal approach is to create unique sounds to work in tandem with the animation, as when a chef adds spices to the pot.

Gags

> *I was beginning to think of comedy in a structural sense . . . its architectural form. Each sequence implied the next sequence. . . .* —Charles Chaplin

Humor in animation is derived from the timing of actions, distortion of shape, the changing of colors, unusual situations, and clever dialogue and narration. The early silent cartoons served up gags one after the other with little thought to continuity or structure. There was time to fill and everything went into the reel just to get it done. If a gag didn't fit the story, it still went in. Once synchronized dialogue and sound effects were possible, gags became integral to the personalities of the characters. By editing out actions that were funny but didn't add to the plot, the cartoons developed more substance. Compare any of the early-1930s animated shorts with those of just a few years later and notice the shift in staging and use of gags. Characters in the later short subjects, such as Mickey Mouse, Donald Duck, and Bugs Bunny, achieved popularity precisely because of the emphasis on personality-based gags integrated with sound and picture.

It is preferable that gags get sketched in as the story develops rather than injected after the plot has been roughed out. Animation humor is best when it is visual and the gags play off the individual traits of the characters. The more that gags fit the nature of the story and the less they appear as if they have been just thrown in, the better they are. To get the most out of a gag, take it to its widest possibilities. Let your imagination soar and stretch it beyond the normal limits. No matter how far-fetched the thought, get it down on paper. Sort through your ideas and find the ones that best develop the gag.

■ Gag Structure

Any attempt to explain what makes something funny or why people laugh at one thing and not at another is a futile exercise. Trying to explain humor is as useless as trying to crack an egg with a feather, but in animation a feather is

A Gag Can Take Many Directions

In this example a character unwittingly causes the destruction of a shelf full of cups. Three possible resolutions are shown.

He nonchalantly replaces the remaining cup.

He smashes the cup.

He hides it in his pocket.

quite capable of cracking an egg. In the creation of gags, some approaches work and some don't.

There must be a *setup*, which establishes the situation, then a *climax*, when something important happens, a *payoff*, and a *reaction* that caps the ending. These are affected by *timing*, the duration of each phase and the lag between them. Pauses create *suspense* and are as effective as action. Timing changes the nature of *surprise* and the *unexpected*—elements that are funny in one case and scary and frightening in another.

■ *Example*

Setup: A vase is shown in constant danger of breaking as it is alternately transported by skiers down a treacherous slope, across a desert on the swaying back of a camel, aboard a ship tossed by huge waves, in a truck over a corrugated road, and finally to its place on the shelf. Nothing happens for a time.

Light payoff: It suddenly shatters into a thousand pieces.

Heavy payoff: The vase slowly dissolves off, revealing a pulsating human heart.

■ The Banana Peel

Examine the structural elements in the stock situation of a character slipping on a banana peel:

Setup: A character, at the far left of the screen, locks a door then turns and walks toward the right of the screen, unaware that he is approaching a banana peel.

Suspense: He walks past the banana peel without noticing it.

Indirection: He stops, runs his hands through his pockets in search of something that he has obviously forgotten, then turns and heads back.

Climax: This time he steps on the banana peel and slips.

Payoff: He falls.

Reaction: The character tosses the offending banana peel out of the scene, slams it to the ground, or reacts in any manner that fits his personality.

■ Timing

Contrast in time is another factor of humor. It becomes important whether the character walks along briskly, slips on a banana peel, flies up and descends in *extreme* slow motion, or if strolling sleepily, he connects with the banana peel and hits the ground fast and hard. In each case the contrast in timing between the start of the action and the final movements heightens tension and accentuates surprise.

■ Study the Works of Others

It's okay to be enamored of the comic styles of different animators (such as the broad takes of Tex Avery or the comic twists of Bill Plympton), but these trademarks are theirs and are easily spotted as such by viewers. Learn from them, but seek your own direction in creating humor.

■ Building Gags

Here is a short sequence using gags that develop out of the structure of the plot. Imagine a character dressed in a new white suit. He stands before a mirror in his room looking pleased and proud. He then strolls out the front door and into the street where a small child is slurping a chocolate ice cream cone. He moves carefully around the kid, avoiding contact with the ice cream. Then he passes a man fixing his car at the curb. The man absently reaches for a cloth to wipe his greasy hands, causing our protagonist, in the white suit, to step deftly aside. Having succeeded in this, he then stands near the curb wiping his forehead in relief. Suddenly a garbage truck careens past, splashing him with a gush of muddy water from a curbside puddle. His once neat suit is now a mess. How he expresses annoyance depends on the personality that has been established. How should this particular character, in this particular place and situation, react?

This incident can be expanded by the inclusion of additional incidents before the arrival of the truck to heighten tension. But this is only a gag sequence and not a story. To make a complete story out of this idea it needs further development. The character could find out where the truck driver lives and do the same to him. How this comes about and what results from this action becomes the basis of the story.

Stories for the Marketplace

Animation story making encompasses more than the worlds of Bugs Bunny, Bart Simpson, or *Finding Nemo*. There is always a demand for videos that focus on the fields of business, advertising, health, and education. Productions for such diverse topics are the mainstay of many small studios, and animators should be alert to the needs of continuity and story for these themes.

■ *Scientific Productions*

Storyboards explaining scientific and medical information should be made as interesting as possible without distorting the facts. Most such storyboards use stylistic symbols to represent complicated elements or those that are invisible to the naked eye. The rule that applies to most storyboards definitely applies here—keep it simple! Keep your designs spare and well defined and avoid a clumsy pastiche of confusing graphics. You don't have to have a doctorate to do scientific storyboards, but it does help to have a small library of related books and articles to keep up on what's happening in the scientific world. Collect magazines that contain illustrations of

other artists' visual solutions; they are very helpful at two o'clock in the morning when you are hung up in depicting an amoebae. This casual research will help you to understand what the specialists are talking about when you go to a preproduction meeting. Knowing just a few scientific terms will give you a sense of what area they are discussing, whether they are out in space among the galaxies, inside the body in a tangle of capillaries, or down among the nuclei of atoms.

■ *Features*

In a feature, the characters and the plot must be welded very solidly, for, if at any time these entities sag, the audience will become bored and inattentive. A feature demands even more attention to continuity and structure than a brief production. An audience that will suffer through three minutes of haphazard animated storytelling will be less gracious when subjected to one and a half hours of poorly connected scenes. Loading the production with songs will do little to help if they do not support the story.

■ *Television Commercials*

Television commercials are a complex, concise, and serious business. Behind the average animated spot, running thirty seconds and costing several thousand dollars for each second, there are about a hundred people—advertisers, writers, artists, and production crews—who labor to give them an offhand charm. Yet any one of these brief sales pitches, made for the purpose of blatantly interrupting popular television programs, will be met with hostility unless it is fashioned as something comforting and unthreatening. To gain this assurance, advertisers turn to animation as a security blanket.

■ Designing Commercial Storyboards

The brevity of television commercials leaves little room for more than the most important information. The power of spots is in language that avoids verbosity. Effective advertising copy side steps weighty dialogue in favor of active words that encourage the viewer to interact. Music and sound effects back up the visuals and aid recall of the brand name when heard again. It is left up to the storyboard artist to convey the essence of a product announced obtusely as "It's like the scent of discovery" while at the same time emphasizing the slogan. The secret is to reread the copy several times to find action words that define the nature of the product.

You would *expect* animated spots to be excruciatingly funny, and some of them truly are, but most commercials are more likely to strive for a smile rather than a guffaw. Commercials are bright, entertaining, and informative, but yucks and howls are frightening to many advertisers. Too big a laugh could represent disapproval, a condition that no product can withstand. Humor and caricature reveal truths, and truth is cleverly fudged in commercials. Telling an audience that a product is "in a new green box" is true, but doesn't say what the product does or whether it does it very well.

Most commercials strike the major note at the very start: "My floors are so dingy"; "Where's the fun in being a teen?"; "I like the new smell"; or "Now you can laugh at hair loss." These slogans are your key to the nature of the commercial, the statement from which all of the visuals flow.

Storyboards . . . Presentation Techniques

■ Size

Rough storyboards are fine for most production purposes, but finished boards define the style and overall look of a production, and are a must when presenting ideas to clients and sponsors. Since they are shown in offices and conference rooms, they should be designed for viewing at a short distance. This rules out thumbnail storyboards but doesn't mean that the artwork must be the size of a refrigerator. Presentations should be lightweight, compact, and easy to carry. Most storyboards are designed with eight to twelve panels on cards no larger than twenty-by-thirty inches. When there is little time to plan the layout of a presentation, choose the size of the panels according to the length of the story. Clearly, a board with oversized artwork calls for time-consuming, detailed drawings, and too large a presentation becomes awkward and clumsy in handling and shipping.

■ *Materials*

Make preliminary roughs and use pencil, ink, or markers to trace them onto good-quality bond paper or Bristol board. You have the choice of outlining everything and then filling in areas with tone, or you can dispense with outlining and just use flat areas of color. If there is enough tonal separation between the colors, the artwork will have clarity and graphic impact.

Pencils, soft or hard, are excellent for scribbling ideas at the moment they strike you, and are easy to erase and alter. It's the most familiar medium and there is no "stage fright" about using a variety of subtle effects of shading.

In direct contrast to pencil is ink. Permanent, bold, and decisive, it offers tremendous variety in line and texture. Ink used with a pen, brush, or a sharpened stick gives a storyboard a confident look.

Pastels come in a range of subdued to bright colors and are fine for shading. Tones put down emphatically give solid hues, but when smeared with a finger or piece of cotton become airy and misty. Highlights are made by putting lighter colors over darker ones, by rubbing out, or by leaving the white of the paper visible. Spray pastel storyboards with a fixative to avoid smearing, but always do this in a well-ventilated area.

Fast-drying felt markers are the most popular medium for presentations

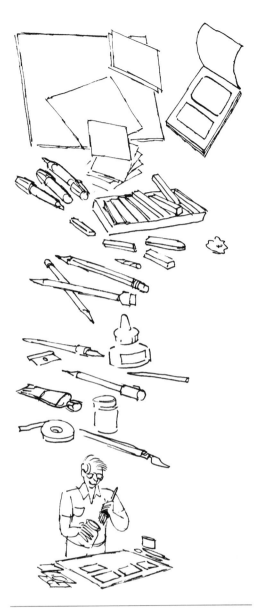

and have become indispensable, considering the many choices of colors in wide, fine, and extra-fine nibs. Most markers have translucent colors allowing for blending by overlaying, but because they are permanent, care must be taken when applying them. There is nothing more exasperating than reaching for a light shade and finding you've accidentally applied a darker one and obliterated a delicate drawing. To prevent this, keep the markers arranged in an organized pattern on your desk.

Some markers bleed through thin paper, marring any artwork that might be underneath. When you trace from a previously drawn panel, sandwich a sheet of disposable storyboard paper or tracing paper between the two drawings to absorb the seeping dyes.

When using markers, watercolors, or inks, always try them out on a scrap sheet before using them on the storyboard. Leaving areas of white paper helps to give the finished work a clear, bright look. Develop subtle tones with watercolors and markers by overlaying separate washes and strokes. Here, too, check effects first on a separate sheet to avoid building up muddy tones that destroy legibility of the artwork.

■ Corrections

Use black ink over areas of marker, and try different white opaque pigments to find which has the best covering ability. Some whites clump, roll off, or become chalky. Others look fine when brushed on, but suddenly the marker color bleeds through. Check them out and if you find one that does the trick, use it and tell other artists about it.

One solution is to adhere scraps of white paper or typewriter correction strips to the artwork. Redraw things you wish to change on scrap paper, then paste them in position on the storyboard panels. When using markers, watercolors, or inks, always try them out on a scrap sheet before using them on the storyboard to avoid building up muddy tones and losing legibility.

■ Backgrounds and Overlays

Ready-made colored and textured papers make good backgrounds for storyboard panels. Buy an assortment of colors in large sheets and cut them up to make many panels. Most papers accept pencil, pen, pastel, or gouache. Light pastel colors or opaque paint on a dark background produces interesting effects. For convenience and variety, make customized color panels by brushing or spraying pigment over large sheets of paper and then cut into individual panels. Use small sponges to make unusual textures.

Attach overlay cels with a thin layer of rubber cement or masking tape. Use thin strips of tape to add neat, uniform lines in white, black, red, or yellow.

■ Rendering

Take advantage of the best of each medium. Use everything at hand: inks, watercolors, markers, and pencil. There are several approaches. One is to start with a watercolor base, ink outlines of figures, then add shading and tonal effects with pencil pastel and marker. Spot in highlights with opaque white or add a touch of airbrush and finish with pressure-sensitive type where needed.

■ Don't Color Every Panel

Fully rendering every panel of a storyboard is rarely necessary. Though a totally rendered board is impressive, it is also confusing and wearying to look at. Avoid overkill, strive to do art that is clear and uncluttered. Color the important panels, those that introduce new elements or ones that have unique pictorial appeal.

An entire storyboard made up of stark black-and-white designs is bold and effective. Add color with markers or by overlaying transparent gels (available from art-supply dealers or theatrical lighting companies). Apply a thin coat of cement and place them over the panels. If a matte is being used, tape the ends of gels so that the tape is tucked under the matte.

■ Time Savers

Save time and effort and make duplicates of storyboard panels in black-and-white or color with Xerox. Use the copying process imaginatively: streak images by moving the original during exposure; use the grainy look of copied photographs as a design motive; experiment by copying small objects as well as your own hand.

Create a style that relates to the subject matter of the final production. Use canceled postage stamps or adapt other related flat materials to create a collage. Use clippings from publications, cigar bands, labels, bits of cloth, thread and string, Band-Aids, rubber stamps, and your own fingerprints in a presentation.

Compose storyboards entirely or in part on a graphics computer. Scan in designs or create them with computer programs. A great advantage is that they can be stored in the computer and called up when needed.

For a production based on existing photographs, make small prints of the shots and use them in the presentation. To add a glossy look to your drawings, copy them with a 35mm still camera, then send the film to the local one-hour-photo processing shop for uniform, standard color prints.

■ Mounting

Framing the panels with die-cut storyboard masks gives the separate panels a uniform look. Art-supply stores carry masks of the same shape and size as pre-printed storyboard pads. Use them in conjunction with matching story panels or as a template to make additional panels.

Tape the sketches, one at a time, to the reverse side of the windows, then check the straightness of each panel from the front. To keep the artwork firm and protected from tearing, back the mask with a same-size black matte board. Adhere the backing with paste, double-faced tape, or strips of black masking tape around the edges.

A less-expensive system is to put individual storyboard panels on sheets of illustration board or foamcore. Use paste instead of rubber cement. Though rubber cement is fast and efficient, it is not a good choice for permanence. Over time the artwork discolors, dries out, and the panels loosen and drop off.

Put narration, spoken dialogue, or descriptions of actions onto self-adhesive labels and position them under each panel. Hand-lettering is fine for short storyboards, but when a lot of wording is called for, use a typewriter or word processor for uniform easy-to-read lines of type.

■ Presenting the Storyboard

When presenting storyboards, be prepared for situations where there are no available walls or bulletin boards to tack them to. Attach the boards together with masking tape to form an accordion fold. This affords easy viewing when placed on a conference table or other firm support. Unfolding it, as the story is revealed, has an added dramatic effect.

For presentation to larger groups, scan storyboard sketches into a computer and paste them into the Microsoft PowerPoint program. Many organizations have the means to project images using the combination of computer and projector. In a darkened room brightly colored drawings are entertaining and strongly suggest the look of the final animated production. This system allows you to jump back and forth to different panels of the storyboard without having to fumble with paper sheets. It is a good idea to call ahead before embarking on this method of presentation to ensure that the meeting room is supplied with projection equipment.

A closer representation of the final film is to make the storyboard into an *animatic*. An animatic is a motion storyboard in which the sketches are scanned or digitized into a computer and shaped into a continuity using software programs like After Effects and Premiere, which can add cuts, fades, dissolves, zooms, pans, and a synchronized soundtrack. Obviously, such preparation is almost as time-consuming as the proposed production, but it is used by advertising agencies to impress clients and to elicit opinions about new products. Copies of the animatic are mailed to others involved in the production.

Presentation boards take many forms in design and execution. Though various methods of preparation have been suggested, there are no hard and fast rules on how finished storyboards must look, except that they should be interesting to view and easy to understand. Keep in mind that you have a wide range of choices in approaching the task and the wonderful opportunity to do something different and innovative each and every time.

OPPOSITE: Storyboards are often needed on short notice.
Here is a way to do good-looking presentations quickly. Prepare small, individual panels using colored pencils, pastels, markers, or inks.

Apply glue to the back of each panel and mount onto sheets of illustration board, foam-board, or black matte board.

You can mount them by eye (see illustration). Place **A** first, then **B**, followed by carefully positioning **C**, **D**, **E**, and **F**. Finish by adding the remaining panels.

Use light, opaque colors over dark areas for sharp contrast.

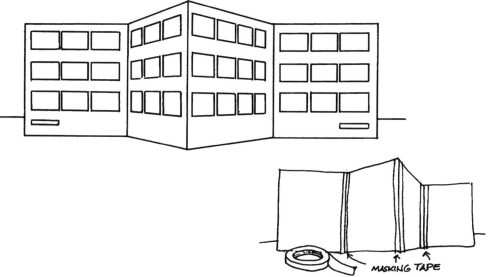

MASKING TAPE

CHAPTER 9

Direction

What I care for, above all, in animation, is the power to master the tempo of thought and emotions in the audience. —Alexandre Alexeieff

The weight of success or failure of a production falls squarely on the director's shoulders. Though surrounded by other capable talents in every phase of production, it is the director who must juggle a surprisingly heavy load of daily problems. When creating your own film, the decisions on story, design, characters, and animation are all yours—you are the director.

What does an animation director do? A director brings a sense of unity to a production and guides the many other talented people involved. Generally, it is the director who keeps the film on track, and keeps the initial theme alive in the minds of the animators. It is the director's point of view and interpretation of the story that becomes the final film. While open to ideas, suggestions, and the insights of others, the director must always take responsibility for the final decisions. Practically, the director oversees the story process and times the scenes, sketches the actions of the characters, and details their every action for the animators.

Unlike live-action filming or stage

production, animation doesn't happen before your eyes. Animators, alone at their desks, develop ideas that have been honed through several meetings and storyboard conferences. They must be given a clear sense of what is expected and made aware of the options available to them. It is the director who brings everything back to center, strengthening the initial idea.

Directing an animated film is similar to forming a lump of clay into an even-sided cube. As each angle is pressed, another curves out of line. With continual attention to each facet, the shape takes on the desired form. If the individual sides are seen as representing *story*, *layout*, *animation*, *camera*, *sound*, and *editing*, then the director's task in fashioning these elements becomes clearer.

A Director's Responsibility

The director is responsible for the substance of the story and strives always to retain the spirit of the original idea. This is necessary whether the work in production is for entertainment, instruction, based on a classic work, or is a brief commercial. The director's concern is always for the essence of the story and the characters being conveyed. The director auditions actors, confers with musicians, and is an active presence at recording sessions. Once the voice and music tracks are analyzed or "broken down" to frame equivalents, the director roughs in actions and indicates these on exposure sheets to guide layout artists and animators.

Communication

A director must communicate ideas and instructions clearly. Words must be chosen thoughtfully. Suggesting to someone that a scene should be handled "loosely" might be interpreted as "sloppily." An animator told to make his work more "stylized" might misconstrue that to mean more "rigid." Be patient, encourage questions, and draw as many explanatory diagrams as needed. Use constructive criticism. Don't tell someone

that his work is no good; instead, explain what it lacks. If an action seems too restricted, suggest ways of making it more supple. Be honest. A director's calm and controlled manner inspires co-workers to enjoy their work and to willingly strive for more exciting results.

Choice of Technique

Directors seek interesting and telling ways to handle the technical and stylistic aspects of their productions. The late John Hubley had an organic style that tightly knit together story, sound, and design. In *The Hat* (1964) in which two soldiers face each other across a boundary, one guard's helmet rolls over the line, and, when he moves to recover it, the other threatens him with his rifle. This absurd situation serves to show how disconnected these two are; a simple act is seen as aggressive. To emphasize this disassociation the characters are designed with separations between parts of their body.

Caroline Leaf is another filmmaker who works in styles that fit the nature of her stories. Leaf eschews the standard methods of large studios and instead chooses techniques that she controls under the camera. In *The Owl That Married a Goose* (1974) she meticulously animated backlighted layers of sand, and in *The Street* (1976), the character's evolving images were lovingly painted on glass.

Normally a director chooses an approach that fits easily into the workings of the studio, using cels or puppets, for instance, because that's what the studio is geared to do. At other times, the nature of the story will suggest techniques best suited to its telling. The following are some of the choices at a director's disposal.

■ *Full Animation*

When characters express themselves in a wide range of emotions, their movements are referred to as *full animation*. The most obvious examples of full animation are to be found in Disney features, where the richness of character acting and the addition of animated atmospheric effects augment the breadth of the medium.

■ *Limited Animation*

Limited animation, also known as *design animation*, is generally seen in educational, health, and business productions, as well as experimental films and children's television. These all take advantage of cycles, pans, holds, and the reuse of drawings in economically planned scenes. The staccato actions of video-arcade games and the constant reliance on lip movements in the *Flintstones*, and similar television shows, are prime examples of limited animation.

■ *"Enough" Animation*

This is a combination of both of the above techniques. Many productions cannot embrace the luxury of full animation, yet the director refuses to bend to the stilted actions of limited animation. To solve the problem, *enough animation* is employed. In this technique an important scene of complicated action is animated fully, but, in the less significant scenes that follow, limited animation is used. In this way the action is planned propor-tionately to meet the budget without jeopardizing story interest.

■ *Animatics and Filmographs*

In the *animatic* technique still photographs and artwork are filmed to simulate movement. Through the manipulation of cuts, dissolves, pans, and zooms, a story is told. Photographs, whether prints or slides, are selected for sharpness and detail and become the basis of a storyboard. The director plots the continuity indicating camera moves and dissolves. The completed storyboard is timed with a stopwatch; an exposure sheet is prepared for the camera operator and the artwork is shot accordingly. As a technique, it is frequently used in conjunction with live-action, as in the Ken Burns's documentary production *The Civil War* (1990).

■ *Cutouts*

Cutouts are used in various ways. Entire productions, requiring few drawings and smaller staffs, are animated with thin, easily cut paper, cardboard, acetate, or aluminum. The most direct method is to position and reposition shapes under the camera for each separate frame. Guides are made to control the paths of action and to serve as a pattern for reshoots. Another approach is to trace the animation drawings onto colored paper and then apply inks and pencil shading. These are carefully cut out and mounted onto cels to match the positions of the drawings. Cutouts have not only been used extensively in independent short films but were the basis of the elaborately conceived feature *Twice Upon a Time* (1983).

Cutouts are not always used flatly but are also animated in relief to cast their own shadows. The paper figures are positioned on a sheet of glass spaced above the tabletop and illuminated for the desired effect. In some instances the cutouts are placed directly on the platen and the lighting is adjusted to throw a shadow onto the artwork below it.

Character animated on paper moves below "background" elements on an overlay cel.

■ Collage

This is another form of cut-paper animation, but one that uses photos, cigar bands, postage stamps, old engravings, etc. The finest examples of this method are the films of Frank and Caroline Mouris. One of these, *Frank Film* (1973), employs elements of magazine advertising to create eye-filling, intermingling images.

■ Drawing on Film

Drawing directly onto clear film bypasses the animation camera completely. Inks, dyes, or markers are applied according to a predetermined pattern of action or merely stroked along the length of the film. Sometimes frame lines are heeded and at other times they are not. The most well-known films using this technique are the works of Len Lye, *A Colour Box* (1935), and Norman McLaren, *Begone Dull Care* (1949) and *Blinkety Blank* (1955).

■ Chalk

This is the earliest drawn animation technique. With chalk, lines are added to, erased, and smeared for a variety of effects. An interesting example, again from Norman McLaren, is his use of colored pastels in *Le Poulet Grise* (1947). The redoubtable McLaren taped a single chalk drawing to a wall and spent several weeks making subtle changes to it, recording most of them with in-camera dissolves.

■ Scratch-Off or Write-On

With this method, signatures, lines, and shapes appear on the screen, as if they were in the process of writing themselves. The complete artwork is prepared on the front of a sheet of glass or cel and is washed or scratched off a frame at a time while the camera shoots in reverse. Removal is done with a wad of cotton or a tortillion, a paper stub used for charcoal renderings. When projected at normal speed the images form as if by their own choosing.

■ Paper

Paper is the handiest material for animation. It is easily found and is inexpensive and comes in a variety of colors. It takes pencil, ink, pastel, watercolor, marker, or crayon. The director has several choices as to how to combine the characters with the backgrounds. The most immediate but time-consuming is to trace the background onto every animation drawing. Though this was how *Gertie the Dinosaur* was done in 1914, it is still used for occasional television commercials and by independent animators who revel in the resulting wavering lines. Another early approach is the *slash system*, in which the character drawings are trimmed so that a simple background appears around them. This differs from cutouts in that the trimmed paper still retains pegholes for registry. The slash method works especially well when the drawings are in stark black and white and are filmed on high-contrast stock. Another way to combine drawings and background is to put the scenery on a cel and place it over the drawings. If it is planned so that the characters don't pass behind any details on the overlay, the impression will be that the cel is in the background. On the other hand, if the artwork cel contains opaque elements intended to conceal, it allows figures to go behind it when necessary. All of these devices were used in the making of the 1920s *Felix the Cat* cartoons.

■ Cels

Cels are the most common professional animation technique, but they are an expensive material and require a sizable number of renderers. Cels offer the most versatile method for combining elements of backgrounds and characters and for introducing various kinds of animation effects. Pencil animation is either hand-traced with ink onto the cels or the drawings are transferred directly by photocopying.

■ Objects

Everyday items that suddenly come to life have a special appeal. Supermarket products, children's toys, buttons, string, block letters, bread, kitchen utensils, and household furnishings can be animated convincingly through stop-motion. Flat objects such as coins, keys, and magnets are easy to light and shoot. Object work in general calls upon knowledge of weight, gravity, elasticity, and other characteristics of materials. Illuminating 3D objects and sets requires an understanding of how light looks in natural surroundings and how to reproduce this appearance on color film.

■ Pixilation

Pixilation, the animating of real people, is an interesting form of stop-motion shooting. Individuals are directed to move through various actions and are filmed a frame at a time. The results have a perky erratic look. Though used primarily for comic effect, the most celebrated film done in this technique, *Neighbors* (1952), by Norman McLaren and Grant Munro, had a serious theme.

■ Clay

Clay is a naturally malleable medium for animation. Though clumsy, brightly colored clay can be made to do interesting things. Some directors, like Will Vinton and Nick Park, have devised impressively pliant characters out of plasticene for commercials, shorts, and full-length features. The advantage of three-dimensional figures is that they can be shot from many angles and reused as they move from background to foreground. Clay has also been used in bas-relief, the details defined by front lighting or, for translucent effects, by back lighting. When used very flat, clay resembles painting. This was employed in Joan Gratz's Oscar-winning short, *Mona Lisa Descending a Staircase* (1992).

■ Sand

Particles of sand, salt, coffee grounds, breadcrumbs, or sugar spread under the camera are accessible materials for stop-motion shooting. Here, too, the lighting can be from above or below. Animation of groupings of larger items such as beans, seeds, and pebbles are also worth considering. This technique was used successfully by Caroline Leaf in *The Owl Who Married a Goose* (1974).

■ Puppets

Puppets are of two kinds, those that are adjusted by moving or twisting their parts and those in which the moving elements are replaced for each shot. There are advantages to each method.

A single articulated figure can be the star of a production, cutting time and expense in fashioning separate models. The work of Ladislav Starevitch is outstanding for this method. In contrast, replacement puppets afford better control of stylized movements, but require the making of hundreds of separate elements. George Pal cartoons are prime examples of replacement puppet animation. Articulated figures and puppets of wood or clay are used by filmmakers not just for children's subjects but as staples in live films where they become King Kong, The Cyclops, Pegasus, or aliens from strange planets. The films of Willis O'Brien and Ray Harryhausen exhibit the high degree of craftsmanship necessary in this area.

■ Pinscreen

Alexandre Alexeieff invented this unusual technique in the early 1930s. It consists of a board containing thousands of small pins. If the board is illuminated from an angle and the pins are slid in and out, shadows will form. When the pins are level with the surface of the board they reflect a full screen of white and when pushed entirely out, over-hanging the board, the shadows form an expanse of black. At the stages in between, the pins form varying tones of gray.

■ Computer

Computer animation is a swiftly expanding area offering directors scores of options. Line drawings are scanned in and colored, or two-dimensional and three-dimensional figures and shapes are created through various computer programs. Evidence of the realism in shading and articulation is demonstrated in the 2002 Pixar production *Monsters, Inc.* In combination with other animation techniques, the variety of computer effects is endless. More important, computers are now involved in every facet of filmmaking, from the recording of sound and the testing of animation drawings to the creation of special effects and the methods of transferring the finished animation to film, video, or disc.

■ *Multimedia*

Video editing has made it possible to combine several techniques into one startling array of images. The director can merge stop-motion, cel animation, and animatics with live footage through optical printing or electronic matting. Colors and shapes are altered, directions on the screen are reversed, actions flopped, and live scenes manipulated to look like animation.

■ *Animation Look-alikes*

Techniques that look like animation but are not recorded a single-frame at a time, are shot with the camera running in *real-time*. These approaches utilize flexible surfaces, such as mirrored cels or sponge rubber. To get the desired effect requires skillful manipulation by one or more operators, twisting and shifting the materials to the rhythms of a soundtrack. Unlike animation, in which synchronization is easily achieved, real-time shooting requires several takes to ensure accuracy in timing.

Art Styles

The style of a production is also the director's decision. The range of elements affected by the style choice is vast, extending from character proportions to the thickness of outlines and to the rendering of backgrounds. Cartoon shorts follow the traditional approach of the Hollywood studios; Saturday morning cartoons ape comic-book art; feature films lend themselves to atmospheric subtleties; and commercials reflect the varied appeal of contemporary illustration and cartoons. The independent filmmaker, freed from these overriding influences, can experiment with style and design a production to match the mood of the story.

Recording

The director is responsible for the auditioning and recording of voices. A wise director uses good actors. In addition to delivering their lines clearly and with variety, the actors must have an understanding of the characters they portray. Their goal should be not only to create funny voices but to express meaning in spoken dialogue. Be aware of actors and comedians who are always "on." Their cute repartee and jokes distract from the business at hand. Not that these people aren't truly funny and wonderful—but that's the problem. They keep you in stitches throughout the recording session, but when you listen to the results in the quiet of your studio, you find that the funny stuff you expected is sadly missing from the track.

The director is there to offer assistance in matters of character, pacing, and expression—but not to teach acting. It is more important for the director to listen during auditions and later at the recording session for contrasts between the voices. Similarity of voices will cause confusion and result in a weak track. Any voice that doesn't match the visual destroys the characterization. Keep your attention on the script reading. If you are easily distracted, listen with your eyes closed. Address anything that doesn't sound as you feel it should— you're the director. If you've gathered

Pacing the Track

Spoken lines are recorded before animation begins, but with scant concern for their definite separation in the actual time sequence.

Once the actor's lines have been selected, the recording is transferred to a digital track, or as shown here, the traditional magnetic coated film stock.

This film has sprocket holes along the edge facilitating its synchronization with animation scenes shot on film with sprocket holes.

It is the director, working with a film or video editor, who paces the dialogue track.

The object is to expand or reduce the spaces between the dialogue lines for the best dramatic or humorous effect.

The director listens to the track and states a preference for a particular section of dialogue. The editor adjusts the spaces between the chosen lines on the track.

The technique often referred to as "slugging the track" is also done electronically by using various computer software.

SCRIPT

SCRAP FOOTAGE

MAG TRACK

MAG TRACK

SPLICER

---

solid professionals about you, they'll know what to do.

■ *Recording Suggestions*

Some directors prefer to keep the recorder going during rehearsals to catch an actor's spontaneous inspiration, since you never know when something special might happen. When recording young children, be prepared to say the lines before hand and have them repeat them.

Since dialogue is not always re-corded in the sequence that it occurs in the script, have an associate check each line as it is spoken. This is a very important job and should be done conscientiously to avoid expensive return trips to the sound studio for lines that were missed.

Bar Sheets

The director plans scenes on printed forms, similar to music sheets, called

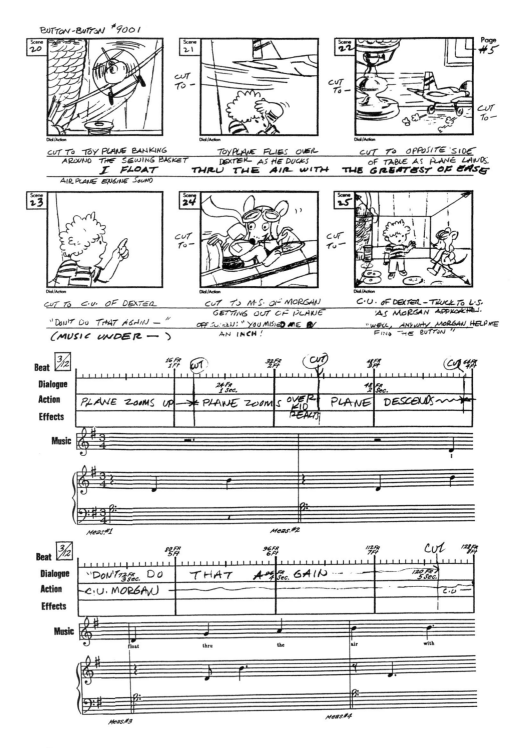

Bar Sheets

Guided by the storyboard (top), the director indicates action and scene lengths in frames and seconds. Staff lines at bottom allow for music scoring.

bar sheets. These aid in establishing the action and music cues over broad segments of the production. The formal pattern of horizontal lines with vertical divisions at convenient intervals represent frames, feet, and seconds. Each long vertical line represents one foot of 35mm film. Screen time is measured in frames and seconds. Since there are twenty-four frames of film for each screen second, the director uses these increments of time to establish a tempo for each sequence. This is done with a stopwatch in one hand while gliding the index finger of the other hand across the individual story panels. The finger moves quickly for fast actions and languorously for slow actions, developing a rhythm that will convey the mood of the story.

For instance: a mouse dashes across the screen, then he comes to a sudden stop and in a few frames, the mouse staggers and falls on his face. Then there is a brief pause before the mouse rights himself and rubs his bruised nose. This action takes just six seconds, 144 frames. The director notes these timing decisions on a bar sheet similar to those used by music composers, except that here the grid is not only spaced for music bars but also for indicating frames.

These directions for character action and scene cuts will eventually be transferred to exposure sheets. Exposure sheets contain not only the necessary indications of key points of the soundtrack, but will eventually be the repository for the numbers of every animation drawing, background, and related camera instruction.

The very short vertical lines along

METRONOME	FRAMES
40	36
45	32
48	30
60 (1 SEC.)	24
72	20
80	18
90	16
120	12
144	10
180	8
240	6

Metronome and Frame Equivalents

To find metronome equivalent, multiply the desired number of frames by a selected metronome number.

If the total equals 1,440 (the amount of film frames in a minute of screen time) then you have selected the correct number.

Example: 80 (metronome number) x 18 (frames) = 1,440 (frames).

the top are individual frames, sixteen of them to the foot. Every eighth frame is indicated with a more pronounced vertical line. Three of these represent one second.

When a prerecorded soundtrack is broken down using a sound reader and a synchronizer, the information is placed on the bar sheets in relation to the numbered frames and feet.

This works well for planning television commercials. For a thirty-second

stop watch

Metronome

WALK TO
THE BEAT—

■ *Tempo*

Beats recur in patterns of two, three, four, six, or more per second. In a group of beats or *measure* of time, the first beat is usually accented. The director chooses a specific set of beats and accents, beginning with a standard march tempo, twelve frames (120 on a metronome), or two steps a second. Since many cartoons are animated before music is added, the director has to imagine changes of tempo that indicate the rhythm of a scene. March tempo is chosen as an average because it reflects not only a walking tempo but serves for other activities like washing dishes or skipping rope. Speeding or slowing the dish washing or the rope skipping means simply quickening or retarding the beat to accommodate varying actions. In the action of the aforementioned mouse, if he were animated without thought to tempo, then each phase of his action might be the same tempo and appear monotonous. By deciding how fast or slow the mouse would move at different points in his action, the director accents the mouse's changing moods and reactions.

■ *Action*

The director separates movement into phases, indicating the exact frames at which action and pauses occur. The footsteps of a walking character are noted with an *X*. If the steps are to be in sync with a predetermined beat, then the *X*s will fall where the beat occurs. If a character is to remove his hat, the director indicates the anticipatory motion of the body dipping with hand poised to grab, then the actual grab fol-

spot (forty-five feet), just three of these sheets are necessary. Many productions require complete musical scoring for recording after the animation is completed. In this case the director plots the tempo of the action as a guide for the animators as well as the composer. To do this, some directors ignore the frame markings at the top of the sheet and use the bottom series of boxes only to represent one second, or twenty-four frames.

lowed by the arm and hat rising above the head, into the follow-through as the hat and hand make a lowering arc, and, finally, the slowing of the figure to a stop with hand and hat at its side.

Tips for Directors

When working with limited budgets and tight deadlines the director must be aware of possible problems and choices.

1. Storyboards don't always originate in the studio. Television commercials and sponsored films are assigned by advertising agencies, government offices, and business corporations, who often prepare their own storyboards. At the start of such an assignment, study the storyboard carefully and ask pertinent questions. Agencies often furnish a tenth-generation copy of a storyboard, which may have dangerous pitfalls lurking among its fuzzy images. Scrutinize each panel several times to make sure you understand the technique or the number of characters involved. Check the length of the spot with a stopwatch as you read the dialogue. In a thirty-second commercial, the dialogue must never overrun the allotted time. If this happens, suggest changes to shorten it. Again, *ask questions!*

2. When calling for the reshooting of unconnected scenes, have the camera operator add a few additional frames at the beginning and end of each scene. The extra frames aid when putting these isolated scenes in sync.

3. When shooting on film where several scenes are connected by dissolves, consider not making the dissolves in the camera. Shoot each scene with additional frames the length of each dissolve and have the scenes combined in optical printing or in video editing. This avoids the necessity of reshooting all of the scenes to correct an error in only one of them.

4. Above all, never lose your sense of humor. What seems an unsolvable problem in the morning will be solved by the close of the day.

CHAPTER 10

Layout: All the World's a Stage

It is Spring, moonless night in the small town, starless and bible-black, the cobblestreets silent. . . . —Dylan Thomas, Under Milk Wood

While storyboards define continuity and plot, they do not supply specific information regarding size relationships and the placement of the components of a scene. This requires full-scale drawings, at the actual size that will be animated, which set the stage for characters and graphic elements. Proper planning smoothes the way for the animator and eliminates unnecessary work.

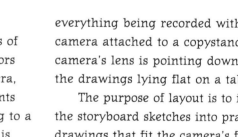

A Quick Overview of Layout

Animation is the least spontaneous of the arts. Though there are animators who work directly under the camera, painting and manipulating pigments and bits of paper without resorting to a prepared scheme, most animation is planned and shaped in a preliminary series of layout drawings.

All of these steps in the animation process lead up to one event: the shoot. Typically, artwork is shot with a film or video camera or scanned into a computer program. For simplicity, think of

everything being recorded with a camera attached to a copystand. The camera's lens is pointing down onto the drawings lying flat on a tabletop.

The purpose of layout is to interpret the storyboard sketches into practical drawings that fit the camera's field of view. The layout artist uses a grid printed on a transparent plastic sheet called a *field guide*, which shows the screen proportion that the camera sees. The camera can move toward or away from this area to create close-ups and long shots, but each view, whether close or distant is of an equal proportion. The artwork can also be physically shifted to create panoramic moves in any direction.

The Frame

The first consideration is the *field size*. The *field* is the frame for the action: it is based on the shape of the aperture in all cameras and projectors, and so it is what the camera "sees." Anything beyond this area is out of view of the lens, though, as a safety measure, experienced layout artists extend artwork beyond the edges of a designated field.

When the movies were invented, any number of shapes could have been chosen for the design of the frame: a circle, a square, a triangle, or even a keyhole. The initial thought may have been to imitate the eight-by-five (1.6:1)* proportion of the *golden section* rectangle, considered aesthetically ideal by the ancient Greeks. Instead, the available area on 35mm was set at four-by-three (1.33:1). It is the proportion still used for television, video, and for 16mm and super-8mm production.

Television introduced a new problem. Transmission reduced the standard frame area approximately 23 percent. Films made before the advent of TV reveal this difference with their annoying lopped-off images. To avoid this, cameras today have a TV-safe area reminder distinctly indicated in the viewfinder. A bigger problem with early television was its popularity, causing film producers to counteract the threat

---

*This is the aspect ratio, found by dividing the width of a rectangle by its height.

of the tiny home screen by widening theater screens.

Wide-Screen Frames

The purpose of the extended view was to create a greater sense of reality, and the names of the wide-screen systems attest to this possibility: Cinerama (2.85:1), Cinemascope (2.35:1), Vistavision (1.66:1), Todd-AO (2.21:1), and Ultra-Panavision (1.25:1 on 65mm). Since these systems demand specialized equipment, most wide-screen films are shot economically within the standard 1.33:1 frame and masked to gain proportions such as 1.66:1, 1.75:1, and 1.85:1.

The Field Guide

To design for the proportions of the film frame, animators use field guides that reflect the aspect ratio of the desired screen size. Most productions require a standard guide, one that is 12 inches wide and 8 11/16 high, but films for the wide screen require guides that are a variation on this.

The width of each field gives it its name; thus a 12 field is twelve inches wide, a 10 field is ten inches wide, and so forth. Fields are also designated in halves and quarters. When extreme accuracy is required, the artwork is placed in front of the camera and the operator projects the actual camera aperture, through the lens, onto it. This is especially necessary when materials not originally intended for shooting are called for, such as storyboard panels, book illustrations, magazine pages, or paintings and photographs.

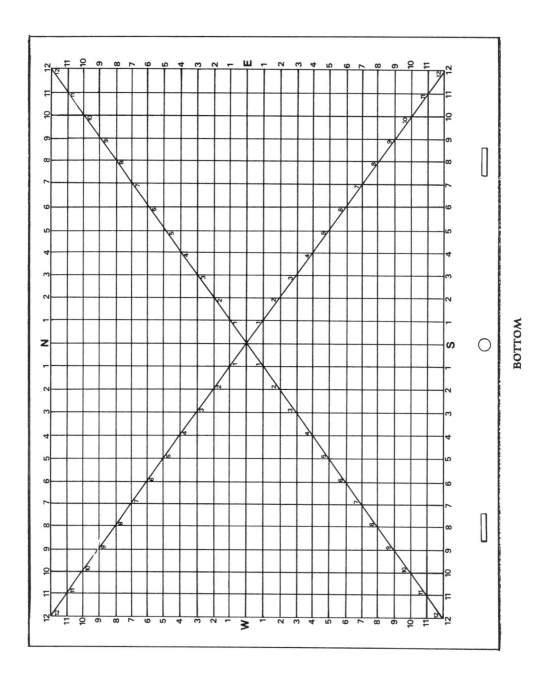

The Field Guide

This is a standard 12-field guide for animation. Its widest area is 12 inches (304.8 mm) across, but this illustration is reduced in size. For use, make an enlarged copy to equal the twelve-inch field proportion.

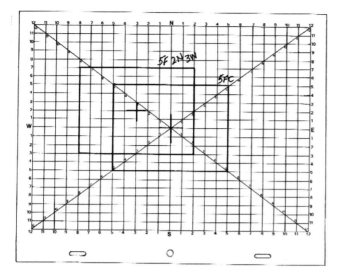

An example of how a center field, in this case a 5 field, and an off-center field, a 5 field, 2 north, and 3 west are indicated.

The same fields as they appear over a scene layout.

Layouts are done using a light board fitted with pegs that match pre-punched holes in animation paper. A field guide is used for the plotting of camera moves toward and away from the artwork as well as across the artwork's surface. The edges of the field guide are defined from our viewpoint. Its top is north, its bottom is south. To our right is east and to our left is west. Its location is determined by where the center cross-mark

falls. For instance, place the field guide on the pegs of your light board and select a field that you feel will accommodate your layout. Put a blank sheet of punched animation paper over it. Trace its contours and include the center crosshair (+). You've just traced a center field. If you traced a 5 field it would be called a 5-field center (written "5 FC"). The guide is like a street map, its overlapping lines akin to the intersecting of

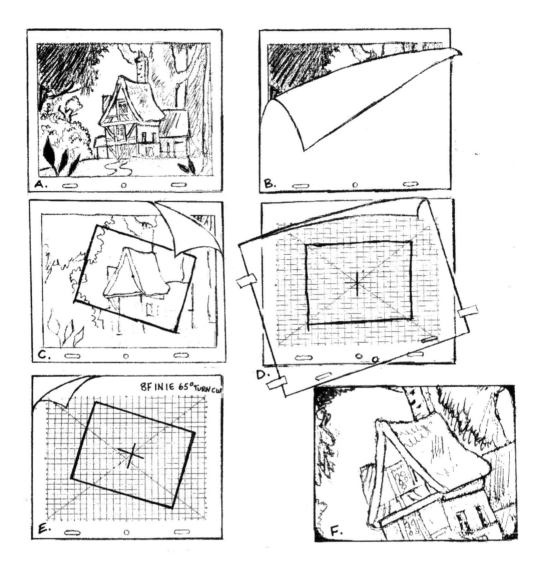

Indicating a Rotated Field

A. Sketch of scene layout on pegs.

B. Place sheet of paper on pegs and over the layout.

C. Make an approximate sketch of your desired rotated field.

D. Center the approximate field over the field chart to find the closest matching field. Secure with tape and make an accurate tracing of the field (this example is an 8 field).

E. Place the accurate drawing on the pegs over the field chart. Label the field. This example is an 8 field, 1 north, 1 east with a 65-degree turn clockwise.

F. This is the field view as it would appear on the screen.

streets and avenues. To find a street corner that is two blocks north and three blocks west of where you are standing you would have to count off each corner to locate your destination on the map. Using the map as an example, count the intersecting points on the field guide to find a 5 field, 2 (intersections) north, and 3 (intersections) west (5F, 2N, 3W).

Fields can also be rotated for various views. To create a rotated field, place your paper sheet over a drawing of your character or background and make a rough sketch of the area you would like to show as a rotated field. Then remove this rough field sketch from the pegs and align it over the field guide. Find the field that approximates your sketch, trace it, and indicate the crosshair. Place the sheet back onto the pegs to see if it is satisfactory. If it is, you can determine the degree of rotation by placing a protractor along the center horizontal line on the field guide.

If you had chosen a 6 field and you found that it was rotated 40 degrees, you would label it as a 6 field with a

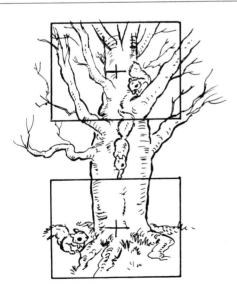

40-degree turn ("6F, 40° turn"). If this sounds too finicky and technical, you can do what many animators do: write the field as a "6-field special." A clearly drawn field so designated will be understood by the camera operator.

Often a field must be positioned with a rotation of 90 degrees for showing movement along a vertical image, such as a tree or a skyscraper. A further indication of direction is *clockwise* or *counterclockwise*, as in an 8-field 90-degree turn, counter-clockwise (8F, 90-degree turn, CCW). These designations ensure that when the artwork is rotated it will be in the correct shooting position and not upside down.

Choosing a Field

A field is selected within an area of the guide that best reflects the action. When laying out a scene don't start with a 12 field but use an 8, 9, or 10 field instead. If you need more area on the 12 field you have nowhere to go, but if you find that the field must be expanded, and you have chosen a 10 field, you can still move to an 11 or 12 field. Starting with an 8, 9, or 10 field also gives you the choice of several smaller field sizes if the action demands it.

A range of views from close-up to long shot is accomplished with one piece of artwork by shooting it at different field sizes. Generally, the smallest area used is between a 3½ and 4 field, since at very close range the slightest imperfections are magnified. Cels reveal visible shadows, scratches, and dust specks, and ink lines appear as wide as the anchor chains of a battleship.

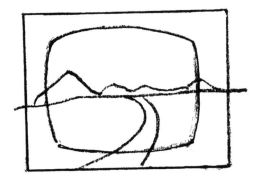

TV Safe Area

All animation finds its way to a television screen or monitor. For this reason, it is necessary to include a TV safe area in your scene designs. To find the proper safety for any field, multiply the field width by 0.77 (see chart). The nearest comfortable whole number is used. For example, an 8 field multiplied by 0.77 equals 6.16, which is then simply adjusted to 6. For a 10 field the safe area becomes an 8 field and for a 6 field the safe area becomes a 4 field, and so on.

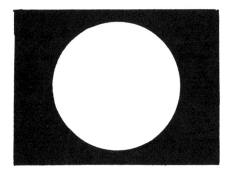

FIELD	SAFETY
3	2½
4	3
5	4
6	4½
7	5
8	6
9	7
10	8
11	8½
12	9

In feature filmmaking larger fields are often used. An example is an 18 field for which the safety area is 13½ field.

Altering the Shape of the Field

Although the contours of the camera and projector aperture cannot be changed, there are creative ways to off-set the rigid limitations of the frame. One obvious way is to reduce the screen area through the use of differently configured masks. A subtler masking is done through natural shapes built into the layout, such as trees, promontory rocks, or architecture. These typical examples direct the audience's attention to what you want to show them.

Designing Scenes

Make thumbnail sketches before attempting the final layouts. This proce-dure aids in weeding out potential prob-lems. Unlike layouts for magazines and newspapers, animation layouts deal with changing compositions. For clarity of action, eliminate all extraneous details and use simple designs to suggest vari-ous moods. Tall vertical lines indicate serenity, extreme angles or jagged lines suggest excitement, agitation, or danger. Shadows reveal the time of day or a hint of mystery. Smooth, round shapes repre-sent warm, friendly, pleasant themes, while distorted images suggest unrest, fear, or disturbing events.

Place prominent elements in the center of the field; in this way there is no confusion about their importance. When a character is offset to one side, the space opposite it indicates that it will either move in that direction or that something will enter into that space.

When laying out an action, you may

START HERE

Plan action at a point where characters and background elements meet. Then work forward or back from there.

have to start at the middle or end of a scene and work backwards and forwards in order to solve all problems. A typical problem is one in which a character walks toward a door, grasps the knob, opens the door, and walks through. This type of information is not carefully developed in the storyboard, but in the layouts it must be made to work: the number of steps taken to arrive at the door; the placement of the doorknob so that it is easily reached; the arc that the door describes as it swings open to avoid hitting any part of the character or anything else in the scene; all are planned precisely.

Start by sketching the character and the doorway to establish relative sizes. Then sketch the action leading back to the character approaching the door and then ahead to where he walks through. Starting at the high point of the action avoids unnecessary re-staging.

A similar situation occurs when a small character has to engage with a larger one. Concentrating on the smaller character may leave insufficient area in the field to show all of the larger one. Draw the bigger figure first.

Character Size

The size of characters and important shapes depends on the requirements of a scene, but when there is a choice, make them large enough for ease of drawing. It is more difficult to draw the in-between positions in tiny drawings. On the other hand, very large drawings require more paint when using cels, longer time in applying the colors, and extended drying periods. Scale creates pictorial problems. An overall view of a dog cannot be shown in the same scene with a tiny flea. To be identified as a flea it requires a close-up, or an action that has the flea leaping from the dog to the forefront of the screen.

The Pose

Characters are blocked in using strong poses, or *keys*, that emphasize the story and the intent of the characters. Here there is no settling for the first sketch, but several drawings are made until a single all-defining drawing results. These key sketches tell the audience what is happening, and tells the animator who will get the scene what to emphasize.

How many character layouts are needed in a scene depends on the nature of the action. A close-up of a hand grabbing an object may need only four layouts: (1) the hand reaching, (2) the fingers spread, (3) the grab, and (4) the hand clutching the object. If the object is a tiny character trying to evade the hand, then more layouts are required as the hand and small figure dart here and there.

Graphics

In designing maps and graphs, include only the elements that match pertinent points in the script and make them as large as possible. On the screen overlapping lines are hard to discern, as when type is placed over roads or rivers.

Picture File

Layouts require the depiction of any number of locales and objects. Knowing how a specific place or thing looks is helpful and comes from hours of sketching indoor and outdoor scenes. Yet even with this experience, photographs, old paintings, and engravings become important as research aids. Create a picture file of places, people, and things to supplement and jog your imagination. Place any accumulated reference material in a folder marked "Scrap." Eventually you can expand this file into additional folders labeled: "People: At Work," "People: Children"; "Animals: Horses," "Animals: Dogs"; "Places: Historic," "Places: Interiors"; "Transportation: Cars," "Transportation: Planes," or any subjects you wish.

PART THREE

The Story Comes to Life

Animation is just doing a lot of simple things . . . one at a time.
—Richard Williams

CHAPTER II

Animation: Moments in Time

. . . have weight in your forms and . . . do whatever you can with
that weight to convey sensation. —Vladimir "Bill" Tytla

All of the foregoing has been necessary preparation for the important task of bringing the story to life. Imparting motion to still drawings brings together a host of skills. These include an aptitude for strong, exaggerated drawing, an understanding of continuity, a distinct sense of timing, and an actor's feel for movement. The animator begins by receiving a scene from the director in a "handout session," in which the director describes the actions to be created. In this session the animator is given the materials related to the scene to be animated. These include a storyboard, character models, layouts, exposure sheets that include a frame-by-frame breakdown of the soundtrack, and a cassette or disc of the track for a close listening of the voices or music for this particular scene. What does the animator do that hasn't been done by the storyboard artist, the layout designer, or the director? The animator deals with the nuances of action, the subtle changes between drawings. A dancing horse, a flying pizza, a visitor from another planet, or a rock-and-roll chorus of skyscrapers are not merely drawings but moments in time expressed through the imagination of the animator.

In a large studio, an animator will do only rough actions and hand these over to another artist to clean up the rough lines and add pertinent details. This is then given to other artists to draw the in-between positions. This procedure allows the animators to put their skills to the best use on other scenes. When working on your own, guess what? Unless you can afford hired help, you have to do it all yourself.

Why Animation Works

Animated movies do not really move but are comprised of a series of still pictures projected at a steady speed to create the illusion of movement. In live-action film, when an image is thrown on a screen we see a recreation of actions that happened in front of a camera. Animation consists of fabricated actions filmed one frame at a time, which, when viewed at a constant speed, give the appearance of motion.

Film runs through a projector at the rate of twenty-four frames a second. It doesn't matter whether these are 8mm, super-8mm, 16mm, or 35mm frames; the size of the film does not change the speed of projection. Since 35mm was the initial animation format, animators find it comfortable to think in terms of 35mm feet and frames no matter which size film is used.

There are 1,440 frames in one minute of screen time. A ten-minute production contains 14,440 frames and an eighty-minute feature eight times that amount, making the animator's job seem daunting. But drawings are rarely made for each and every frame. Instead, various tactics are used to simplify the task. One is to shoot on *twos*, giving each drawing two frames of exposure, so that one minute—1,440 frames—is dramatically cut to 720 drawings. It takes eight frames for an action to register; anything less than that is too fast for comprehension. Things don't have to be moving all the time, but anything held for more than twelve frames appears flat and static.

Cycle actions such as walks, water drops, a swinging pendulum, or a turning wheel are actions that are drawn only once and then repeated, further cutting into the total number of drawings. There are *held* poses in which characters remain still, and these help to lighten the workload as well. Legitimate held positions occur when figures and objects hesitate, come to a stop to stand, lean, sit, or lie still. Then there is the *reuse* of drawings, in which the same action is shot over at a different point. So, in actual practice, one minute of

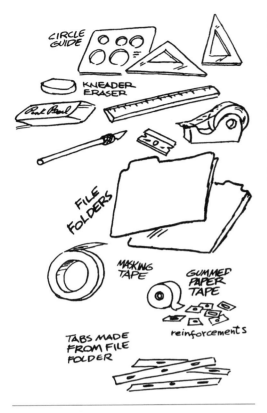

CIRCLE GUIDE

KNEADER ERASER

FILE FOLDERS

MASKING TAPE

GUMMED PAPER TAPE

reinforcements

TABS MADE FROM FILE FOLDER

in appendix E.) It is very white, translucent, and takes pencil, pen, and markers. Any lightweight bond of convenient size, such as loose-leaf paper, serves the same purpose. Bond papers are used in conjunction with a lightboard, but some animators forego this necessity by working on tracing paper. Whatever paper you choose, if you intend to use it for final shooting rather than cels, make sure the sheets are free of spots and creases.

■ Pencils

Anything that will make a line is fine for animation, but most animation is done in pencil, usually medium soft (2B) to soft (4B). Inexpensive number-two pencils work fine but another choice would be standard mechanical lead pencils. A handful of these, loaded with HB, 2B black, red, or blue leads are always ready with an easy twirl of the eraser tip.

For drawings that will be copied to cels by xerography, a pencil with a medium soft (2B, 3B), dense, black lead is necessary. Colored pencils, such as the Col-Erase, work well on paper and

animation on twos, with cycles, holds, and repeats requires many less drawings to fill 1,440 frames.

This changes when animation is shot with video systems. NTSC requires thirty frames per second and PAL twenty-five frames per second. When film is transferred to video, the twenty-four frames are automatically translated into thirty or twenty-five frames per second.

Animation Supplies

■ Paper

Standard animation paper is called "animation bond." It is available through dealers, precut to 10½ by 13½ inches for the industry. (See the "List of Suppliers"

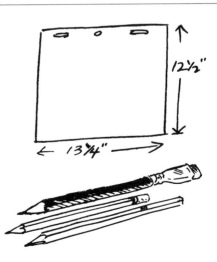

12½"

← 13¾" →

exposure sheets and are erased easily. For sharpening points, get a good electric sharpener, but the old standby of using a razor blade and then honing the point with a sandpaper block works well for defining lines.

■ Erasers

Use both a Pink Pearl and a kneaded eraser for corrections. The first is excellent for totally removing pencil marks and the second for toning down rough lines prior to making *cleanups*. Although they never wear out, you should get several kneaded erasers as they have the annoying characteristic of bouncing silently off into the dark corners under your desk.

■ Adhesive Tapes

Animators use transparent tape for cutting and repairing animation paper, brown masking tape for attaching peg strips to cels, black masking tape (black on both sides) for making opaque mattes, and gummed paper tape for punching peghole reinforcements for animation paper.

■ Miscellaneous

A sharp scissors, a single-edged razor blade, or an X-Acto knife with a handle are used for trimming and cutting paper and cels. For drawing straight lines, use a twelve-inch metal ruler, a forty-five-degree triangle and a ninety-degree triangle.

■ File Folders

You'll be amazed how out-of-hand things can get. A production starts with a batch of sketches that lie snugly on a shelf, but one day you look around and find that drawings, cels, and exposure sheets have multiplied, filling the room. Without a cataloging system, drawings are lost, time is squandered looking for things, and the pile of materials becomes a jumble.

Buy about two-dozen file folders and label them. Each will be for a specific purpose—"Storyboards," "Model Sheets," "Layouts," "Scene 1," "Scene 2," and so on.

■ The Animation Desk

Animators work over a light box consisting of a glass or plastic top illuminated from underneath. The glass fits into a metal disc that swivels for ease of drawing, and the desk is supplemented with storage shelves and drawers placed above or to the side.

■ Desert Island Animation

You can do animation without resorting to expensive equipment. To use the preposterous example of being stranded on a desert island and suddenly getting the desire to make a film, you would have to take advantage of the limited resources at hand. Many individuals and schools are without funds or lacking proper tools to create an animation program. They might as well be on a desert island. Yet with imagination anyone can make serviceable equipment out of everyday items.

A transparent plastic-box picture frame, of the type found in art-supply stores or variety shops, makes an inexpensive light board. Remove the cardboard insert, tilt the box against a table, and rest it on your lap. Place a sheet of white paper on the tabletop,

Items from the local hardware or variety store serve as inexpensive animation equipment. For example, a plastic-box picture frame becomes a convenient light box.

directly *under* the box, and reflect the light of a small desk lamp off of the paper to create sufficient illumination for seeing through four or five sheets of paper. If it isn't bright enough for you, substitute a small fluorescent fixture. When not in use the box becomes a handy storage container and carryall for paper, pencils, and pegbar. If a box frame is unobtainable, a sheet of clear plastic one-eighth- or one-quarter-inch thick can serve as well.

■ Pegbars

Animation drawings, on paper or cels, are held in place on the animator's desk (and also while shooting or scanning) by *pegbars*, upright metal, wood, or plastic pegs set into a strip of similar material that fit punched holes along one edge of the desk. This system of registry is necessary to keep all of the drawings in a relative position to each other so that when Popeye reaches for a can of spinach it will be where it is supposed to be.

Professional pegbars come in two systems, Acme and Oxberry.* Made of metal, they sell for around $30 or $40. (There is a low-cost plastic Acme pegbar available for about $5.) For less, you can fashion a set from wood or bits of

---

*A few studios may still use the U.S. Army Signal Corp system, a holdover from World War II.

aluminum. Wooden dowels, sold at lumber yards and many hardware stores, are cheap, easy to cut, and serve very well when glued onto a thin strip of wood and then taped to your animation board.

The width of the pegs must coincide with the hole made by the punch you are using. Pegs made from quarter-inch dowels make a snug fit for the hole produced by a standard office punch. Sandpaper the pegs lightly until the paper slips over them easily without damaging the punched hole. To eliminate the necessity of buying a punch use standard two- or three-hole unlined loose-leaf paper.

Studios use three-hole registration (paper punched with two holes works just as well), a round center hole between two rectangular ones. Stress on the holes, as the paper is put on and taken off the pegs, is lessened by the small open spaces at the corners of the rectangles.

Mount the pegs on a thin strip of wood, similar to that found at the bottom edge of a window shade. Punch a set of holes in a strip of thin cardboard or cel and place it over the pegs to check for straightness and the distance between each peg.

Starting to Animate

■ *Top Pegs, Bottom Pegs*

Studios originally placed the drawings on two upright pins. The constant threat of impalement on a couple of sharp points no doubt encouraged the positioning of the pins at the top of the desk, a practice that continued when they were replaced with pegs. The Disney studio championed the practice of using bottom pegs because it speeded the shooting of cels, since the operator could slip them in and out under the glass platen that kept the drawings lying flat without raising it to its full height.

Bottom pegs offer an important advantage for the animator. With one hand the animator can grasp the tops of five sheets that are held in alignment by the bottom pegs. While rolling through the sheets with the fingers of one hand, in order to see how well the sequence of pictures works together, the animator can make adjustments with a pencil held in the other hand. There are animators who only use top pegs and others who only use bottom pegs. For a while in the United States these preferences indicated whether an animator came from the East Coast, where animation started on top pegs, or the West Coast, where bottom pegs were synonymous with advances in animation technique. Animators, no matter what their geographic location, must be adept at using either set of pegs.

■ *Exposure Sheets*

You can't just go to the camera with a cardboard box stuffed with cels, cutouts, and backgrounds, and expect anyone to instinctively understand what you want done with it. There has got to be a system, a method for keeping track of drawings and scenes and their shooting sequence. Before sound film, animators scribbled notes on the corners of drawings, but synchronization required precise animation camera instructions. For this reason, ruled forms, variously

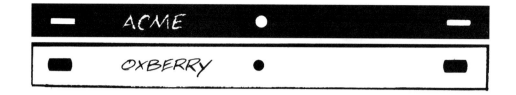

referred to as *dope sheets, exposure sheets,* or simply *X-sheets* were instituted. In an earlier chapter we discussed how the exposure sheets for each scene originate with the director; as we shall see, they are then augmented by the animator.

Look at the blank exposure sheet in the illustration on page 172. Notice that along the top are listed important data such as picture title and number, the section and scene, the total footage, the page number, and the animator's name. All of this information is written in a clearly defined manner.

Each horizontal line indicates one frame of the picture—sixteen to the foot, totaling eighty frames, or five feet of 35mm film to a page. This equals three and a quarter seconds of screen time per page, requiring eighteen of these pages for a total of one minute. Camera operators prefer the easy adding of digits in sheets containing one hundred frames, but the eighty-frame sheets are superior for animating since each sheet has a consistent pattern of heavy lines at every sixteenth frame. These serve as reference points and offer a visual break in the uniform, eye-numbing pattern of lines. The emphasis on 35mm feet is practical whether you are shooting in 16mm, with forty frames to the foot, or super-8mm, with seventy-two frames to the foot. When animating, the frames are the chief concern, not footage.

The right side of the sheet is for prior information. This includes a column for dialogue, narration, and music beats, a second column for the director's instructions, and a column of *frame* or *dial numbers.* Since each horizontal space on the sheets equals one frame, these numbers are simply accounting for this, and are indicated from one to zero, eight times down the length of the page. At the beginning of a scene, consecutive numbers are written at every zero designation to equal multiples of eighty on every page. The accumulative numbering will reach 720 on the ninth sheet (thirty seconds) and 1,440 on the eighteenth (sixty seconds).

The wider center portion of the page shows five or more narrow columns. One column marked "BG" is for the *background.* The others are for listing individual cels and the levels they occupy. Cels, the transparent sheets that contain characters and other elements of the scene, are placed over each other. Together they create the illusion of a single picture. Normally, four cel levels are considered the limit before dust, scratches, shadows, and decreasing density take their toll. Since no one can foresee what situations will arise during production, extra columns are provided on some exposure sheets for additional levels, *cutouts* (CO), and *overlays* (OL). Cels are not perfectly transparent; there is always

| TITLE: | SCENE: | FEET FRAMES | ANIMATOR: | | SHEET # |

TRACK	DIAL	ACTION	4	3	2	1	BG	DIAL	PAN	FLD	CAMERA

Blank Exposure Sheet

There are eighty frames per page. Eighteen sheets equal one minute of screen time.

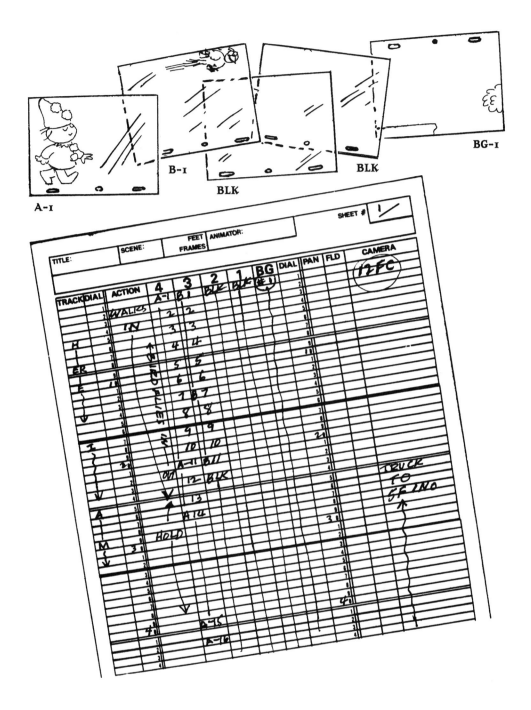

Exposure Sheet

Dialogue is indicated on the far left. The next column to the right, labeled "Action," carries director's notations, and the columns marked "4, 3, 2, 1" are for listing drawings in proper sequence and according to level over background (BG).

All camera instructions (fades, dissolves, trucks, and pans) are written on the far right.

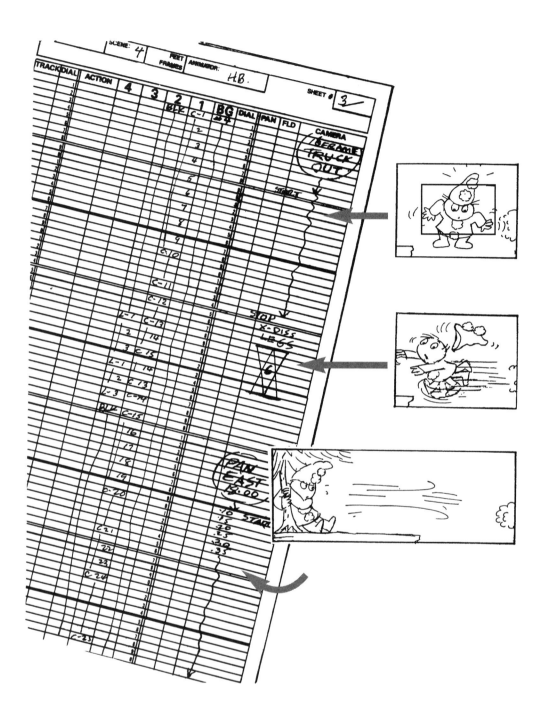

Exposure Sheet (continued)

Camera instructions include: field changes such as a truck from 12 field center to a 6 field, 1 north, a cross-dissolve for a blurred running action, and background pan increments to show the character's action across the background.

a darkening of colors, noticeable when they are placed over each other. For this reason, a *blank cel* (BLK) must be carried as a density balance whenever there is no cel on a specific level. If this is not done, there will be a noticeable flickering and color shift in elements of the scene.

A circle around a number signals an intentionally repeated drawing or drawing numbers purposely out of sequence.

At the right of the exposure sheet, next to a second strip of dial numbers, is a wide column for camera instructions. Even when shooting your own work you will discover that anything not written down results in minutes and hours wasted while trying to recall what was intended. The foremost notation is the field size, without which nothing can be shot. It is a sound practice to write the field, even when it hasn't changed, at the top of every sheet. This avoids lost time in going back page after page to see which field is required.

Other information for this column includes fades, dissolves, pan moves, and numbers pertaining to the manipulation of cutouts. Fades and dissolves are expressed in even numbers of frames (4, 6, 8, 10, 12, 14, 16, 24, 60, 80, 100, 200, and so on). Cutouts are differentiated from cels by indicating them in blue or red pencil. Make indications legible and consistent. One approach is to place a circle around all field numbers, a square to indicate a pan, and a rectangle for a camera or table move. Special instructions should be highlighted in red or blue and those that require complex descriptions are best written or typed on a separate sheet of paper and stapled to the exposure sheet.

To guarantee the proper start of a pan or a truck, draw a line to the exact frame where these begin and write "START" on that frame and "END" on the last frame of the move.

■ *Creative Uses of Exposure Sheets*

Exposure sheets serve practical organizational and time-saving purposes. They are used for plotting the length of a scene as well as the points where action takes place, before any anmation begins. They are also used for doing animation without making drawings. It is not unusual for animators to spend hours and even days working out scenes on exposure sheets and doing little or no new animation. Drawings from other scenes or previous pictures are reused and rearranged to fit a new scene. Cycles are exposed in selected ways, each new timing is worked out by flipping the drawings and noting the different sequences on the sheets, and entire sequences are created with pans and zooms. For instance, one drawing of a background of a row of skyscrapers can serve in many ways. It can be shown as a long shot with a truck in to a close-up of one building, or it can be panned under the camera to create a move across the entire view, and it can be filmed at a dramatic angle to create excitement. Though only one drawing is involved, the various notes on the exposure sheet give it a substantial role.

Here is a way to use the exposure sheets to increase the rainfall in a scene. Animate a cycle of rain with, say, twelve drawings. In column three, write the drawing numbers one through twelve,

TITLE: "CITY" **SCENE:** 12 **FEET** 8 **FRAMES** 0 **ANIMATOR:** Roy **SHEET #** 21

TRACK	DIAL	ACTION	4	3	2	1	BG	DIAL	PAN	FLD	CAMERA
				1			BLK BLK BG-12				8FC
		RAIN		2							
		CYCLE		3							
				4		1					
				5	2						
				6	3	1					
				7	4	2					
				8	5	3					
sound				9	6	4					
				10	7	5					
				11	8	6					
effects				12	9	7					
		(REPEAT)		1	10	8					
				2	11	9					
				3	12	10					
				4	1	11					
				5	2	12					
				6	3	1					
				7	4	2					
				8	5	3					

Creative Uses of Exposure Sheets

Increasing the intensity of rain animation without making extra drawings.

using one drawing for every two frames. Now we are going to reuse the drawings by overlaying them to enhance the total effect. In column two, write "BLK" at the first frame, run a line down to frame six and begin the twelve-drawing rain cycle again. At the start of column one, write "BLK," run a line down to frame ten and add the twelve-drawing cycle here too. The same cels are used on succeeding levels to create a denser rain effect. Since the drawings in the cycles are used on each level *after* they have been shot on a previous level, this is an economical method of making a simple action more interesting.

■ Arcs

All actions are defined in arcs. If you were to twirl a small flashlight in a darkened room you would see the line of an arc as the light darts about. In animation arcs are indicated by lightly sketching paths for whatever is being

animated—a figure, a head, a finger, or a flag. When drawings do not follow the lines of the arc, the resulting movement is jerky and unconvincing. Arcs indicate the direction that an animated shape will follow and should be sketched in at the start of an action to plot the move. Once the drawings are roughed in, the animator checks to see if the drawings match the arcs.

■ Keys and Extremes

In any scene there will be just a few initial drawings, depending on the length of the scene, that indicate the overall movement and story points. These are called *key* drawings and are established by the director, the layout artist, or the animator. No matter where they originate, the key drawings express what the scene is about. At this stage, the action pose takes precedence over small details of style or outline. The animator uses the keys as a starting point and then defines the action further by drawing a series of *extreme* poses. Extremes are the drawings that represent shifts in the action and like the keys are clearly stated. When creating keys and extremes make sure that the characters are uncluttered and strongly silhouetted. No part of an

action should be obscured by other elements in the scene. As you work, flip the drawings frequently and make adjustments as you proceed.

Working with extremes of a movement and then adding necessary in-betweens is called *working from extreme to extreme*. Some actions, however, are best created *straight ahead*. In the straight-ahead method the animator begins with drawing number one and then does those that follow. This method works well for walks, runs, or actions where subtle changes occur on every frame. In practice animators employ both techniques to their best advantage.

■ In-betweens

The animator places a *timing chart* on each extreme along the right edge of the paper. This acts as a guide for the in-betweener, indicating the number of drawings needed and the spacing between each. In-between positions are either directly in the middle or closer to one or the other extremes. To follow these charts, place two extremes on the pegs over the light board with the lower number on the bottom. Over these place a clean sheet of paper. With the under-light on, lightly sketch in the arcs of the

In-betweens

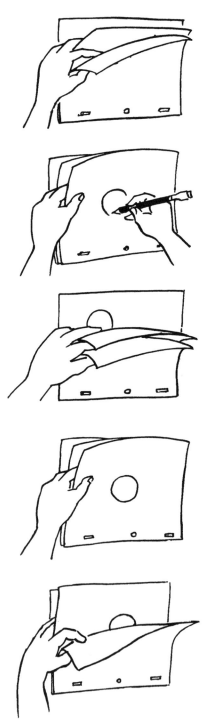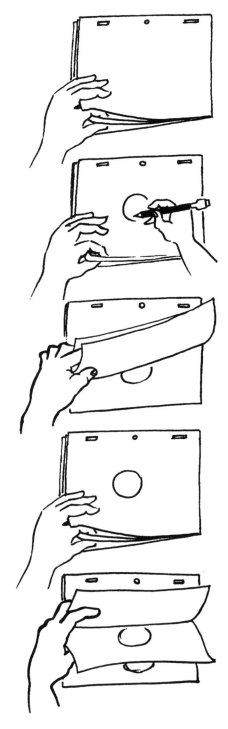

Proper finger positions for flipping in-betweens on bottom pegs.

Finger positions for flipping in-betweens on top pegs.

action, then rough in the basic forms so that they fall in-between the shapes of the two extremes. As you sketch, flip the drawings with the other hand. Work without the underlight at this stage to enhance the solidity of the character. When the rough is completed, rub it with a kneaded eraser to tone it down. It is best to erase with the drawing off the pegs to avoid tearing the pegholes. Also rub the opposite side of the sheet with the eraser to remove pencil impressions from the drawing underneath. Now, clean up the drawing with a definite, dark line. Again, flip the drawings to find drawing errors. To check the accuracy of the in-betweens, and to see if they agree with the timing charts, place them on the pegs in numerical order, including the extremes (usually four to eight drawings). Then, with the underlight on, run the point of a pencil lightly along the prescribed arcs. If some drawn shapes have gone outside of an arc or missed it in some way, correct the drawing. Give special attention to the spacings between each drawing to see if the middles are properly located and if the drawings intended to be closer to an extreme actually are.

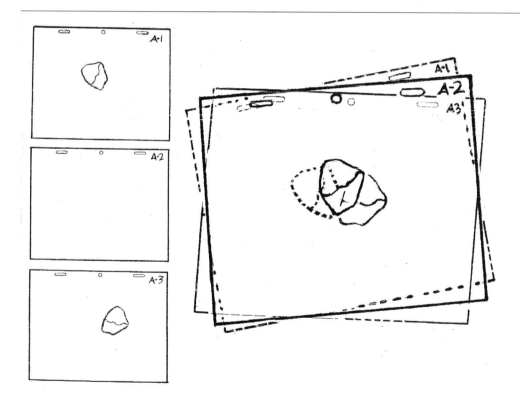

Middling Drawings

A-1 and A-3 are extremes. To make the in-between (A-2), A-1 and A-3 are taken off the pegs and overlapped so that the drawings are closer together. Then blank sheet A-2 is positioned on top of the other drawings so that its corners and pegholes are centered between A-1 and A-3. The in-between A-2 is then drawn in this position.

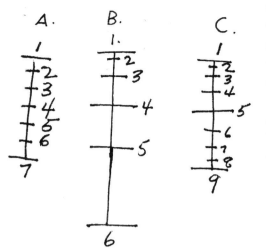

Animator's timing instructions for the in-betweener. (A) is an evenly spaced move, (B) is an accelerated move, and (C) is a move that starts slow, gathers speed, and then slows to a stop.

■ Middling

The above method of drawing in-betweens is the accepted way for working with characters. It allows for creative adjustments of facial expressions and gestures of hands and figures. For rigid shapes, spaced far apart, such as a falling rock, in-betweening is easier to do with a method sometimes referred to as *middling*. This is done by removing the two extremes from the pegs and positioning them over each other on the light board so that the drawings are as

close as possible. Secure the papers with masking tape then tape a clean sheet so that its edges fall between the two extremes and the pegholes are equidistant.

In this way the configurations are easier to in-between. When a set of in-betweens are complete, place them on the pegs and check to see that the arcs and spacing have been maintained.

■ Numbering

Each drawing is given a number, placed in the corner of the paper to the right of the pegholes. The numbers for separate levels of animation require identifying letters, either A, B, C, or D for each level, or B for "boy," G for "girl," C for "cat," D for "dog," and so on. Imagine a camera operator toiling alone, far into the night, holding your drawings up to the camera lights attempting to decipher your numbering. These are not secret code. Make them large and legible on the drawings and on the exposure sheets so that they are easily read.

■ Slow–Out and Slow–In

Actions do not occur at a consistent speed but go through shifts in pacing. An object moving from a static position will start out slowly, the positions close together but becoming proportionately further apart as the speed increases. It then slows gradually to a stopped position. A falling object gathers momentum, reaches a steady speed, and hits the ground without a slow-in. A descending balloon or a leaf is affected by air currents causing it to circle and drift slowly to the ground. An airplane

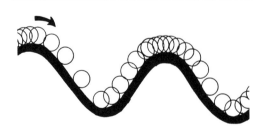

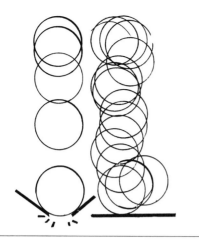

has control over its speed and direction, a quality that at times is injected into cartoon characters to guarantee a soft landing.

■ Objects Have Weight

Credible action in animation is achieved by showing the effects of gravity and balance. Observe athletes and notice how they position themselves before pitching or hitting a ball. They are very aware of their body mass and avoid weak stances. Try this: Draw two identical circles opposite each other and about six inches above a horizontal ground line. Use no shading on the circles to indicate surface texture, but assume one to represent a very heavy object and the other a lightweight balloon. How would the heavy circle descend in comparison to the balloon circle?

■ Squash and Stretch

Animation that is stiff and rigid is tedious to watch. To soften the actions and to gain flexibility, animators *squash* and *stretch* drawings. The degree to which anything is compressed or elongated depends on what it is made of and the speed at which it is traveling. A soft rubber ball would have a natural tendency to flatten when hit forcefully with a tennis racket. It would also change its shape as it increased its speed through the air. In contrast, a ping-pong ball would squash and stretch very little due to its lighter weight and harder consistency. The amount of squashing and stretching of objects and characters depends also on fashions in animation. Examine the full animation of the 1930s and 1940s, when squash and stretch were used extensively, and compare it with 1950s limited-animation examples that reflect less flexibility.

■ Anticipation

In animation simple actions are exaggerated because movement that takes place without a forewarning or buildup is ineffectual and is lost on the screen. In throwing a ball, for instance, an arm goes back before it is thrust forward. The retracting arm sets up the throwing action to follow. This is called

anticipation and it can also be detected in a reaching hand that opens inches away from the object it will pick up or a leaping figure that crouches before it springs into action.

■ *Follow Through*

If anticipation precedes an action, indicating that something is about to take place, there is an equal activity at the completion of a movement to show that something has occurred. One example is the swing of a golfer. The figure anticipates the action by raising the club above one shoulder then bringing it down toward the ball. The *follow through* occurs after the ball is hit and the club continues its motion to a point above the opposite shoulder. This is normal and is found in all activities. In animation follow through is given added emphasis.

■ *Overlapping Action*

Characters are made up of jointed arms and legs and items of clothing. All of these elements move at different rates of speed, and animation that fails to show this looks dull and static. When a cartoon rabbit turns, his ears follow slightly behind the head action and his coat continues on past his body movement before coming to rest.

■ *Emphasis*

To insure that an action is seen, it must be highlighted, or emphasized. To do this, animate an object past its apparent destination and then bring it back to that spot. This is used for a sharply pointing index finger or another familiar form of cartoon emphasis, the figure that runs in place before it dashes off the screen.

Overlapping Action

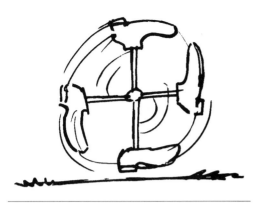

■ *Cycles*

Any repeat action, such as the swing of a pendulum, a walk, a run, or a dripping faucet is a *cycle*. If a pendulum swing requires eight drawings in one direction, the same eight drawings are repeated, in reverse, for the opposite direction. In a ten-drawing walk cycle, the first drawing would be repeated after drawing number ten. Any cycle repeated too many times becomes monotonous, so its frequency must be limited or changes in the action should be added for variety.

■ *Holds*

Characters in constant motion are tiresome to watch and need moments of rest, as in music, to create rhythm and interest. When used effectively, *held* drawings highlight other movements. There are legitimate holds: a figure leaning against a wall, a startled character brought suddenly to a halt, or the hesitation of a figure before it leaps.

■ *What Moves What?*

Does a finger initiate a move or do the hand and arm play equal roles in the action? To raise an arm, a shoulder must be activated first, yet at times a hand will move without the arm and at other times it is the arm that raises the hand. A finger can wiggle by itself, but to accomplish most things it depends on the hand and the arm. Action is not as important as the character's *thought process*, which governs all motivation and the resulting moves.

■ *Action and Reaction*

Actions by themselves are not exciting, but become so when they create a *reaction*. A snowball passing through a scene excites little interest, but gains importance if it splatters against an obstacle. The interest lies in the combination of the initial action and its consequences, such as the snowball knocking a hat off of someone's head. Interest is elevated to a higher level when the owner of the hat, enraged by the loss of his dignity, reacts with a show of emotion.

■ *Takes*

When a character registers obvious shock or surprise, it is referred to as a *take*. A *double take* is a reaction where

Wave Action

the character looks at something, turns away, and suddenly looks at it again. An *extreme take* relies on extreme distortion to get it across. Such a take occurring without sufficient cause is less effective than one in reaction to something truly startling.

■ *Wave Action*

Figures in motion form patterns of opposing actions. As you stand with your full weight on one foot, your shoulders and hips slant at opposite angles. Shift your weight to the other foot and the slant of shoulders and hips reverses. Observe people in action and see how they curve toward and away from each other. Using *wave action* is effective in giving life to characters and objects. Flowing hair, tails, whips, and flags are all wave actions, and the path of

each of these cycle movements forms a figure-eight.

■ *Timing*

Action happens in time. Deciding the rhythm or timing of an action is a major part of the art of animation. Movement loses significance if it lacks a pattern of accents, rhythm, or graduated spacing. Whatever time sequence is indicated at the start of a scene the viewer will accept throughout the scene. So whether the action is slow and steady or fast and frenzied does not matter, unless it fails to relate to the story or is mindlessly repetitious. As an experiment in timing, try the following exercise:

> Place a paper cup on a flat surface and then pick it up several times, imagining each time that the condition of the cup has changed.

1. It is enormously heavy.
2. It is burning hot.
3. It has an electric current running through it.
4. It has been glued to the table.
5. It's covered with a sticky substance.
6. It turns into a snake.

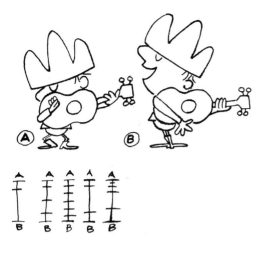

Timing is based on the amount of drawings and the spacing of these drawings between extremes A and B.

You will see that these basic actions are actually very complex. If you followed the above suggestions, you probably hesitated before picking up the electrified or very hot cup. Did you struggle to pick up the very heavy cup or the one glued to the desk? The timing of any action is affected by such conditions, as well as by subtleties of mood and unusual events occurring in the story.

■ *Acting*

Action deals with mechanics but acting reflects feelings—jealousy, irritation, happiness, joy—or any number of human feelings. If an animated character slips on a banana peel, and that character remains calm and unfazed by his fall, the animator has missed an opportunity to display the emotional range of the character. Imagine a play in which the actors stand around just being calm and "cool." Hardly exciting theater. When someone trips or falls, he experi-

ences embarrassment, and, to maintain his dignity, he shields his true feelings from onlookers. The animator, like the actor on stage, must express the character's true feelings of annoyance, frustration, anger, or pain. If character action is detailed in storyboards and layouts, what influence does the animator have?

Take a close look at a scene from *The Wabbit Who Came to Dinner* (1942), in which Bugs Bunny, who normally goes unclothed, is shown stepping out of a shower with a towel around his waist. As he walks forward he modestly adjusts the towel. It is unlikely that this subtle towel action was in the storyboard and probably not even in the layouts, but the animator, well versed in Bugs's persona, added this telling action. The animation could have been done without it, but the animator's acting sense enhanced the total effect.

■ *Blurred Movement*

Wave your hand in front of your eyes and you'll see that the fingers blur. If you study live films one frame at a time, you'll notice blurs as the actors turn and extreme blurring when they get very active. Drawn animation normally lacks this distinction and the inked outlines remain sharp and distinct. This seeming

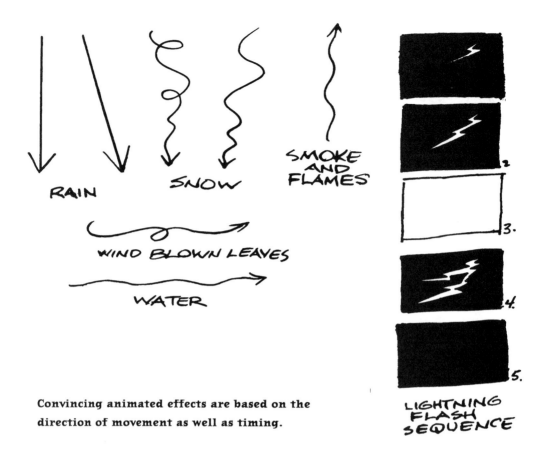

Convincing animated effects are based on the direction of movement as well as timing.

advantage of clear-cut images actually works against animation, leading to a *jitter* or an annoying *stroboscopic* effect, but there are specific ways to soften the image.

In a fast move, when drawings are spaced far apart, *speed lines* are added to fill in for the poses left out. Speed lines are drawn in a definite path. If they are drawn without concern for a path or arc, but loose and wavy, they look like trailing hair rather then indications of blurred speed. These lines should move continuously away from the speeding object. Other techniques for subduing the outline include drawing a soft edge

or using short dissolves between each frame.

■ Effects

Animated *effects* include natural elements like water, rain, snow, mist, smoke, and fire, as well as sparkles, fireworks, and explosions. Each of these is worth studying individually, either in nature or through live-action footage. Strive for your personal impressions rather than a duplication of reality. Look for contrasts between a flickering candle and a roaring log fire; rippling pond water and crashing ocean surf; curling cigar smoke and a blast from a steam engine. Each effect has a unique design and contour, but it is through timing that drawings achieve credibility.

Wind is invisible but shows itself in the objects it touches. The reaction of leaves, sailing ships, flags, or a character's hair and clothing attests to the intensity of the wind. Falling snow and rain, unless being whipped by wind, follow defined paths. Raindrops move in steady, straight paths, whether directly downward or slanted. Contrary to cartoon logic, a falling drop of water is not tear shaped, but is actually round with a flattened bottom. A splash resembles a crown, each point moving upward in separate but similar arcs, then curving and falling in a straight downward path. Snow falls slower than rain and with a floating, swirling action.

Fire moves upward in a changing configuration, flinging off small flames and sparks. Each flame ascends in an undulating arc.

Smoke appears in various densities from vaporous fog to cottony clouds. Air currents affect the timing of smoke and steam so that light smoke curls and wavers more gently than dense rain-filled clouds, while sand-laden dust is heavier still.

EXPLOSIONS

SPARKLES

Sparkles, explosions, and fireworks all radiate from a central point, everything expanding outward in separate straight lines. Fireworks start the same way, but then the remnants arc and fall earthward in straight lines.

■ Animating with Verve

Animation is basically the moving of lines and shapes in space. You must begin by thinking only of the overriding form and not be concerned with insignificant details. Imagine that you are drawing a simple lump of clay without face, hands, feet, or clothing. Clay is flexible and can be manipulated into any form. Just sketch what you feel best expresses these shapes. Examine a lump of clay; hold it in your hand. Fill several sheets of paper with drawings of clay-like forms. Draw the shapes so that they appear to have weight.

Now, take about thirty or forty sheets of punched paper and animate a lump of clay. Show it hopping, bouncing, stretching, twisting, and flattening.

Draw quickly. A feeling of looseness, as found in flowing water or a flexible clock spring, is the point of this exercise. Don't erase, just continue to put down immediate impressions, flipping your drawings frequently. You can rearrange them and then flip the stack to find different accents. Maintain the character of a flexible, undulating lump of clay. Number the sheets and add in-betweens. Make the in-betweens just as rough as the extreme drawings.

■ Roughing In

To discover the possibilities in a movement, visualize, in rough form, the accents, dips, and twists. The sparring of two fighters contains all the basic animation principles of squash and stretch. Their actions, crouching and weaving, are fast and full of surprises.

As one drawing follows another, a pattern is formed, discernible by constantly flipping the stack of papers. If the action looks flat and without emphasis, make adjustments in the drawings to accent or soften the dip and weave of the figures. Working with roughs allows you to experiment, see results quickly, try different approaches, or simply discard any drawings that don't work.

■ Swatching

To speed the drawing process for stylized actions or for blocking in complicated designs, a swatch of a character is placed under the paper and traced in various positions. It is best to indicate an arc first, then trace the swatch, and when the action is complete, add the necessary details.

■ When Characters Interact

Animating two or more characters acting together requires careful planning. Whether they are wrestling or shaking hands, the handling of such scenes is much the same.

Start by sketching the key drawing of the moment of contact between the characters. Try different stagings by making several thumbnail roughs. When you find a satisfactory contact pose, make sketches of the action leading into it. These small roughs are the basis for the full-size drawings.

On the exposure sheets, in the column marked "action," establish what is taking place. Note the number of frames required for each character to approach and then connect with the other. Eye contact strengthens their intent.

Number these drawings and mark their location on the exposure sheet. If there is a soundtrack, find the approximate point of dialogue or musical beat for each layout. Match the action for each character. To get an idea of the length of the combined actions, act it out with someone and time the movements with a stopwatch.

Now, with the action roughed in, add the extremes that set the relationship between the interacting figures. Flip the drawings several times to find spots that need emphasis, such as the direction of a hand or the positioning of a nose. Study the space between the characters. Is it too wide? Too narrow? Are they overlapping each other and blocking parts of the action?

■ Distortion

Distortion is a unique property of animation and gives it its special appeal, but it must be handled carefully to retain the identity of forms and established volumes. A character, no matter how disfigured, must remain recognizable, in some way, as that character.

■ Metamorphosis

In *metamorphosis*, images evolve into other forms. Merely in-betweening one shape into another makes for tedium on the screen, since once the process begins it becomes obvious where it is going. Think of shapes not as flat entities, but as objects full of life and determination. Show them twisting and

Character interaction requires planning.

revolving into one or more shapes before they settle into their final form. For emphasis, go beyond the final shape and then back into it. Some examples of this would be the everchanging Genie in *Aladdin* and Jim Carrey's facial distortions in *The Mask*.

■ *Clean-ups*

Animation drawings begin as roughs, and then details and outlines are defined in the *clean-up* stage. The purpose of this procedure is to approximate the character model with sureness while striving for accuracy of shape, perspective, and foreshortening.

Clean-ups are made with a dense line for photocopying onto cels or for scanning into a computer. To avoid reproducing unerased lines and stains, make a clean tracing of the original rough sketch. Drawings to be inked do not have to be as dense, only distinct enough to be followed by the inker. For computer scanning, check to see that contour lines connect to each other. This is important, because almost all animation drawings today are scanned into a computer. Shapes must have closed lines, otherwise when a fill tool is used to color objects in many computer programs the color will go beyond the broken lines and color the entire screen.

Begin by cleaning up key extremes in a scene. Do the first and last drawing and then every fifth, eighth, or tenth drawing, and then do the ones in-between those. In this way you maintain accuracy in the look of the character more than if the clean-ups were done straight ahead.

When tracing over a character, draw as if you were hugging the *outside* of the line. This doesn't mean that you don't draw over the lines accurately, it's just that favoring the *inside* of the lines weakens the drawings, making them appear less robust.

■ *Drawing from a Model Chart*

Characters in films are drawn by many animators, yet they must appear to come from one hand. For this reason a chart showing the proportions of a character and how that character looks in different views and poses is created to aid the artists. When copying from a model chart try to feel the form of the character. The best approach is to make several rough sketches, leaving out small details. Compare the sizes of the head and body and note the distance between the eyes and nose, the size of the hands compared to the head, and so on. Once you've learned the proportions, turn your attention to the shape of individual features. Don't get discouraged; this process takes time and you'll have to make more sketches than you first thought. Keep in mind that everyone draws differently and that you are attempting to replicate someone else's concept. While there are characters that will be difficult for you, there are others that will be ready-made for your style.

Frames Per Second

Seconds		Frames
	1	24
	2	48
	3	72
	4	96
	5	120
	6	144
	7	168
	8	192
	9	216
	10	240
	15	360
	20	480
	30	720
	40	960
	50	1,200
(1 min)	60	1,440
(2 min)	120	2,880
(3 min)	180	4,320
(5 min)	300	7,200
(10 min)	600	14,400

 Locomotion: The Illusion of Movement

*Walking is a unique activity during which the body, step by step,
teeters on the verge of catastrophe.* —John Napier

When we walk we reflect the conditions of our upright, two-legged gait. We have eyes that face forward, affording a stereo-scopic view of the terrain, and a special relationship between our hips and feet that contributes to smooth locomotion over and around obstacles.

Walk around the room and observe the series of actions your legs and arms make. You will find that your arms swing opposite to your legs, right arm forward with left leg back, then left arm forward with right leg back. You might also become aware of a slight up-and-down movement of the body. If you could put a small light bulb on the top of your head and observe it while walk-ing in a darkened room you would see that the light describes a rising and falling arc. In animation these specific aspects of human locomotion are exag-gerated for emphasis.

Animated walks should be consid-ered a distillation of actual movements, a stylization and caricature, and not a carbon copy of the real thing. The basic walking action, with slight adjustments,

becomes a run, a sneak, a skip, or a dance. Body posture and timing denote the differences.

The cycle of walking starts with a pushing off at the toe with, say, the left foot, resulting in the muscles of the right thigh contracting and tilting the left side of the pelvis so that the weight is lessened on the left leg. This leg lifts, bending the knee as it passes the oppo-site knee at about a twenty-degree angle. During this advance, the body rises and leans forward.

The right leg remains straight while the left leg, its muscles relaxed, swings forward and, as gravity takes hold,

The walk, and its variations as a run, a jump, a careful step backward, and a silly step.

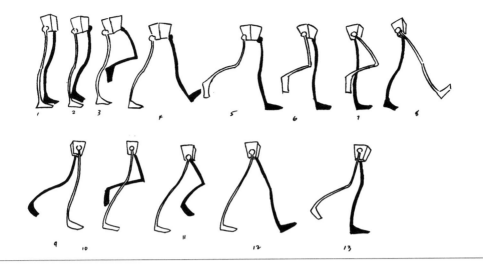

descends, and straightens till the left heel hits the ground.

The body's weight rolls from the heel to the full support of the ball of the foot. With balance assured, it is now the right foot's turn to repeat the process.

At the point where either foot is flat on the ground, just before the push-off, the knee above that foot is rigid. As the leg rises the opposite knee bends slightly and the foot is flattened perceptibly to absorb the weight of the body.

The forward swing of the leg depends on a concerted rotation of the pelvis. This shift is balanced by an opposite rotation of the shoulders and an outward rotation of the thigh. These actions are necessary to keep the feet from tripping over each other, as would happen if they stepped in a straight line directly under the pelvis.

The degree of bounce emphasizes the intensity of a walk. A cartoon figure would have a pronounced squash and stretch, while an approximation of a real person walking would be less exaggerated. There is a natural squash of the soft pads of the bottom of the foot, and accenting this adds a sense of weight to the animated figure.

As one leg passes the other, if the angle of the passing knee changes in any way, so will the character of the walk. Pointing the knee outward or inward, or bringing it in front of the other knee adds humor and interest. Act it out yourself, have fun, but watch your balance.

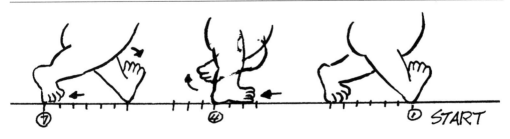

Cycle or Treadmill Walk

Cycle Walks

A figure walking over a pan background requires cycled drawings. The effect is similar to that of a live actor being tracked by a camera mounted on wheels. The walk imitates a treadmill action, with the contact foot sliding back at a steady calibration, while the background moves in the opposite direction in which the figure is facing. The speed of the pan is determined by the exact distance between the heel of the foot in contact with the ground and the heel on the following drawing. The walk can be shot on twos, but the background should move on ones at one half the distance of a single move of the foot.

Animating Animals

> . . . animators have to have, in their mind, a clear picture of how a chipmunk rolls over in the snow . . . . —Stephen Spielberg

Animal life is so varied that to make bears, horses, kangaroos, ducks, and insects look believable requires study and observation. Spend time drawing animals at the zoo and the aquarium, on farms and in natural science museums. For your personal library, obtain an edition of the classic *Animals in Motion* with photographs by Edweard Muybridge, and use it as a guide.

The movements of a running horse or a bird in flight are actions too fast for the eye to register, but what you see will impress you in a specific way. Draw what you think you saw, making several fast sketches. By combining your reac-

tions with observations at the zoo, anatomy charts, and the Muybridge photos, you will develop a feel and a personal style in animating animals.

■ *Characteristics of Animals*

In animating animals, strive for rhythm and a solid structure, but caricature and exaggerate them. Look for distinguishing physical traits. Bears are pigeon-toed; cats' paws tend to spread; and baby animals, such as colts and fawns, are knockneed. The rhino has great flexibility at the knee, elbow, hip, and shoulder and bounces as these joints compress in walks and runs. A squirrel undulates, the action flowing through the body and continuing through the bushy tail. The legs of elephants and large dinosaurs are placed directly under their bodies to support their great weight. Scientists have surmised, from studying fossilized footprints, that dinosaurs moved as elephants do. Before animating an animal, try to imagine its mood; is it hungry or tired, cold or frightened?

■ *How Animals Move*

Animals get around in a variety of ways. They step, paddle, flap, wiggle, swing, hop, etc. Each type of locomotion is similar in that it is a push backward against the surrounding area, creating a force equal to the resulting forward movement. Each animal alters its shape in some way as it pits itself against the air, water, or ground.

Animal movement depends on firm supports, flexible joints, and opposing muscles. When a foot pushes against the ground, it receives the force of the bent leg above it bearing the weight of the

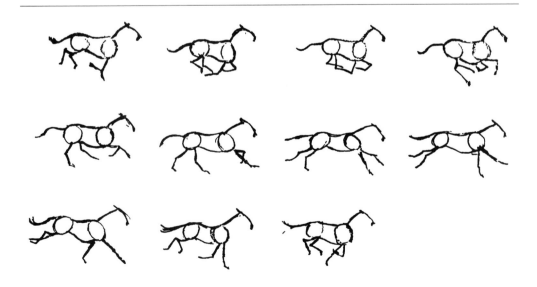

START WITH RIGHT REAR AND RIGHT FRONT LEGS OFF THE GROUND

RIGHT REAR CONTACTS GROUND FIRST

FOLLOWED BY RIGHT FRONT AS LEFT REAR LEG IS LIFTED.

NOW LEFT REAR AND LEFT FRONT LEGS ARE OFF THE GROUND

LEFT REAR HOOF CONTACTS GROUND AS LEFT FRONT PHASES INTO Ⓐ

animal. When this tension is released, like that of a spring uncoiling, the leg moves away from the ground. This is the start of a step or a hop. If the foot is positioned on a flexible base, then the base will move away from the foot as it pushes against it.

A standing horse is a lot like a four-legged table and has the same problems of balance. A pile of books placed in the center of the table will be secure, but lift one of the legs slightly and the weight of the books will force the table down. If the books are placed off to one end of the table and a leg is lifted on the opposite side, they will act as a counter-balance, as when a bear rises up on

two legs. (Actually, the books would probably fall off the table, but we're using our imagination here.) The location of this weight is referred to as the *center of mass*. Some animals have their center of mass near the hind legs and others have it closer to the forelegs.

As a horse walks, its weight shifts for balance. It raises a rear leg and then places the foot on the ground, shifting weight to the front leg, which lifts just before the hind foot hits the ground. A foot lands slightly ahead of the shoulder if it is a front leg or in front of the hip joint if it is a rear leg. Each foot remains stationary until the shoulder or hip joint shifts forward of the foot, then the foot

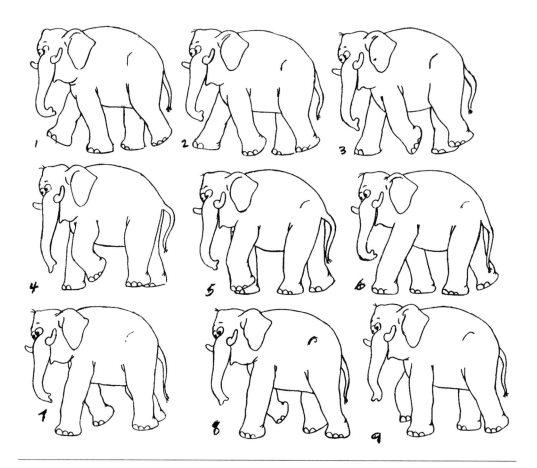

is lifted and swung and brought down in the follow-up step. A walking animal moves in a definite sequence, a pattern that ensures that the animal will be balanced as it advances—and is a boon to animators for the creation of cycle actions.

What happens during the faster pace of a run when more than one foot is off the ground? Though there is a quick stage where all feet are in the air, the animal must retain balance at another point when two feet rise simultaneously and the other two supporting feet take their proper positions fast enough to keep the animal from falling over.

■ Birds

How many times must a bird flap its wings to stay aloft? That depends on the individual species. The following times per *second* are based on notes from the American Museum of Natural History: pelican, about one; stork, two; owl, five; pigeon, seven; sparrow, thirteen; and humming bird, twenty to fifty.

But all bird flight is not involved with flapping. Soaring action, when the wings are spread and the body turns slowly and gracefully, is a necessary component of animating birds.

Perspective Walk

nal line from the bottom left corner to where the horizontal line intersects with the right side of the triangle. Wherever this crosses the other lines, draw a horizontal line. These horizontal lines will become the positions for each step.

Expressions

The three areas of the figure that present the greatest array of emotion are the eyes, the mouth, and the hands. It is through these that feelings and attitudes are expressed.

Entire stories can be told with just the hands, but it is easy to fall into the habit of animating them in boring and clichéd motions. There are more interesting actions than the "point," the typical solution for most situations. Observe people around you to see how they use their hands for emphasis.

A nervous character has hands that fidget with props: neckties, tight clothing, eyeglasses, or pencils. Characters in thought twirl a lock of hair, stroke their chins, run their fingers along the edges of furniture. Exasperated types fling

Perspective Walks

To avoid misplaced feet in perspective walks, first decide how many steps will be taken, then establish the scale of the background and relate the changing size of the character to the height of objects it will pass. Draw a triangle to indicate the diminishing angle and measure equal points for each step along its front end. Rule lines to the vanishing point. Draw a horizontal line just below the apex of the triangle, then draw a diago-

objects in all directions. Gruff individuals stuff their fists into their pockets or grab the lapels of others. Genteel types hold objects with one pinky raised. These also become clichés when overdone, but even more important, to avoid a frenzied effect it is best to do less with the hands and more with the eyes.

The movements of the eyes reveal a great deal about personality. Earlier film actors knew this. Watch Laurence Olivier's entrance in the film *Richard III* (1955) as he defines this devious character with nervously darting eyes. Marlene Dietrich could look seductive by merely dipping her head and peering up from under her eyelids, and Cary Grant's acting style depended a great deal on the intensity with which he gazed into the eyes of the other players as he exhibited concerned interest or comic disbelief.

The large eyes of many cartoon characters attest to the eyes' importance in expressing feeling and emotion, but eyes, whether tiny or gigantic, should be placed on the head with care. Handled too casually, without consistent positioning, the eyes can look as though they are swimming around the face.

The most often-used eye reaction is the blink, and it has many advantages. It adds emphasis to action and dialogue and keeps the eye from looking dead. Certain eye actions have become signatures. Chuck Jones liked to use delayed action. The character apparently does not understand that he has suffered a terrible blow and just stands there looking at the audience. Suddenly his eyes open wide and then squint in painful recognition before he crumples to the ground. Tex Avery became known for the eye-bulging takes his characters experienced, the eyeballs extending beyond the whites as a pattern of veins forms on the surface of the cornea.

■ *Lip Sync*

Animation is the perfect pantomime medium, so it is surprising that so many productions depend on talking, singing, and shouting. Most of the noise coming out of the mouths of characters serves to keep the story in the minds of the audience. Disney's *Bambi* (1942) is an example of a long film with strong animation and very little dialogue. By contrast, oversimplified television animation consists of nonstop explanatory dialogue as the characters continually explain every action:

"What'll we do tonight, Barney?"
"I dunno, Fred."
"Say, Barney, why don't we go bowling?"
"That's a great idea, Fred."

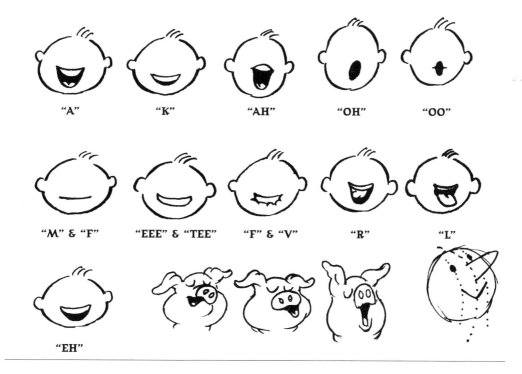

"A"   "K"   "AH"   "OH"   "OO"

"M" & "F"   "EEE" & "TEE"   "F" & "V"   "R"   "L"

"EH"

This approach opens the story up to humorous interchange, is cheaper than full animation, and keeps viewers apprised of what Fred and Barney are going to do. Chuck Jones has referred to this as "animated radio."

Some productions avoid lip sync altogether. In Jiri Trnka's puppet version of *The Good Soldier Schweik* (1954) the characters engage in dialogue, but when one is talking the camera is on the face of the one listening. It works so smoothly that viewers are unaware that there are no moving mouths. Another effective device is a shot from behind a speaker as his body actions accent the dialogue. This brings us to the first major concern of lip sync—the stance of the figure. Grim Natwick, whose experience as an animator spanned more than sixty years, always stressed the accents of the body over the mouth. He pointed

out that with funny dialogue, "Posture is the thing, always."

Listen to a recording of the dialogue several times, and visualize or act out the accompanying action. Listen repeatedly to the phrase to locate the key to the action, the word or words that stress the character's intent. Concentrate also on the rhythm or cadence of the dialogue, feel the action and then sketch in the high points. Once this is done, place the approximate mouth shapes on these key drawings.

Mouths, as with the eyes, reflect the personality of a character, and even if a mouth is represented by a simple outline it should adhere to mouthlike shapes. To avoid a "swimming" effect think of the head as a solid, with a center line, and draw the mouth to fit the total perspective of this shape. Think of an open mouth as a shape that has been scooped out of the solid form of the head.

The mouth actions coincide with the track reading on the exposure sheets and the matching drawings are numbered accordingly. Each mouth coincides with the frame of sound it relates to, but synchronization is an elusive thing. It has been found that exposing mouths one or two frames (sometimes three or four frames) ahead of the sound enhances synchronization. Why? Well, no one knows for sure, though the reason may be that a mouth must first open to speak, and this is more acceptable than sound arriving by the time the mouth is closed. Many experienced animators adhere to the general rule of exposing mouth actions one frame ahead of the sync, while others prefer to expose the drawings on the exact sync frame and then have the film or video editor make slight adjustments by shifting the soundtrack.

Music Beats

As with syncing dialogue, the rhythms of music create accents (beats) for the animator. Accents are established by the director on *bar sheets* in advance of the actual recording, and a *click track* is made for the musicians to listen to through earphones.

If the action is fast, then an accent every eight frames (an "eight beat") is indicated. If the pace is moderate, a beat every twelve frames (a "twelve beat") is established, and if it is very slow, then every twenty frames (a "twenty beat"). Accenting every beat* becomes tedious

---

*Often referred to as *Mickey Mousing*.

and obvious, so animators seek variety by accentuating the action just before the beat, exactly on the beat, between beats, or they ignore them completely. Depending on the action, an accent can arrive a few frames late, when you least expect it, as in a double take.

Before beginning to animate, listen to the music many times, to find the less obvious but interesting accents. Sometimes a beat is lost in a mélange of aural effects and can only be determined by repeated playing of the track. A dancing horse, hitting the downbeats with its feet, creates comic accents in sync with upbeats in other parts of its body.

Analyzing Action

Use a home-video player to review live scenes to analyze movement and sketch what you see. The simplest actions are just as active as the most violent movements. For instance, observe the extreme bending of the body in a person sitting or rising from a chair.

When you decide to take these action sketches to the next level, avoid the tendency to go directly to detailed, full-size drawings. Instead, first experiment with the movements in thumbnail sketches and try several approaches. Enlarge the best of these for use as extremes.

Believability

How important is accuracy in movement? Animation need not ape reality, but while it is possible to do interesting animation without paying strict attention to proper locomotion of a walk or the beat of a wing, there's good reason for thoroughly understanding the actual sequencing of such actions. The working animator has to indicate accurate movements for believability. In everyday practice an action such as a man rowing a boat will show the rate of movement of the arms in a pattern that fits the needs of the story. In such an example, no offhand sequence of drawings or manipulations of a puppet can supply the necessary subtleties. Even if the character is drawn as a stick figure, the body positions, arm movements, and tilt of the head should reflect the mood of the character and the concept of rowing.

Rotoscope

It occurs to everyone at some time or other that the tedious and time-consuming process of drawing every frame of a film could be avoided simply by projecting live-action footage and tracing the actions of real people. This revelation struck Max Fleischer back in 1917 when he received a patent for such a technique. He called it the *rotoscope* and it continues to be used for its original purpose, but it is now more frequently employed as a guide for creating scenes where elements of animation, live-action, and graphics are combined.

In rotoscoping, quality suffers tremendously and there are strong reasons for and against its use. It has an economic advantage in getting drawings done very quickly, but the technique lacks the spark of actual animation. A direct tracing of a photograph appears lifeless as compared to a sketch made of a live model. Tracing emphasizes con-

tours, and unless the person doing it knows where to add important accents, the results will be flat and wooden.

Cartoon characters do not follow human proportions and their charm lies in the fact that they look very different from live actors. Photographs often contain distortions, the figures obscured by shadows, wrinkles, and foreshortening, and live-action frames are marred by blurring. When slavish copying is demanded to render figures "realistic," the result is neither animation nor live-action, but a hybrid that lacks the appeal of either. It's like trying to pass off plastic forks for real silverware. An animator's sharp observations reveal more about life than any outlining of photos can accomplish. What we like about animation is that it is not real.

Pans

Pans are derived from the sliding scenics and figures of nineteenth-century dioramas and toy theaters. A pan, short for "panorama," creates the illusion of moving across a view and is also used for sliding elements over a background, as when you pass your hand in front of your eyes. Its use in animation conserves effort by adding movement with less drawing. The first sliding animation background was fashioned by William C. Nolan in the 1910s from shelving paper borrowed from a local shopkeeper.

Pans lie flat under the camera and slide in any direction. They are typically used to create the illusion of walking forward in a *treadmill action*. Here a character animates in place, in a cycle, while the background moves in the

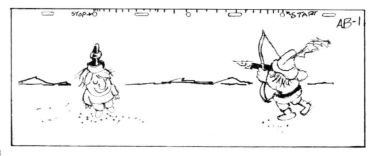

Pan Moves

Penciled spacing marks, indicating the speed of movement of a pan, can be placed adjacent to the peg holes, along the edge of the artwork.

---

opposite direction to that in which the figure is facing. If the elements are reversed, the background held stationary, and the drawings placed on panning cels, the character appears to be passing in and out of the scene.

Pans can be any length, but extremely long pans are unwieldy and cumbersome to work with. On rare occasions, artwork of snakelike proportions has been made that extends off the camera table and out the door as in some features where pans of thirty feet or more have been used. The average pan, however, is less than thirty inches and is easy to prepare and shoot.

■ Establishing a Pan's Length

Pans are indicated in fields, usually from the center peg of one field to the center peg of another. A 2-field pan covers two field areas, a 3-field pan spans three fields, a 4-field pan encompasses four fields, and so on. It's easy to measure a pan when using standard pegs by counting the holes along the length of the artwork. Multiply the total by four (which is the distance in inches between the centers of each peg).

Pan moves are either scribed directly on the artwork or noted as numbers on

an exposure sheet. The speed is indicated by marks spaced closer for a slow move and wider apart for faster moves. A start mark is placed just below the center peg hole and the distance it is to travel is indicated by another mark at the stop position. To simplify figuring, use the center pegs as start or stop positions. With the distance decided, the next consideration is the speed of the pan.

■ Panning Bars

The panning bars on studio drawing discs are calibrated in twentieths of an inch and correspond to sliding pegs on the camera table. The moves are marked on the exposure sheet as decimals: an eight-inch pan is written as "8.00." A twenty-two-inch pan is noted as "22.00." Frame moves are shown at various speeds from very slow (.01, .02, .03, .04, .05), to moderate (.10, .15, .20, .25, .30), to very fast (.50, .60, .75, 1.00). These same spacings can be indicated with pencil marks directly onto the bottom of the pan.

■ Figuring Pans

Pans move in a graduated pattern: slowing out, arriving at a consistent speed, and then slowing to a stop. Abrupt moves that lack a gradual increase and then a decrease of speed are used only for sudden, jarring actions. To figure the degree of movement per frame, using a scale of twenty moves to an inch, and to arrive at gradually accelerated and decelerated movements, plot the moves with a simple grid:

100 (FRAMES)	RATE OF MOVEMENT	12.00 (INCHES)
15	@ .20 =	3.00
10	@ .12 =	1.20
65	@ .08 =	5.20
6	@ .20 =	1.20
4	@ .05 =	0.20
100		10.80

In the first try the total frames work out right but the distance is too short. Try again.

100 (FRAMES)	RATE OF MOVEMENT	12.00 (INCHES)
15	@ .25 =	3.75
10	@ .10 =	1.00
30	@ .08 =	2.40
34	@ .10 =	3.40
6	@ .20 =	1.20
5	@ .05 =	0.25
100		12.00

With a few adjustments, the desired totals are reached.

To move a car, the cel can be still against a panning background or the car can slide over a still background. In either case the same accelerating and decelerating moves are employed for the car or for the background.

If both elements move at the same time, the car in one direction and the background in the opposite direction, the car will appear to be moving faster. If the car pans across the screen at a constant speed and another vehicle enters in the opposite direction, both will appear to increase in speed as they pass each other. To compensate for this, the speeds of both vehicles are slowly reduced until their combined moves equal the original speed.

If, in figuring a pan move, you find that you have to add faster speeds to make up the difference, always keep these numbers clustered in the middle of the move to maintain a gradual increase and decrease in speed; for example: .05, .05, .05, .08, .08, .10, .10, .10, .15, .15, .20, .20, .25, .30, .40, .50, .40, .30, .25, .20, .15, .15, .10, .10, .10, .08, .08, .05, .05, .05.

■ Limited Animation Pans

Pans are a boon to limited animation. A revolving barber pole is suggested by a *window* arrangement. A portion of the pole is left open while everything else around it is opaque, and a repeat pattern of the stripes is panned behind the opening. The effect works best when it is on the screen briefly.

Pencil Tests

Flipping a stack of drawings is the most immediate method of reviewing an action, but flipping lacks the important element of actual screen time. To see how an action or a scene plays out, the drawings are shot as a *pencil test* (also called a *line test*), usually by the studio camera operator, but with the advent of video test equipment animators or their assistants can make quick tests of their

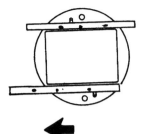
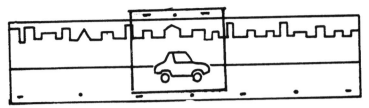

A background panning to the left under a stationary car.

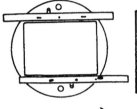
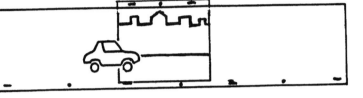

A car on a long cel panning to the right, over a still background.

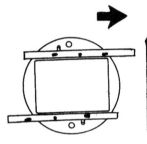

Two vehicles on long cels panning in opposite directions, on top and bottom pegs over a still background.

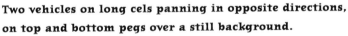

A repeat or hook-up pan is a short pan with matching images on each end that, when cycled, seems much longer.

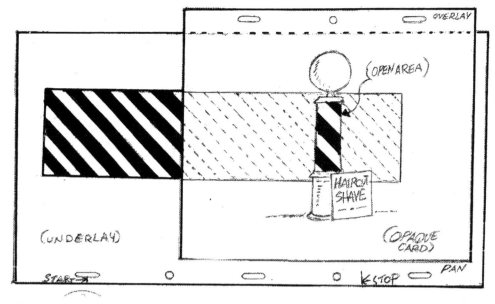

Animating with Pans

An opaque overlay with an opening for the barber pole shows diagonal stripes as they slide underneath, creating a "rotating" effect.

---

work and view it instantly. The drawings are filmed with an underlight, the background and the various levels showing through. The shooting follows the exact numbering on the exposure sheet. If it is a partial test to study a single movement, then only the action series is shot. But if the purpose is to

get the sense of everything working together, the pencil test will include pan moves, trucks, and dissolves. Pencil tests are made on film or video and in computer programs, and are played back in sync with the soundtrack. Since most work is done according to the standard projection speed of twenty-four frames per second, animators use equipment that is designed to record and play back at that speed rather than at the video rate of thirty frames per second. When a

total video or computer presentation is planned and no film is involved at any-time, pencil tests are made at the higher speed, on equipment that works at thirty frames per second.*

How an Animator Works

The director explains the nature of the sequence and makes suggestions as to the playing of the scene, giving the animator the storyboard, character models, exposure sheets, layouts, and the necessary portion of the soundtrack.

The animator does not go directly to final drawings, but instead thinks about all of this information. This is the time

---

*The increased speed requires additional drawings.

to organize the facts and to consider the best approach to the characters and their place in the story. The important thing is not how many drawings the animator will have to make, but that they be the right ones, the ones that will put over the action. The animator studies the storyboard and the layouts, listens to the track many times, and asks, "What makes this scene unique? Is this

Using a mirror for mouth actions.
Figures in motion constantly shift their weight to keep from falling over.

the only way to stage the action? What is the high point of the scene?" By making several thumbnail doodles the animator finds the poses that work best and discovers any hidden technical problems in scale or perspective.

Using the doodles as a guide, the animator roughs in the action over the background layout. Details are not important a this stage, only the large masses. As the animator works, one drawing is flipped against another. By flipping or rolling five drawings at a time, the animator checks for actions that lack emphasis. Like a sculptor with clay, the animator makes slight adjustments, extending a character's arm or exaggerating a pointing toe. Any drawings that weaken the action are discarded. The animator must also decide how much squash and stretch to put into the action and if effects such as flashes, smoke, or speed lines would enhance or detract from it.

Once a series of drawings is roughed in, the animator numbers them and indicates these numbers on the exposure sheet. Throughout the roughing-in stage, the animator refers to the storyboard and the layouts and listens again and again to the soundtrack. This continues until the scene is completed and all of the drawings and camera instructions have been clearly written on the exposure sheet.

In brief, the work of a competent animator entails these qualities:

- The presence of rhythm and weight in each action
- Normal movements, like speaking, hands tying a shoelace, a figure climbing a ladder, and such, appear believable
- Purposeful distortion of shapes
- Effective timing
- Characters appearing to think
- An economical number of drawings
- Clearly stated, systematic instructions for those who do the follow-up work

Tips for Animators

Here are some additional pointers on solving animation problems:

1. When you are animating an erratic action, such as a character excitedly waving his arms, and you are dissatisfied with it, try this: number each drawing and then disturb their order by mixing and shuffling the sheets. Flip the result. If the action still doesn't feel right, shuffle them again. When you get the effect you are looking for, add any necessary in-betweens and write the numbered sequence on the exposure sheets.

2. If you have a scene in which several characters enter simultaneously from various directions, each with a distinctive walking action, animate each character separately, straight ahead, or animate the action backwards beginning with the final grouping and working back to where they enter the scene.

3. Design actions so that you can work back through some of the same movements. This adds stability to the animation and cuts down on the total amount of drawings.

4. Think like an actor and vary the

timing of actions to create interest.

5. This is a technique used effectively by David Ehrlich for making drawn fades. Tracing paper overlays are made and shot in a continuously growing stack. As the drawings pile up, the sheets on the bottom become fainter. It can also be done with about six or eight cels before the lowest must be removed. The cels should constantly be checked for dust.

6. If one scene must be reshot and it is joined by dissolves to several other scenes, all of the connecting scenes will also have to be reshot. To avoid this, shoot the scene minus dissolves and then add them through optical printing or video editing.

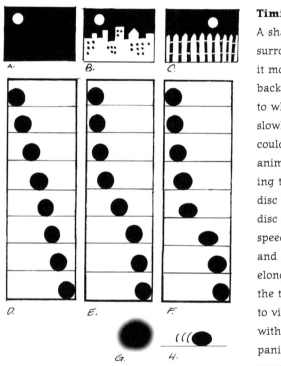

Timing: Association and Scale

A shape takes on meaning by its associated surroundings and the relative speed at which it moves. In (**A**) a disc moving against a background lacking in detail offers no clue as to what it represents. In (**B**) the disc moves slowly across a skyline indicating that it could be the sun or the moon. In (**C**) the disc animates quickly over a picket fence suggesting that it might be a baseball. In (**D**) the disc is moving with even spacing. In (**E**) the disc starts with an acceleration, picks up speed, then decelerates. In (**F**) the disc starts and ends similarly to (**E**) but in the middle it elongates its shape. This distortion reduces the tendency of hard-edged animated shapes to vibrate or strobe. The circle (**G**) is drawn with fuzzy edges and the shape (**H**) is accompanied by speed lines. Both approaches compensate for drawings left out in a fast move.

CHAPTER 13

Using Color

Color is life; for a world without color appears to us dead.

—Johannes Itten, *The Art of Color*

Color arrangements are decided in the storyboard stage and further defined in the layouts. This is preferable to just throwing in colors after the animation is done. Avoid surprises by considering things that are similar in hue, or elements of importance being upstaged by vibrantly colored minor items. If a specific color is necessary to the story, such as a pink cow, then all other colors in a scene should relate to it.

Simplify the selection process by making thumbnail color sketches of characters and scenes. Think of the scene in terms of white, gray, and black with one or two colors added. Maintain separation between elements by starting with a basic overall background tone—white, gray, black, pale blue, or green—and then adding the colors of the key shapes or characters. These could be a red cape, a blue horse, or a magenta automobile. Once you are satisfied with this rough combination of background and key characters, add small color patches of details such as hands, face, a collar, the hubcaps on a car, and so on.

In this way you maintain control of the amount of color actually needed and avoid muddying the image with similar tones and shades.

Use color as an entity for storytelling and to develop your own style. John Culhane has noted that the basic color for McLaren is red and the colors for the Hubley's are blues and greens. "In *The Tender Game*," he points out, "as the young woman and man become aware of each other, the colors get deeper and deeper. They start out fairly light and keep going into deep purple all during the scene. It's a nice way to indicate emotion, showing how the couple is getting heated up."

Color and Light

The appearance of a color changes according to its relationship with other colors. In nature objects reflect their surroundings, and a brown tree trunk looks blue, green, red, or black depending on the light filtering through to its surface or reflections from nearby objects. The Gaugin painting *The White Horse* reveals that the horse is anything but white as it reflects the colors of the pool of water it is standing in and the trees overhanging it. The colors of objects on cloudy days or at night look different than they do in bright sunshine. Since we accept these actual appearances in nature, it is possible to render objects any colors we wish. A tree with blue leaves and a purple trunk is still a tree, and with other parts of the background in complementary hues the effect is much more interesting than it would be with so-called realistic coloring.

How colors are illuminated affects their appearance when photographed. Pigments in artwork, seen by reflective light, react according to the color temperature of that light. True rendition of colors occurs when the light falling on the pigments is close to pure white. Light that has more yellow in it will shift the colors in that direction, just as lights closer to the red or blue end of the spectrum also affect the overall color balance.

Colored gels and transparencies are illuminated from behind and are therefore affected by the whiteness of the light. Make tests of the range of pigments, gels, and the lighting before final shooting. When film is transferred to video, or when animation is recorded electronically, subdued hues become brighter while red tends to "bloom," making it necessary to limit its use to small areas.

Backgrounds

Backgrounds are the stages on which the characters perform. They set the

Painting Backgrounds

style of the production and establish locale and mood.

The background artist, schooled in color and painting techniques, understands the characteristics of surfaces and the effects of light and texture. A polished apple, the rough bark of a tree, a glossy sheet of steel, a sunwashed sidewalk, a fluffy pillow, or the effect of water or steam on plate glass are the daily concerns of the background painter. But knowledge of the natural world is only part of the artist's concerns, since these subjects also must be depicted in a variety of design styles, and working under time constraints, as well as creative ones, the background painter uses techniques that offer quick and effective solutions.

Background shapes and colors should complement, not conflict with, the overlaid designs. If the colors are too similar, the characters will disappear into the scenery. Confusing shapes, lines, and colors on the background interfere with the smooth flow of action. This is avoided in the layout stage by

reflect cohesion between backgrounds and character styles.

To ensure clear-cut, consistent renderings, plan the tonal scheme of a film with small color sketches or take snippets of magazine advertisements and form easily rearrangeable color patterns. It is not advisable to use all of the colors of the rainbow, even though modern film and video reproduce them accurately.

Inking Cels

---

composing backgrounds and characters as a unit.

Backgrounds often appear vacant when the characters are absent; they resemble abandoned stage sets waiting for actors to bring them to life. An example of this is the small corner in the forest where Elmer Fudd and Bugs Bunny converge.

Reason would suggest that the style of backgrounds mirror the style of the characters placed over them, but the cel method has defied this for decades. Audiences have always accepted, and admired, the strange sandwiching of a modeled, light-and-dark rendering behind outlined, flatly painted figures.

There have been attempts to change this, bringing the backgrounds to center stage. In *Plague Dogs* (1982) backgrounds and characters are equally sharp, forming a harsh reality through detailed hard-edged renderings. In *Grendel, Grendel, Grendel* (1980) or the *Samarai Jack* television series the backgrounds and the characters are of one stylistic design, just as Bill Plympton's films

Inking and Painting

Great results are attained by the pressure . . .
or delicacy with which the stroke is made.
—Robert Henri

Inking and painting cels may seem unnecessary now that other techniques are usurping this process. Forewarnings of a change in the system of transferring pencil drawings to cels came in the 1950s with the introduction of photocopying. Still, the colors had to be applied by skilled hands. Now even that is passing with the advent of computer paint programs in which animation drawings receive colors by simply pointing at areas on a monitor display. Yet for many filmmakers, inking and painting cels offers control of classic artistic styles without resorting to costly computer equipment and software.

■ *Cels*

The animator's clean-ups are inked with pen or brush onto clear acetate sheets, called cels. These come in varying degrees of thickness, but the .005 gauge is the standard in the field. Most art-supply outlets stock them in large sheets or in pads of graduated sizes. Companies specializing in animation materials cut and package them in lengths required for filming, which includes the standard twelve-inch field cel and longer sheets for pans.

Cels are sensitive to sharp objects, dust, and grease (never handle cels while eating tuna fish sandwiches). The use of white cotton gloves is recommended since fingerprints and perspiration affect the application of pigments. These are available in large and small sizes at supply houses catering to photographers and film editors. For ease in handling pens and brushes, inkers snip off the thumb and forefinger of one glove (before putting it on, of course).

■ Inking

The inker works at a standard animation desk fitted with pegs or on a portable board to which pegs have been mounted. The latter is used to avoid the cost of an additional light table, but also for ease in turning the work. For the application of colors (*opaquing*), some studios use light tables to guarantee that the pigments are applied in the proper opacity, while others avoid the under-light and rely simply on reflective white tabletops. In either case there is sure to be a set of shelves above the desk or on a handy wheeled cart for holding newly painted cels.

The inker is expected to trace the animator's lines, in black, with extreme accuracy and without deviating from the original. The lines are often rendered in a distinctive style, such as a broken or dotted line, a heavy or rough outline, a thick-and-thin stroke, or any of a number of contours possible with pen or brush.

■ Materials

Waterproof India ink is best if used with traditional dip points and non-waterproof ink for mechanical pens. Colored inks are made in the studio by diluting a few small drops of clean water with a glob of cel paint in a mixing cup. Avoid too watery a mixture. The correct combination is arrived at when the paint has lost its thickness but is still opaque.

The choice of pen size relates to the style of line required. In the color cartoons of the 1930s and 1940s, thin contours were used mainly to designate the areas of color and included outlining with the same hue as the paint areas they defined (*self-line*). This required a constant thin line and to do this the inkers had to master control of fine crow-quill pens. This was long before the advent of graded sets of mechanical pens like the Rapidograph that are used

Inking Cels

Inking and Painting

(**A**) Cels held with cotton gloves. (**B**) Inking. (**C**) Cels drying. (**D**) Stir paint with brush handle. (**E**) Small portion of color. (**F**) Painting the reverse side of the cel (inset) shows circular method of applying colors. (**G**) Pointed brush handle for gently removing excess paint. (**H**) Polishing cels over a black card to remove stains and fingerprints. (**I**) Special effects and shading added on top of cel with grease crayons.

today. Lettering pens or watercolor brushes are also used when wide lines and strokes of varied weight are required.

Inking on the slippery surface of a cel demands hours of practice. This is necessary for developing the skill and consistency in following the contours of pencil animation. There are other mediums that adhere to the cel surface and that are less demanding than pen and ink, such as grease pencils and markers. Kohinoor (#1555) and Stabilo pencils adhere easily to glossy surfaces and come in several colors. Unlike India ink, these do not require drying time, but they should be handled carefully to avoid smearing. Each technique results in a different effect and must be given serious thought in regards to its graphic strength, cost, and ease of application. Practice and experiment with each before embarking on a long-range effort.

■ Scratch-off

To achieve the effect of lines writing themselves magically (*scratch-off*), the lines must be drawn for easy removal under the camera. For this purpose, add a drop of soap to a small portion of cel color. Apply this mixture, with a brush, to the front of the cel. When dry it can be carefully scratched away with the end of a pointed paper stump or a sharpened stick.

■ Opaquing

Cel paints must be opaque and specially formulated to adhere to plastic surfaces. They are applied to the back of the cel to avoid obliterating the ink line, and

when viewed through the front of the cel, the normally unpolished surface of the paint appears flat, smooth, and consistent.

Originally, poster colors were used with the addition of a sticky substance, such as glycerin, to make them adhere to the cel surface. Too much glycerin and the paint would remain tacky; too little and it would not adhere at all. Since paint manufacturers gained little profit putting out a line of cel paints for the then-small animation industry, early studios mixed their own. Today, companies in the United States and Europe specialize in the preparation of a wide range of colors strictly for the animation field. These paints are generally vinyl acrylic and cling to plastic material without any additional preparation. They are sold in plastic bottles of two, four, eight, sixteen, and thirty-two ounces. The two-ounce size is usually sufficient for painting one character, in one color, in an average thirty-second commercial. The price per bottle is comparable to a tube of standard watercolors and comes in more than seven hundred shades, tints, and grays.

The proper consistency of cel paints could be compared to that of condensed milk. After standing unused for a time, the pigments lodge at the bottle bottom and the water rises to the top. To regain the proper uniformity, they must be stirred and for this the wooden handle of a brush serves perfectly. If the pigment in the bottle has become a dried mass, add a few drops of water, and with the top screwed on tightly, shake the container vigorously. Then remove the cap and stir until it is soft and

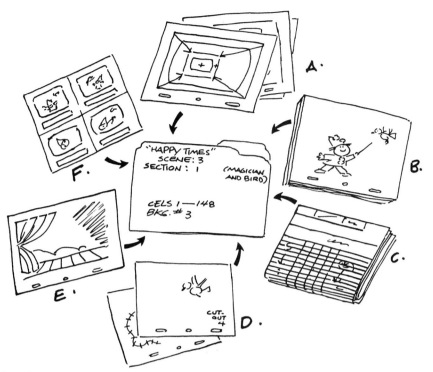

Ready for Camera

Each scene folder should contain all of the elements of a scene: (**A**) camera fields, (**B**) drawings and cels, (**C**) exposure sheets, (**D**) cutout guides, (**E**) backgrounds, (**F**) layouts or storyboard of the scene.

smooth. For use, pour a small portion of the pigment into a small container, then recap the bottle.

The colors are applied with watercolor brushes, most commonly #0, #1, #2, and #3, and for large areas, #4 and #5. The brushes should be good, but needn't be of the highest quality, since the vinyl acrylic paints play havoc with them in the course of a production. Choose inexpensive brushes, but ones that have a well-formed point. Get several of them for opaquing and save your expensive brushes for painting backgrounds.

Applying cel colors is not like painting a picture, nor is it like painting a wall. You don't stroke the pigment on. Instead, starting with the darkest colors, dip the brush just to its ferrule and avoid dragging it across the edge of the container as you remove it. Apply it directly to the cel, in a puddle, and *push* it carefully around with the brush. Paint in a circular motion, nudging the inside edge of the inked line without going beyond it. Pause periodically to check for opacity by turning up the edge of the cel slightly to view the front. A group of cels from a scene, a *set*, are painted one color at a time and each cel is placed on a shelf to dry. The darker colors are applied first to avoid overlapping white or yellow and creating a noticeable gray area, visible through the front of the cel.

Once the paint has dried, check the colors again for opacity. To do this, place the cel over a black card. If the colors look streaky they will require additional coats. As noted, white and yellow require extra attention and unless they have been laid down with sufficient care, you can expect to give them a second coat.

Never contaminate paint from one bottle with paint from another. This interferes with the carefully formulated system for maintaining consistent colors from cel to cel. A separate brush for black paint helps to avoid accidental mixing. Extremely important: *Wash all brushes thoroughly in clean water immediately after use.* Also, don't leave them overnight in a jar of water, unless you enjoy the frustrating experience of painting with bent brushes.

■ *Mixing Colors*

You can mix your own colors as needed. Pour off small quantities of the desired tints into a clean mixing cup. The castoff canisters from 35mm still-camera films are fine for this and they have the advantage of tight-fitting covers. Label each canister or bottle to avoid confusion. Many colors appear lighter when wet, so test your mixture on a cel and check it once it has dried. In use, stir the pigment periodically to keep it from separating.

■ *Corrections and Cleaning*

To remove paint that has gone over the line or that has accidentally splattered

Scene Checking

on the cel, moisten it with the corner of a wet cloth or tissue. After a few seconds, scrape it gently with a paper stump, the sort used for shading charcoal drawings. Experienced cel painters sharpen the back of a brush handle to a point and very carefully flick off spots of dried paint. Always remove paint at an angle and never, never dig or gouge into the cel, since scratches show. After a set of cels has dried, place each over a black card and *polish* them with a clean, soft cloth using a gentle side-to-side motion across the surface of the cel. Up and down strokes, going against the grain of the cel, could create visible scratches. After the cels are cleaned they are stacked, each with its drawing behind it, and placed in the scene folder ready for camera.

All of these warnings about care are important, but don't be put off by them (given time you will develop the necessary good habits). If cels had to be super perfect, considering the conditions under which many productions have been made, there never would have been animated films in the first place.

■ *Checking*

Before going to camera, the scenes are checked for accuracy. Frame by frame the cels are placed over the background in a run-through that imitates final shooting. Any discrepancy between the numbering on the exposure sheets and the cels is corrected. Damaged drawings, or those with missing details, are repaired. At the completion of this rehearsal, the scene folders are ready for camera.

Computer Color Program

Coloring outline animation is now the province of the computer. Drawings with clean lines are scanned into a computer program, where they are adjusted further for size and alignment and outlines are checked for breaks and repaired. There are various specialized animation programs that allow for coloring drawings and creating backgrounds. The line drawings are scanned as grayscale images and then each is given a designated file name followed by a unique number. The scanned drawings are assigned a labeled folder. The mode is shifted to RGB and the drawings are ready for coloring.

When using inks or paint you are working with reflected light, but when choosing colors in a computer paint program you are working with transmitted light. The primary colors of reflected pigments are red, blue, and yellow, which when mixed together result in black. These are called *subtractive colors*, unlike the primary colors of light—the red, green, and blue (RGB) of the computer monitor—called additive colors. When these three colors are combined the result is white light.

To select computer-based colors you simply click on the palette presented in the paint program. A preferred color palette can be selected from the many color choices and with a fill or brush tool the colors are placed by pointing a mouse or a stylus.

When the coloring is complete, the art is exported to an effects or editing program, where the colored drawings are then combined with backgrounds or live-action, assigned proper time lengths, and then output to video or DVD.

A.

AA.

B.

C.

D.

E.   EE.

F.

SKY

TREES   G.

H.

FF.

HH.

Painting Backgrounds Using Opaque Watercolors.

A. Watercolor paper comes in various weights and surfaces. Use semi-rough paper (hot pressed), 100 to 140 lb. weight. It lies flat when placed under the cels.

AA. Some papers should be soaked or dampened and dried first.

B. Attach the wet paper firmly to a board with masking tape and allow to dry.

C. Background layout drawing.

D. Rub soft pencil over animation paper. This penciled area will serve as less greasy "carbon paper" for copying your layout drawing onto the watercolor paper.

E. Place the carbon over the dried watercolor paper, penciled side down.

EE. Put your layout drawing on top of the carbon and the watercolor paper. Using a hard pencil (2H), trace the outlines of the layout drawing. The lines will appear lightly on the watercolor paper.

F. Before starting to paint, check your color scheme by trying the colors on a scrap sheet. Think of the background in layers of distance. Brush in the most distant areas, such as the sky, with a wide brush. This will be the faintest area. When that is dry, paint the next layer, then the next, coming closer to the front of the scene. Much of this can be done with a #4 brush, or whatever size works best for you. Background tones are less saturated than the colors of characters that are placed over them. Reduce the intensity of the background colors by adding white to the pigments. Again, check your color scheme by trying the colors on a scrap sheet.

FF. As you proceed, hold cels of character models over the background to check for separation between the background tones and the character colors. Remember, though cels are transparent they have a density that darkens background tones. Adjust these tones in relation to the cel levels. (Painted backgrounds can also be scanned into Photoshop®.)

G. To keep consistency of color throughout a production, mix a quantity of pigment in containers for use in other scenes. Keep these covered.

H. When the painting is finished, match the background to the layout drawing and cut file folders into strips for pegholes.

HH. Attach to the background with masking tape. Keep the tape outside the field area.

CHAPTER 14

Filming, Frame by Frame

Among other things, I raised the height of the table which held the artwork, because, as a tall guy I was constantly bumping my knees on the old stands. —John Oxberry

There are three basic methods for shooting animation artwork: on film, on video, and by scanning or digitizing on a computer. Yet no matter which road is taken, knowing the basic workings of the camera stand is essential for getting your efforts to the screen. This knowledge, put to best advantage, opens the way for the creation of unusual effects, avoids excess work, and holds down costs.

A Roll of Film

Film has a transparent base of acetate, with one surface covered with a light-sensitive emulsion. Of the many emulsions available, some are much better for animation than others. The professional film sizes are 35mm, 65mm, 16mm, and also super-16mm, but the standard film used in production is thirty-five millimeters wide, has sprocket holes along the inside of both edges, and is made of slow-burning cellulose triacetate.

Until the 1950s, this support was made of cellulose nitrate, a highly flammable material and was the cause of numerous fires in studios and theaters. Photographs of old editing rooms show light bulbs shielded with wire frame guards to protect film from any direct contact with heat. Stored cans of the material must be opened with extreme caution, as any spark caused in removal of the metal cover could ignite the contents. Nitrate materials that have lain unattended for many years are often reduced to a jellied state, a dangerous condition that calls for fire department assistance for removal.

Narrow-Gauge Films

Sixteen millimeter, introduced in 1923 as an amateur format, has always been made with an acetate safety base considerably less flammable than the cellulose nitrate material used for the early 35mm film. Like the larger gauge, 16mm productions rely on specialized processing labs in major cities. To cut production costs, films are often made in 16mm and then enlarged to 35mm for theatrical release or transferred to videotape for television.

Sixteen millimeter was just one result of the many early attempts to develop a convenient film for home use. In France, in 1922, Pathé issued a narrower 9.5mm film. It achieved a broad frame area by the elimination of sprocket holes along the edges, but had a cleverly placed single hole between each frame. Though this gauge remained in use in Europe for many years, interest in 9.5mm diminished in 1932, when Kodak introduced the even narrower 8mm.

Essentially 16mm film with sprocket holes along both edges, 8mm recorded two narrow strips of images side by side. To accomplish this, the film was run through the camera twice, necessitating removal of the spool after one side was shot and flipping it over to record the second strip. At the lab, this "double-8" roll would be slit down the middle and spliced at one end. The result was a small reel running as long as a 16mm roll twice its length. It was economical, but lacked the sharpness of 16mm.

In 1965 Kodak unveiled super-8mm, a vast improvement on the earlier 8mm. Super-8 film is the same width as the old 8mm, but with smaller sprocket holes. The result is a 50 percent increase in picture area and a larger, sharper projected image. The space vacated by the smaller holes allows for the inclusion of a slim magnetic soundtrack, an addition that had been tried less successfully on the standard 8mm film. The super-8 cameras are designed to be loaded with cartridges that don't have to be flipped over as in the 8mm cameras. Though the format is still in use by many filmmakers and the cameras are handily capable of shooting single frames, it has been pushed into a corner by the wave of video camcorders that are capable of taking hours of live-action pictures with sound and color.

The Negative

In the manufacture of film an emulsion of halide crystals suspended in gelatin is applied to one surface of an acetate base. The other side contains an antihalation backing as protection against the scattering of stray light in the base that might reflect back onto the emulsion. When exposed to light, the emulsion responds with a latent image that becomes visible after chemical development. Since crystals still sensitive to light remain and could destroy the permanency of the image, it is necessary to remove all unexposed crystals by placing the film in a *stop bath* to stop the action of the developer and then a *fixing* solution to keep the image from fading.

The darkest, most opaque areas of a negative are those that have received the strongest light, while the clearest spaces are those that have had little exposure to light. Prints made from the negative show the areas of black, gray, and clear portions in reverse, like the original subjects. Negative film stocks provide the greatest flexibility and latitude in exposure during shooting and in printing.

Reversal Stock

Some films yield a positive image when developed; these are called *reversal* stocks. After exposure the film is developed into a negative, but through reexposure to light or after placement in a special developer the negative image turns positive. This has been the general method in the processing of amateur films, but reversal films have also been used for shooting professional 16mm color animation.

Film Speed and Depth of Field

Each film has its own *speed* in relation to exposure. The faster a film the more it responds to low light conditions, but the image is grainier and more contrasty. With slower film speeds, more light is required to capture the image, but the results are finer grained. Live cinematography, performed under changing light conditions, requires a wide range of film speeds, but animation shot under constant and manageable illumination is best served by slower film stocks. With a controlled light supply and a small diaphragm opening, the results are images that are sharp and of normal contrast.

Films for animation include black-and-white panchromatic stocks for pencil tests, with an average exposure index of EI 64, and color stocks with an exposure index of EI 100. The EI reflects the standard lens and shutter settings for controlled results for shooting and processing. High-contrast stock used for bipack and optical printing mattes are of such slow speeds that a test strip, called a cinex, should be made prior to final shooting. This is done by filming single-frame exposures at quarter stops of the lens diaphragm openings, from the smallest to the largest. New improved emulsions are issued periodically by Kodak, Fuji, and Agfa. Contact local suppliers for the latest information.

Videotape

Videotaping of live scenes has been available since 1956, but frame-by-frame recording has only recently come into serious use. The gears of a movie camera are easily set to shoot single frames, but to accomplish the same feat with video requires a tricky combination of mechanics and electronics. In the 1970s, video was successfully incorporated into studio use as a pencil-test system. Since then, technical improvements in electronic frame-by-frame recording have moved to videotape and discs as well as new versatile digital recorders.

Videotape Gauges

Early videotapes were two inches wide. By the 1970s, one inch had become the standard for studio production and three-quarter-inch for use in portable cassettes. Lower-cost, high-quality half-inch and 8mm cassettes and digital discs are now widely used.

The Animation Stand or Rostrum

The *animation stand* consists of sturdy, durable, precision components. The

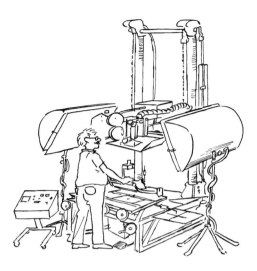

Animation Stand
Camera operator adjusts glass platen over artwork. Movement of camera and table is controlled by switches on panel at far left.

artwork is placed on a *compound table*, which shifts horizontally, vertically, diagonally, and in a complete circle. Rigid columns support the *camera* above the table. The camera tracks vertically along these columns to approach or move away from the artwork. Trucks and pans are planned through coordinated control of the camera and tabletop.

All camera and table moves are managed from a panel of buttons and switches positioned to the side of the stand. An *on/off power switch* starts the *stop-action motor* that drives the camera motor. A *forward/reverse switch* selects the direction of the film in the camera while a touch of the *single frame button* does exactly that—exposes just one frame of film. A *continuous run switch* allows for the running of many frames of a single setup, such as a title, more quickly than resorting to the single-frame button.

Inside the camera, behind the lens, is a *shuttle* containing a *gate* for positioning the film and *registration pins* to ensure precise alignment of each frame as it comes into position for exposure. This is especially necessary for repeated runs through the camera when combining images. Included in the mechanism is a *variable shutter* that opens and closes in progressive phases for making fades and dissolves.

To sight accurately on the artwork, two techniques are commonly used, *reflex viewing* or a *rackover system*. The first method employs a prism that allows viewing directly through the lens, while in the second method the main camera body is slid to one side, bringing the viewfinder in line with the film aperture. Once the artwork is composed in the viewfinder, the camera is racked back to shooting position. There is a *follow focus guide* or *cam system* that keeps the lens in focus as the camera moves up or down. The cam, a metal bar with one edge fashioned in a gentle curve, fits along the length of the rear of the column. A *connecting arm* between the cam and the lens tracks the curve and moves the lens barrel, focusing the lens elements as the camera trucks up and down on the the supporting columns.

Film, loaded into a four-hundred-foot *magazine*, feeds through the top of the camera. The operator checks for dirt and hairs in the camera and the gate, and then threads the film carefully around the sprockets and positions it in the gate. Before securing the door two or three feet of film are run to ensure that it has been properly threaded and wound onto the *take-up spool*. Only then is the door closed and locked.

Larger magazines are used for extended shots of still artwork, but for standard single framing it is not good to keep film in the camera, exposed or unexposed, over long periods. Sensitive emulsions are adversely affected by humidity and changing room temperatures. After a day or two of shooting, film should be removed and sent for processing.

Attached to the camera is a *frame counter*, which accumulatively records every frame shot. The camera operator relies on it to ensure that the frames on the exposure sheet are being shot in correct order. It is necessary as a visual tally of frame numbers, as when the film is moved forward and rewound in making dissolves and other effects.

To block reflections of the camera in cels and the overlying glass platen, a *shadowboard* is affixed under the camera lens.

The Compound Table

During filming artwork is positioned in front of the camera on a flat, sturdy surface, geared to slide on a double set of tracks, go in any horizontal direction, and rotate 360 degrees.

A platen of water white glass is hinged to the table. This glass is made with less of the impurities found in window glass, and is therefore clearer. Its full weight does not fall on the cels, but rather is adjusted to lie over them with even pressure. Below the artwork is a *foam rubber insert* that presses softly upwards, sandwiching cels and back-ground between the insert and the platen. This insert, when removed and replaced with a sheet of glass, opens the area to a light box for backlighting effects and projected images.

Above and below the shooting area are four sliding pegbars which, like the table, move generally in increments of one hundred to an inch. These table adjustments, once made strictly by hand-operated wheels, are now generally done by computer-controlled motors that can move precisely at one thousand increments to an inch.

Lighting

For best results in shooting flat artwork lighting must fall evenly. The lighting units of small copystands are attached by flexible arms and are adjusted for overall coverage. With the larger rigs, the units are supported by sturdy floorstands. In either case the lighting consists of two reflectors, evenly spaced and at an angle of 45 degrees. Lamps for general use are 250-watt photofloods arranged in groups of four; also suitable in reflectors are two 300-watt tungsten lamps or tungsten-halogen quartz lamps. For color shooting these must be 3200 Kelvin.

Underlighting

Pencil-test artwork and color transparencies are placed over a milk-white glass and illuminated from underneath. The lights are arranged in clusters of two to four bulbs and cooled by an electric fan trained continually on them. This build-up of heat is avoided by exclusively using fluorescent bulbs.

Dimensional Effects

The illusion of depth, the way scenes appear in nature, depends on the passing of elements over each other. Imagine a view of telephone poles from the window of a moving train. The ones closest to you whiz by, those in the middle distance pass at a slower speed, and the poles on the horizon seem to be standing still. By splitting the elements of a scene into different levels and panning them at appropriate increments (each attached to a separate sliding peg-bar), the flatness of the artwork disappears and the eye is fooled into perceiving depth. To create such an illusion, establish a speed for the bottom level, move the one above twice as fast, and the top level three times faster than the bottom level. Of course, the illusion ceases as soon as the panning stops, and continues once it is resumed.

The Multiplane Setup

To gain an increased illusion of depth calls for a *multiplane stand*. Though advances in technology have brought multiplane effects into the area of computer functions, it is important to know how photography of several levels works. In a multiplane arrangement there are actual spaces between the layers of artwork, representing foreground, middleground, and horizon. Such a rig was constructed at the Disney studio in the 1930s and consisted of six levels. It stood eleven-feet, fourteen-inches high, cost tens of thousands and required several people to operate it. To compensate for the shooting distance and to maintain sharpness, longer exposures and a great deal of light were needed. To gain the proper depth of field for encompassing the various levels, a 117mm lens was used. Such a structure made it possible to recreate the desired depth illusion not only horizontally, but also when moving in or out, as in a moonlit scene.

When out walking at night, you may have noticed that the moon kept the same distance away no matter how far you strolled. Your house got closer, but the moon remained 240,000 miles out in space. If, for animation, you plan this as a flat illustration of your house and the moon, the effect would lack the natural illusion because both elements would approach the camera at the same rate as you moved the camera toward the artwork. With the multiplane camera, the separate levels of foreground, house, sky, and moon are moved independently to maintain their comparative distances. A smaller multiplane setup accomplishes pretty much the same thing with less cost, but still requires very careful planning.

Today, these same effects are obtained either by scanning the various planes into a computer or creating them directly in a computer program where

A single letter A becomes many images when shot with multiple exposures and overlapping camera trucks.

Double Exposure

A sparkle effect is created by double exposing a pinhole made in a black card. A star filter over the lens creates points of light, while overexposure of the pinhole results in a glow.

they are layered and moved in the desired relationship.

In-Camera Effects

Fades, dissolves, and double exposures can be done in the camera during animation shooting. This requires a camera with automated shutters and frame counters. It is not impossible to do these effects with cameras lacking such controls, but the task is more difficult and demands patience in governing exposure and keeping track of frames. A fade-out is made by gradually limiting the amount of light on each frame and a fade-in reverses the procedure. A dissolve is a combination of a fade-out and a fade-in. The exposures are made by first running the camera ahead as one scene is faded out, then with the lens covered rewinding the film to the start of the fade-out, uncapping the lens and fading in on a new scene. To avoid flash frames during a dissolve, each frame of the fade-out must be compensated for in the exposure of the equivalent frame of the fade-in.

Electronic Shooting

The film camera on an animation stand can be replaced with one that records onto tape, disc, or computer. The artwork is *digitized* into the system, and depending on the capabilities of the computer program being used, the action is viewed immediately, colored, and given visual enhancements. These are important advantages over traditional photography, which requires overnight laboratory work before any results can be seen.

Optical Printing

Optical printing is the rephotographing of film frames for making fades, dissolves, repositioning, blow-ups, freeze frames, atmospheric effects, and combining live-action and animation. The optical printer consists of a projector and a camera, aligned facing each other, each with stop-frame functions. One or more strips of film containing images to be combined are loaded into the projector. The camera's lens is focused directly through the projector lens onto the filmstrip image. A fade-out can be made

Effects

Double exposure of mattes allows one scene to "wipe" off another.

by rephotographing a filmed scene and setting the camera's diaphragm to close one frame at a time. Glass filters of varying color or pattern can also be interposed between projector and camera to create color and distortion effects.

Developed in the 1930s, optical printing technique remains the same today, but in the decades since the mechanism's design has become increasingly precise in handling multiple exposures. The addition of electronic controls in the 1970s made possible the stunning special effects in a wave of science-fiction productions.

Shooting 35mm or 16mm frames demands film equipment with construction tolerances and lens sharpness that place optical printers among the most expensive of professional equipment. Independent firms that own and operate these tools cater to the needs of filmmakers. Presently, optical printing is losing out to computer-effects techniques.

Inexpensive, fully operable optical printers are available for 16mm work from equipment suppliers, and homemade units can be constructed by building a steady rig that holds a cast-off projector and camera. Some effects can also be achieved without an optical printer by running strips of film through a camera in *bi-pack*. A typical bi-pack subject would be a cartoon sequence of a view through the black circle of a telescope. To have the scene go in and out of focus cannot be achieved by making the lens go out of focus and then refocusing the lens, because the black circle would also go out of focus. By threading a prefilmed

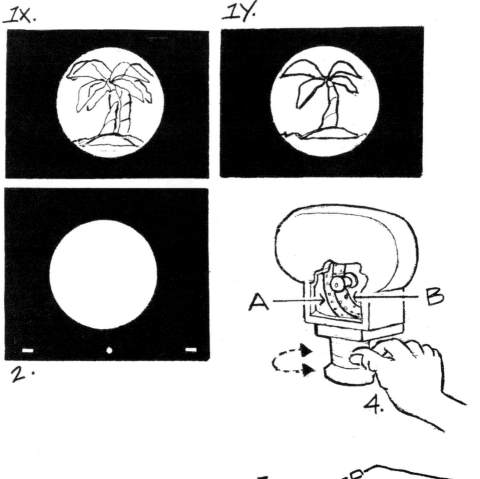

Bi-pack Filming

To create a view through a telescope where the palm tree goes in and out of focus (**1X** and **1Y**) but the edge of the circle remains in sharp focus, two separate strips of film are run simultaneously through the camera.

A black circle art matte is made (**2**) and is shot on high-contrast black-and-white film. The resulting filmstrip (**A**) is solid black except for a clear center area and is threaded through the camera. Unexposed color film (**B**) is then threaded in behind it.

Color artwork (**3**) is filmed as the operator (**4**) adjusts the focus of the camera lens. Since the matte filmstrip is behind the lens, only artwork in front of the lens is affected by any lens adjustments.

The final effect, recorded through the matte's clear center onto color film, will show the palm tree coming into focus while the telescope circle remains sharp.

matte strip of the black circle into the camera so that the matte runs in front of the raw stock and behind the lens, the scene is filmed and placed out of focus while the black matte remains in focus, and both are recorded onto the raw film simultaneously.

The most crucial of the optical printer uses is the combining of varied footage to create fantasy scenes. In practice the diverse elements include animated characters, animated effects, models, live actors, and live backgrounds. To make these combinations, each phase requires the use of film masks called *traveling mattes*.

For combining live scenes with animation, the live-action is shot first. The scenes are then rotoscoped by positioning a strip of film in an animation camera and projecting through it one frame at a time. The projections are either traced by hand or photographed onto full-field positive photographic paper. The rotoscoped frames are then used by the animator as a guide for locating the drawings.

Since live-action is on ones—one frame for each move—all matching animation, that is animation that makes direct contact with live-action elements, must also be shot on ones. Animation on twos, where two frames are shot of each drawing, can be done when it functions independently of live actors or moving props. Sometimes, when delicate, slow-moving live-action is combined with drawings that are *not* shot on ones, the animation seems out of sync. This can only be found out through testing, by shooting the translucent photographic "roto" copies in conjunction with the animation drawings. The rule is: When in doubt, do the animation on ones.

The matte of the animation is made by shooting the cels twice. First they are recorded on color stock against a black background, then they are shot on *high-contrast* black-and-white film. In this case the cels are backlit and placed on an opal glass. It is extremely important to shoot the two strips identically according to the frame-by-frame notations on the exposure sheet, and preferably on the same camera stand.

The films are processed and the black-and-white high-con material is printed to obtain separate negative and positive strips. The positive strip, called the *core* or *male* matte, shows the cartoon figure in silhouette. The negative matte is the *counter* or *female* matte, and is black except for the character area that is clear. These strips are loaded into the optical printer for combining with the live-action sequence. First the live footage with the male black-and-white matte in front of it is run through the projector. This is filmed by the camera. If the film were processed at this point the resulting image would be a live-action scene with just a silhouetted black shape of the character. Instead, the sequence is rewound to the beginning and the strip of live-action film and the black-and-white strip with the male matte of the character is replaced with the film bearing the female matte and the strip with the color character.

These are run in combination and recorded with the camera a second time. Now when the camera negative is developed and printed, the black silhouette has been filled in by the color cartoon

Effects

Combining live-action and animation. Mattes are used to block areas of the film emulsion holding back exposure until a second run through the camera.

A live-action scene (**A**) is projected and traced (**B**) for positioning animation.

Color cels of the animation (**C**) are shot against a black background.

A high-contrast matte strip (**D**) is made from the same cels shot with a backlight. The result is a solid black figure surrounded by a clear area.

From this a reverse matte (**E**) is printed resulting in a clear figure surrounded by solid black. The live-action negative is printed in combination with the solid black figure (**D**), then in the next run the negative of the color animation (**C**) is printed with the clear figure matte (**E**) to obtain the final frame (**F**).

character and the counter matte has protected the refilmed live strip from being exposed. The match of the live actor and the cartoon is realized.

Other Techniques

Special effects must be given storytelling emphasis through intercutting to maintain a convincing illusion. If an actor is to fly, then the effect, whether done with animation, miniatures, or matting, is enhanced through close-ups of the actor followed by reaction shots of other actors in the scene.

The creation of imaginative or historical locales can be achieved through rear projection, front projection, hanging miniatures, perspective set construction, and lighting and exposure control. In each of these techniques the actors must be positioned carefully. Similarly, with a static matte, the actors' movements are restricted to avoid disappearing behind the matte. With traveling mattes, the action area is broader.

Video Effects

The greatest boon to the creation of special effects has been the development of video techniques. When film is employed, as in optical printing, several days elapse for the chemical processing of negatives and prints. In video, though the same preliminary care is necessary for preparing the elements, the actual compositing is seen in a matter of minutes.

There is no physical cutting and splicing of videotape (although this was a necessary procedure in the early days of tape production). The stored images, instead, are rearranged or discarded by re-recording. The addition of effects and titles is managed the same way and, if a facility has all of the specialized electronic gear, all in one place.

The studio cameras, optical printers, and editing machines used in film special effects have definite and recognizable silhouettes. Not so in the video world of rectangular boxes. Each has a different purpose and a special magic all its own. To flip or rotate an image, technicians turn to one rectangular box; to composite shots, they'll call upon another box; and to introduce animation into the mix, there are still more special boxes. Before assigning work to any effects company, find out the range of their equipment. It is not uncommon for a producer to find, after the work has begun, that the chosen studio lacks the capability to do a certain effect because they do not have the correct rectangular box.

Doing It Yourself

Filming animation requires a camera able to shoot one frame at a time. Once strictly the province of film, this method is now increasingly upstaged by electronic imaging.

Video cameras that can be used for single-frame shooting require sophisticated equipment. There are inexpensive cameras that record four to eight frames with a quick tap or squeeze of the run button, but this limitation gets in the way of creating smooth, single-frame animation. To shoot frame by frame on video, a camera must be con-

Camera Stand Made from Plywood

The table accepts a standard animation disc and is fitted with fluorescent fixtures for underlighting.

The table slides on channel aluminum. The camera is positioned to shoot in proper alignment with the artwork.

Counterbalanced with sash weights, the camera trucks up and down on metal rods.

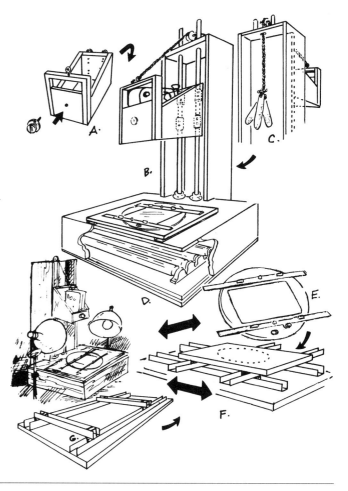

nected to a versatile recorder or a computer program.

Video recording offers instant replay, a rewarding and desirable advantage when testing action. The technology is constantly upgraded, and one day it will have the high image quality, sharpness, and large-screen projectability of film. Still, there are advantages in the simplest film cameras that cannot be realized in video shooting. With 16mm or super-8mm it is possible to make multiple exposures and dissolves in the camera, but in video this must be done in post-editing.

The super-8mm format, like the 16mm before it, has moved into a highly specialized area. It has been maintained on a professional level by specialized supply houses that sell new super-8mm equipment and stock the film in a variety of black-and-white and color emulsions. Bargains in used 16mm and super-8mm cameras are available if you are on the lookout for those forgotten in attics, on closet shelves, or at flea markets. Though of little use to the average home moviemaker in an age of video, this equipment is still viable for shooting animation.

Types of Stands

Once you've obtained a camera, the next concern is finding a steady support to hold it. The most direct method of shooting animation is to set a camera on a tripod and focus the lens on artwork positioned on the wall or floor. An even simpler approach is to use a clamp with an attached tripod screw and secure it to a shelf above your drawing board, the edge of a table, or the back of a chair. Many darkroom photo enlargers have been enlisted in the service of animation by substituting a camera, on the post, for the enlarger. Discarded parts, such as the stand used for supporting an X-ray camera or similar medical equipment, can be found through classified ads. Professional photo-supply dealers sell copystands specifically made for film and video cameras.

None of the aforementioned supports, including the special equipment made for copying, mount the camera so that the artwork is shot right-side-up as you face the front of the setup. This happens because the tripod screw is in the base,

the sturdiest part of the camera. If the stand is rugged enough to accept it, a support can be built to accept the camera in a turned-around position.

Many copystands use a single, round pole causing the camera to swing from side to side when sliding it up and down, but some stands incorporate double posts or a single square post to keep the camera in line. These supports are adequate for shooting simple animation tests, but for more advanced work, a professional stand is needed. The large, expensive units, standbys of the commercial houses, have all the versatile means of handling animation art, and if you can't buy one you can rent the services of companies that will shoot your work for an agreed-upon price. If you are shooting for your own pleasure, you can probably get away with using one of the stands mentioned above, or constructing your own.

Focusing

Centering a camera over the artwork is easy if it is equipped with a through-

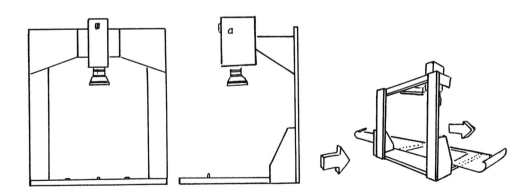

A simple stand for a lightweight video camcorder that allows for panning artwork in north, south, east, and west directions.

the-lens viewfinder. If you have an older camera that lacks this feature, various methods can be used for centering. The problem with cameras that don't focus directly through the lens is that at close distances the viewfinder image does not match the position of the lens. This off-set view is known as *parallax*.

One way to solve this is to make a special guide by accurately measuring and drawing the front of the camera and finding the centers for the lens and the viewfinder. Then, by scaling up the drawing so that it matches the shooting field of your artwork, you will have a guide that corrects for parallax, allowing you to focus through the viewfinder while positioning the artwork in line with the center of the lens.

Another solution is to open the camera and then remove the pressure plate of the film gate. Then position a small, bright flashlight behind the film-gate aperture. For the light to hit the shooting table, the camera's shutter must be in the open position. To do this, run the camera and stop in an open position or, if this doesn't work, manually open the shutter gently. With the room darkened the shape of the aperture is projected onto the table. This area, when traced, is where the artwork should be placed to fall under the lens.

Most super-8 cameras have a single-frame release, but many older cameras lack this feature. You can practice on these cameras to roll off one frame at a time. With the camera open, give the run button a quick tap and observe the claw movement. Repeat this until you develop a consistent touch that moves the mechanism one frame every time.

The worst that can happen is that you occasionally run off two frames.

Alignment Tests

Start by making tests. Shooting work that you've spent untold hours on and neglecting to check your equipment for exposure, light balance, proper focus, and camera alignment is not good sense.

Use two lamps set at a forty-five-degree angle. For black-and-white shooting with Plus-X or Tri-X stock, two 100-watt household bulbs will work fine. For color films, match the lamps with the color temperature requirements stated by the manufacturer. To check for even distribution of light, stand a pencil on its flat end in the center of your camera table and adjust the lights so that the pencil's shadows fall to equal lengths, with even density on both sides.

Load the camera, in dim light, and run off about two feet of film to check the threading. Close the camera door and run 150 frames to bypass any footage that may have been fogged in loading. The doors of cameras that have been used frequently develop an imperfect fit. Immediately after loading and closing the camera door, put black tape around the edge of the door where it meets the camera body.

With the camera in position, expose four frames at each f-stop opening, slating each shot accordingly. The lens openings are calibrated on the outside of the barrel of the lens in degrees ranging from f-22 to f-1.4. Then run another 150 or 200 frames as protection leader. When the processed film is returned from the lab, study it for proper focus, evenness of lighting, correct exposure, and alignment of the image. Establish a relationship with a lab that you expect to use on a regular basis so that a standard is maintained.

Developing Black-and-White Pencil Tests

You can develop short black-and-white, Plus-X or Tri-X 16mm strips yourself, in just a few minutes, to check for centering or to view your animation. You'll need a space that can be made perfectly dark. Film your test and then, with the lights out, open the camera and cut the film at a point below the gate, remove the take-up spool from the camera, and place it in a black bag or a covered film can.

Prepare the necessary chemicals, developer, stop bath, and fixer. Once they are mixed, pour each into separate trays. The chemicals should be about 68 degrees Fahrenheit (20 degrees Celsius). Set a timer for about five minutes and then in complete darkness immerse the film in the developer bath. Immediately unwind the roll by twirling the opposite end into another roll. Once this is formed, unwind it and twirl it the other way. Keep doing this till the warning bell of the timer rings. Then place the strip into the stop bath (plain water can also be used), continuing the same winding and unwinding technique for thirty seconds. After this, place the roll into the hypo fix and repeat the rolling and unrolling for another five minutes. The roll can now be examined by the illumination of a dim green safelight. If the image has not completely cleared

and appears milky white, return it to the hypo fix for another two minutes or until it clears. (At this point you can turn on a dark-green safelight.) After the required development and fix times, wash the film in a tray with running water, or several changes of clean water, for fifteen to twenty minutes. Hang the strip in a dust-free place for drying. To protect your skin from any caustic substances, use plastic gloves. Use paper towels and soap to wash your hands and all surfaces when you are finished.

Computer Controls

Computers arrived at an opportune moment, when the field was ready for something new. Early animated films had been done with chalk on a blackboard, then on paper, and finally on cels. Animation stands were originally manually operated and advanced to being motor driven; with the increased demand for intricate special effects in the 1970s, stands were given computer controls. This made it possible to accurately repeat exacting moves hour after hour, and the procedure was not subjected to the interruptions and distractions that plague humans on the job. When the phone rings, the camera operator answers it while the computerized camera continues shooting the scene unperturbed.

Then, of course, there are the multitude of computer programs that accept scanned or digitized drawings for coloring, adding textures, and for putting it all in motion. A complete track can be scored with music, voice, and sound effects, and synchronized with your

DROP
PLASTER
ON BACK
OF FIGURE
TO FORM
SECOND
PART
OF
MOLD.

Making a mold is a time-consuming and messy procedure. Cover the work area with plastic sheets and have running water at hand. When mixing and molding with plaster, wear a dust mask and old clothes. Before you start, decide if you are going to need more than one copy.

If only one is required, then a waste mold is made. As the name implies, it cannot be used again; for more than one copy, a reusable latex mold will be necessary.

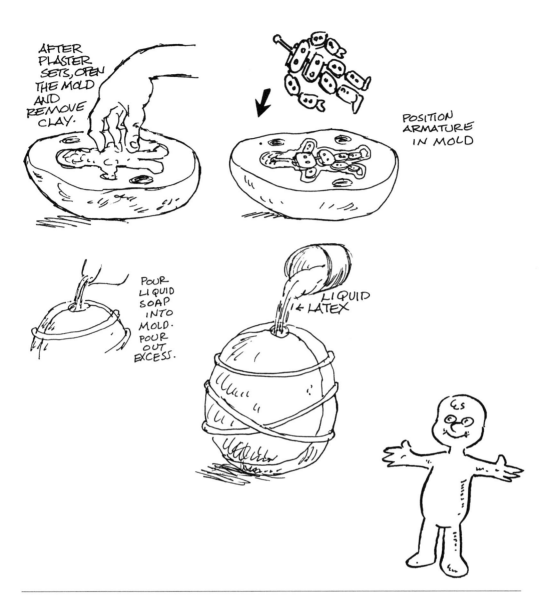

AFTER PLASTER SETS, OPEN THE MOLD AND REMOVE CLAY.

POSITION ARMATURE IN MOLD

POUR LIQUID SOAP INTO MOLD. POUR OUT EXCESS.

LIQUID LATEX

character's actions. In the process there are no spilled ink bottles, no gargantuan camera stand, no going out into the storm to rush the film to the lab—just you and your mouse and some millions of pixels. You can even send it to another computer on the other side of the globe for viewing. And all of this can be done in the privacy of your own home on a rainy day, and you won't get wet.

Stop Motion

The appeal of stop-motion is the challenge, the performance and the magic in the search for what makes us happy. —John Gati

There has always been an appeal in seeing stationary objects come to life. It is magical to watch a light bulb twist out of one lamp, bounce across the screen,

Stop-motion Shooting

and screw itself into another. Objects filmed in stop-motion are solid and cast their own shadows. They are also reusable and can be shot from several angles, compared to cel animation where every shape, shadow, and angle must be drawn.

Not everything in stop-motion has a comic purpose. Live films have always depended on the photography of objects, especially for the illusion of sailing ships, trains, grand palaces, ancient castles, or Greek mythology's Mount Olympus. However, more and more stop-motion specialists are being asked to inject intricately modeled figures of horses, people, and, if the script calls for it, sea serpents, dinosaurs, and angels into realistic scenes.

■ *Some Pointers on Puppet Filming*

Puppets and figures are created out of plasticine, wood, metal, foam rubber, fiberglass, and plastics. Much of what you will need, though, can be found around the home.

Scenes shot intuitively may look fine, but they cannot be duplicated in a reshoot. In commercial production, where precise timing and placement is required and where reshoots are expected, exposure sheets and guides must be followed.

Here are some suggestions from stop-motion filmmakers Becky Wible, John Gati, and Jimmy Picker:

1. Design figures and sets for ease of manipulation. When using wire armatures, double the wire and twist it around itself for strength.
2. Light your subject so there is separation between background and foreground elements. Expert lighting of 3D sets is based on a familiarity with natural conditions and then skillfully reinterpreting this to a tabletop setup. Imagine a room at twilight as it slowly darkens. Recreating the same effect for a stop-motion production demands meticulous lighting.
3. After a period of shooting, clay puppets acquire a layer of dust. You can't always detect this on the set, but when projected, the change in coloring is obvious. To avoid this, make duplicate puppets, place them in plastic bags, and store them in a refrigerator.
4. For close-ups, use larger heads.
5. Subtle moves create greater wear on a figure than fast actions, such as running and jumping.

Lighting of Objects

Combining puppets with foreground props and rear-projected scenery.

The Soundtrack and Editing

Music is like a small flame put under a screen to warm it. . . . —Aaron Copland

Music for animation has its roots in the days of live piano accompaniment for film. The sound heightened the dramatic action and served to drown out audience noise. Although some studios provided sheet music to accompany their films (which could get lost in transit), the choice of appropriate melodies to enhance the action was placed in the skilled hands of the pianists themselves. Themes ran from pleasant, joyous flourishes for happy moments to somber, dramatic chords for scenes of mystery and conflict. A projectionist who wanted to go home early cranked the projector faster and the piano player picked up the tempo. When talkies arrived, some of these musicians joined the staffs of cartoon studios and transferred their silent-movie experience to recorded soundtracks.

Movies and Sound

Over the decades, each step in the recording of movie sound has been heralded as a wondrous invention. In 1927 sound for film was recorded and synchronized to theater projectors by a needle traversing the grooves of a disc. Soon after, optical soundtracks with voices and music were being recorded directly onto the edge of motion-picture film as a scraggly line drawn by light, triggered by electrons. The sound, however, could not be listened to until the film was developed overnight at a lab.

In the 1950s when improved magnetic film was introduced it was seen as the ultimate advance in sound quality and could be listened to immediately. At present, there are innumerable ways of recording sound and multiple ways of employing it. Sound is still recorded onto tape, but now the tape track is a tiny digital audiotape (DAT), or a shiny compact disc (CD). Though movies are still shot on film, they are more likely to be transferred to video, usually a Beta tape, and edited in computer systems where the scenes are synchronized to sound. Depending on what the release destination for the production is—television, video (VHS or DVD), or movie theater (35mm, or 70mm)—it will be copied out as a tape or disc, or meticulously recorded back onto motion picture film to cheer the audience at a theater near you.

Recording Sound

The editing of an animated film begins at the recording session, and since the track must adhere to the completed animation, the recording should be given scrupulous attention. Read again the guidelines about recording actors in chapter 9 on direction. Some additional points are important to remember: Use separate microphones for recording more than one actor to avoid the overlapping of voices. Record a few seconds of silence to get the "room tone." The quiet "sound" of the room is inserted during editing to maintain acoustic consistency when filling silent spaces on the track.

When your recording is complete and you are satisfied with it, make one or two protection copies of the original. If these copies are in tape format, they should include digital sync control tracks. This is almost automatic today with the cassettes and discs used in digital computer and video-editing systems.

Choosing and Using Music

The purpose of adding music to a film is to amplify the action. The right music propels the story; music wrongly chosen distracts. Don't just think that you can take a disc of your favorite music and slap it onto the animation. If you are really serious about such copyrighted materials, permission must be obtained from the composer, recording artist, or the American Society of Composers, Authors and Publishers (ASCAP). Rights can be expensive, especially if they include theatrical, educational, television, home video, and other outlets.

There are music libraries that offer a wide range of prerecorded musical styles at various prices. It is possible to get a break on the cost of library music if you explain that it is for an independent, educational, or student production. You could use public domain music, songs and tunes that no longer fall under copyright laws, such as folk music, nursery rhymes, and compositions from the nineteenth-century and earlier. Be careful though: "Yankee Doodle" is copyright free, but "Happy Birthday to You" is still under copyright. Contemporary recordings of such selections are protected for performances and arrangements, but the melodies are available to anyone. Whatever your choice, make sure that the music does not conflict with dialogue or obscure the nature of your story. Screen classic films like UPA's *Gerald McBoing-Boing*, *The Unicorn in the Garden,* or shorts from Disney and Warner Bros., and listen.

Sound Effects

Sounds create strong images and are essential to animated productions. You can gather actual street noises, parades, motorboats, construction sounds, or clocks and bell rings yourself, but, unfortunately, many sounds don't record the way we hear them. A day of roaming around the zoo carries no guarantee that a lion will roar or that the seals will bark on cue. Outdoor recordings have distracting crowd and traffic noises and a tape of a home washing machine will sound like an automobile factory at full tilt. For realistic effects, use recordings made by professionals who capture sounds under controlled conditions with sophisticated microphones and filters. Effects have an advantage over music in that they are not copyrighted and royalty payments are not imposed on their use. Recordings of effects are found at sound libraries and most music-editing facilities, and are also available on tape and disc and on the Internet. If you do make your own effects, you should know that the best sounds are not realistic, but the ones specially created to fit the needs of the animation. These can be made using simple props.

A more "homey" washing machine sound is made by tipping an overturned glass in a bucket of water while someone else twangs a metal spring. The kerplunk of the landing of a cartoon spaceship is accomplished by dropping a couple of heavy telephone books on the floor. Distorting sounds by re-recording taped noises at varying speeds or playing them backwards is one way to get offbeat effects. Bill Plympton used a woman's voice at a slower speed to get it to sound like a man's in the film *Your Face* (1986).

Here are some other easily managed sound effects:

- *Footsteps:* Hold a microphone close to the floor as someone walks in place. Different floor surfaces give different results. For the sound of walking through twigs and leaves combine actual steps with a straw broom being twisted and squeezed close to the microphone.
- *Walking in snow:* To simulate someone trudging in deep snow, press a packet of granular material like rice near the microphone. Pressing slowly creates the pattern of labored walking.
- *Fire or frying bacon:* Crinkle a sheet of cellophane.
- *Crashing through a wooden door:* Crush pieces of thin wood a short distance from the mike.

Reading the Track

- *Horse's hoofs:* Alternately tap a pair of paper cups, open side down, in a box of gravel.
- *Waves, rolling surf:* Slide ball bearings or grains of rice back and forth in a cardboard box.

Analyzing a Soundtrack

Now, with the recording completed, the track is ready to be analyzed. This is done in several ways. A standard method is to transfer the recording to magnetic film, 35mm, or 16mm wide, with sprocket holes along the edges, both sides for 35mm and one side for 16mm. The sprockets allow for the film to be pulled manually over a *synchronizer* wheel, which activates a counter with numbers like a speedometer but in frames and feet, not miles or kilometers. Also connected to the synchronizer is a magnetic pickup wired to an amplifier and a loudspeaker. The magnetic soundtrack is then run slowly through the synchronizer until the first audible sound comes through the loudspeaker. The track is rolled back forty-eight frames, a large X is placed at that point on the film, and a small piece of tape with an audible "beep" is also adhered to the frame. These indications will aid in synchronizing the sound with the picture once the animation is completed.

Now the reading proceeds. The start and end of each word is found by holding the magnetic track with the fingers of both hands and slowly rolling it back and forth past the magnetic pickup on the synchronizer. The numbers on the frame counter correspond to dial counts on the exposure sheet, and as each syl-

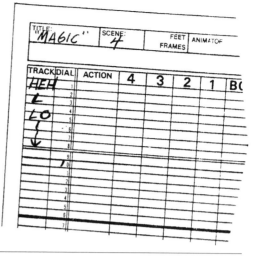

lable or portion of a word is heard, the information is jotted down next to the matching frame number on the sheets. This means that if the first word is *hello*, and it takes eight frames to say it, the editor marks the start of the word at frame number one on the exposure sheet and then marks the end of the word eight frames later. For accurate lip sync, the rolling procedure continues over the word until every syllable has been discerned. The word *hello* would be marked as starting on frame one with the sound "heh," then the sound "el" would be placed at frame three, and at frame five the sound "lo" is marked and a line is added to indicate the trailing off of the last syllable to frame eight.

When done properly, track analysis with magnetic film is very exact, and many filmmakers still rely on this method. However, others in the field are now using digital software that shows a visual graph of the soundtrack on a monitor, so that music or dialogue can be analyzed on the computer. When playing music or voice with the proper

Electronic Computing

1. Background painting.
2. Actor performing in specified area on a Chroma Key painted set.
3. Model of aircraft on pedestal placed against a Chroma Key (a color that will be removed later) backdrop. Model remains stationary as a camera, operated by motion-control, moves past it, simulating the shifts and turns of an actual aircraft.
4. Animated effects filmed against a Chroma Key backing.
5. Extraneous rigging, such as pedestals and wires, is painted out by matching the background color, using computer software.
6. The separate elements are assembled on videotape. A matte is created electronically, and the background color drops out and is replaced by the combined images to create a scene that could not have been accomplished through live-action shooting. The final illusion is reinforced if the scale of objects, shadows, and highlights have been carefully integrated.

software installed, at a normal listening mode or reduced speed, important points in the track can be indicated by tapping the computer's keyboard spacebar. This information is then written onto exposure sheets, but the track, copied into the computer program, can be referred to throughout the production, and is ready for synchronizing with scanned-in animation later on.

The Sound Mix

Sound for films is recorded on separate tracks: one for voice, another for music, and a third for effects. In a global market it is likely that your production will go into distribution in other countries, and if the voice, music, and effects are not separated, foreign language dubs cannot be made. However, if these three tracks were played simultaneously at equal volume, as they had been recorded, these sounds would drown each other out.

Imagine a night scene in a churchyard. Two characters are walking and whispering to each other as their footsteps indicate their movements. The

Video Editing by Computer

Recording and playback machines for video- and audiocassettes (**A**) respond to commands from an editing controller.

A computer program (**B**) lists all of the available scenes on one monitor (**C**) from which the editor selects sequences.

The assembled scenes are listed in screening order on a second monitor (**D**). To view a sequence, the editor uses the controller to signal the playback machines, and the results are screened on the monitor (**E**).

The controller also allows for the addition and mixing of previously recorded music, voice, and sound effects.

church bell tolls, and an owl hoots. Eerie music on the track heightens the suspense. If all of these sounds are played at the same volume, the atmospheric quality of the soundtrack will be destroyed. To correct this lack of balance, and for proper emphasis of voice, effects, and music, the tracks must be re-recorded at a *mix* or, as it is also called, *dub* session.

For those independent animators who like doing everything themselves, I've got a suggestion: take a break. Don't do the mix yourself. Unless you've worked as a sound mixer in the past, go to a professional studio for this. It's comparable to when you hire actors to do voices. You don't want to employ amateurs. Your brother-in-law may have a comic voice, but chances are he can't read lines. Actors know how to breathe and where to add emphasis and character to a word or phrase.

Sound engineers, many of whom are musically trained, have the experience and sensitivity, as well as the proper equipment, for the job. It will cost you a few bucks but, believe me, it's worth it.

To prepare for a mix, a log of the contents of each track is placed onto a *cue sheet* to alert the recording engineer as to what frame these sounds should sync with, which sounds to emphasize, and which to diminish. A short production can be mixed in two to four hours. A feature could take several days or weeks. The final track can be combined with your visuals as a video, CD, DVD, or as an optical negative for making a film print.

PART FOUR

The Story Goes Forth

*Technical skill . . . can take you where you want to go
but it can't tell you where to go.*

—Alan Reynolds Thompson

CHAPTER 16

Computer Animation

The image revolution that movies represented has now been overhauled by the television evolution, and is approaching the next visual stage—to computer graphics, to computer controls of environment, to a new cybernetic 'movie art.' —Stan Vanderbeek

No matter how well rendered a cannonball may be, it does not look like a cannonball if it does not behave like one when animated. —John Lasseter

Computers and animation are natural partners brought together by the animation process itself. Advanced studios now equip each animator with not only a drawing table but a computer with a scanner or digitizer as well. This is not because the animators' job has changed; it's just that computers free the artist to perform old tasks in a new way.

Computers, Art, and Animation

Producing images by activating thousands of tiny pixels on a computer screen is not far from the dot patterns of the pointillist paintings of Georges Seurat and the experimental pinscreen animations of Alexandre Alexeieff and Claire Parker. Forty years ago, experiments with *oscilloscopes* gave animators an opportunity to trace instantaneous pictures of electron motion on a cathode ray tube. Images were triggered by speaking into an attached microphone and patterns were generated to illustrate what voices "looked like." It was usually pointed out that the word *spaghetti* resembled what it was—thin, squiggly strands. Mary Ellen Bute's *Abstronic* (1954) and Norman McLaren's *Begone Dull Care* (1949) are two examples of animated productions that included the photography of oscilloscopes. Finally, in the late 1960s and early 1970s, Peter Foldes, John Whitney, Lillian Schwartz, and Ken Knowlton pioneered computer animation by wrestling with equipment that dwarfs today's compact units. In the 1980s companies like Digital Productions, Magi, Robert Abel Associates, Pixar, and Pacific Data Images produced elaborate animated images for live-action feature films and television commercials. By the 1990s their legacy of quality had become evident in the Disney-Pixar feature collaboration *Toy Story* (1995) and Dreamworks's SKG's *Shrek* (2001).

Getting Acquainted

Information about computer graphics changes quickly. Anything written two or three years ago is as stale as last week's *TV Guide*. To learn the basics of computers and become familiar with current software, choose a reputable school. In the fast-moving electronic world, even the top schools find it difficult to keep up with the constant upgrading of equipment. One solution, serve as an apprentice at a professional studio and gain experience with high-end equipment.

What You Need to Start: Hardware, Software, and Underwear

Since everything related to computers will be obsolete before you read this I must paraphrase an old adage: Don't put the computer before the horse! The way I see it, before tackling reams of technical information, concentrate on developing your storytelling, drawing, and animation skills—all of the subjects dealt with in earlier chapters. Thus armed, you will bring something of importance to the computer, rather than be overwhelmed by it.

Still, you might want to experiment. The basic machinery, or *hardware*, consists of the computer itself, a monitor, a scanner, a keyboard, pointing devices such as a mouse or stylus, a graphics card, and capabilities for burning a DVD or for sending images to a videocassette recorder. These devices accommodate the *programs* or *software*, the tools that support all of the things you're hankering to do on the computer. Gathering it all together can be fun (and expensive) but when you get down to work be sure you've got comfortable surroundings and loose-fitting underwear for the many long hours you will be seated at the computer.

Recording Pencil Animation

There is still one predominant tool for creating action on the computer: the pencil. Without the pencil there are no storyboards, no character designs, and no animation. Computers are handy tools, but they know nothing of aesthetics and are not as smart as you are. Just as you command the pencil, so will you command the computer.

Some skilled artists use a stylus or a mouse to draw directly into the computer. However, you may find that doing animation drawings at your desk and timing the action by constant flipping satisfies you best. When ready, scan your drawings into the computer for rendering in a broad range of opaque and transparent colors and tints. For this, the drawings should have clean, dark, connected outlines. Breaks in the strokes are a problem, as the most trivial opening causes any chosen color to spread itself over the entire screen.

Creating Images on the Computer

Specialization is important to a production and one person rarely does it all. Complex 3D scenes require modelmakers, texture artists, figure animators, facial

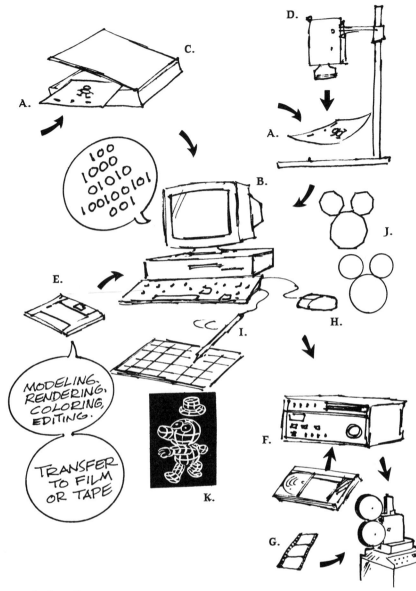

Computer Animation

Pencil drawings (**A**) are entered into a computer (**B**) by scanning (**C**) or by video capture (**D**).

A rendering program (**E**) allows the drawings to be enlarged, reduced, and embellished with color and tonal effects. The action can be replayed on the computer and transferred to tape (**F**) or film (**G**).

Animation is created in the computer with a mouse (**H**) or a stylus (**I**), and is either 2D (**J**) or 3D (**K**). The 3D images are constructed as a wire frame to which an outer skin covering of color is applied.

Animation of 2D or 3D is adjusted through computer commands, and then transferred to tape, disc, or film.

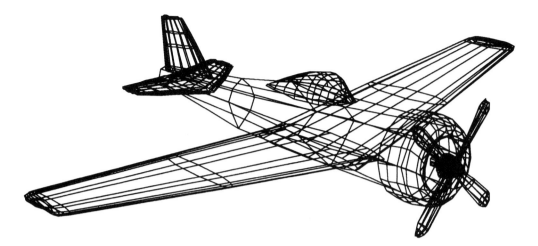

A wire frame construction, the basis of 3D computer design. (Created by Adrian Sinott.)

animators, graphic designers, and experts for developing atmospheric effects.

There are programs that imitate flat 2D pictures, and others that turn your request for a solid 3D shape into a form that looks as if it could be held in your hand. To create perspective shapes on a 2D system you draw on a tablet with a stylus or a mouse, but in the 3D programs you type in the information. The suggestion of a square directs the program to create an accurate shape. Computer-generated solids achieve the look of stop-motion figures, and though real puppets have a special appeal, the electronic forms have at least one advantage over the real thing: computer puppets don't fall over.

Dimensional shapes are built as a *wire frame* image—a picture of rudimentary coordinates or a geometric skeleton on which the surface is attached. A head, a pencil, or an automobile is developed by using the actual subject as a guide, or by making a clay model of it.

This is carefully marked with overlapping longitudinal and latitudinal lines. The intersections of the lines are the points for digitizing spatial information into the computer. For filling in the outline form, a palette of thousands of colors is available, while shadow effects are created with a chosen point of light, with rays projecting through the body of the drawn shape. When done properly the effect is a believable simulation of shadows and highlights. The completed animation is then transferred to a video recorder or photographed onto motion picture film one frame at a time. Through all of this the wire frame image remains intact and is stored in the computer, where it is available for restructuring as a new character in another story.

Prominent studios use their own software to generate images, which gives each a distinctive look, but they also require store-bought programs and integrate them into their own highly developed applications. Pixar, PDI,

Rhythm and Hues, Blue Sky, and R/Greenberg have all developed their own applications or have tweaked commercial products, as have the Disney artists who, when confronted with the tantalizing problem of animating vast crowd scenes in *The Hunchback of Notre Dame* (1996), developed unique commands for the versatile *Softimage* program, and in doing so advanced the possibilities of the art of animation.

Computer Pencil Tests

Use easily acquired programs to make pencil tests of your drawings, such as Flipbook by Digicel or Quick Checker by Celsys, Inc. These both offer sample programs on the Internet. There are other less sophisticated, lower-priced programs, such as Stop Motion Studio by Loud By Design, Inc., for Mac users, which is simple to use and can be very satisfying.

A popular way to view your animation is through the combined forces of Adobe Photoshop and Adobe After Effects. Scan your drawings into Photoshop then export them to After Effects, where you assign the drawings a time sequence and view the results on your monitor. That's the idea in a nutshell, but what are the basic steps for doing this?

First, animate a series of drawings on paper. Make sure the lines are dark and that any line breaks are closed up. This helps when coloring with Photoshop's Magic Wand tool. Tape a set of pegs to the edge of your scanner. Now open Photoshop. Set your scanner to grayscale and the output resolution to 72 dpi. Scan each drawing, naming each with a successive number, such as "cat-01," "cat-02," "cat-03," through "cat-24" and beyond, and save each to your Desktop. Close Photoshop and create a new folder on the Desktop called "Cat." Drag each drawing from the desktop to the folder.

Open After Effects. Click on New Project. Click File > Import File. Then open the "Cat" folder. Click only the first frame of the sequence. In this case that would be "cat-01." Go to the bottom of the dialogue box and select Generic EPS Sequence and click on the name of the sequence as it appears in the New Project window and drag it to the Composition window. The first frame of your sequence will appear. Press the space bar and your series will animate in the composition window.

The frame rate is preset, but you can change this and also loop your animation by clicking on the name of your file in the Project Window and then clicking File > Interpret Main. A dialogue box will appear with screening choices as for further embellishments. With the drawings now nestled in your computer, they are available for coloring or for receiving other visual effects in Photoshop and After Effects.

CHAPTER 17

The Business of Animation

I've never called it art—it's show business. —Walt Disney

No matter how much animation is viewed as an art form, it is impossible to ignore that it is also a business. Animation is a business that experiences periodic highs and lows and has rarely been a source of wealth for those that bend over the drawing boards. Still, it has afforded a decent living for many artists whose creative efforts have brought millions in revenues to producers, distributors, advertisers, stockholders, and the thousands of manufacturers of related licensed products. What follows are a few hints to smooth the way to becoming a responsible salaried worker, a free-lancer, or an independent filmmaker.

Finding Work

In the United States, most studios are in Los Angeles, New York, Chicago, and San Francisco, and in any place with a fair-sized television outlet. But Los Angeles is where the bulk of animation originates. Studios are listed in the telephone yellow pages under Motion Picture and Video Producers. Some companies' names indi-

cate that they do animation. Others may include animation in their list of services. Most small shops create commercials and productions for television, education, and business as well as entertainment reels. These are the places to head for. A phone call is always advisable, but be brief and to the point. State the purpose of your call and don't say that you are "into animation." (If a pipe bursts in your home, would you hire someone who is "into plumbing"? You'd want a real plumber.) So it is with animation studios; they require people who are skilled in very special categories. If you have artwork or animation samples, mention this. They might request to see certain types of samples. Some studios are informal and a conversation might develop. If there is no work at one place, a considerate employee might point you in the direction of other more active firms, ones that you would not have known about otherwise.

Your Portfolio

Experienced animators seeking work know where the studios are—not just those that are highly publicized, but the smaller service shops as well. They know they are expected to have sample reels— three-quarter-inch or half-inch video-cassettes or DVDs of their previous assignments, running less than five minutes. Only their very best work, a few commercials, or brief excerpts from longer productions are included. When they must be mailed, these lightweight vidoes are shipped in padded envelopes along with a short introductory letter, a résumé, and a stamped, self-addressed envelope to guarantee the video's return. For story work, originals or copies of sample storyboards go into a presentation binding and are shown to the studios. Each page is marked with a copyright symbol (©), the name of the author, and the current year. For submissions by mail, only copies are sent. The originals are kept on file.

Starting Out

For the newcomer, a portfolio of drawings is more important than a sample reel. The studio wants to know what skills you have, since they need people for in-betweening and assistant positions. When looking at a reel, they can't be sure whether you did it all or others helped you. But a selection of art

samples shows them exactly what you are capable of and how well you draw and design. The Disney studio has special requirements for prospective interns, trainees, and experienced artists. They are interested in on-the-spot sketches of people and animals and an indication of your awareness of figure movement, attitude, and mood. They want to *see* good drawings and not cartooning samples, although a few of your best can be included. They are seeking artists who can "think with a pencil." For up-to-date requirements, check their Web site at *http://disneycareers.newjobs.com*.

Television

Television programming for children begins in the studios in and around Hollywood and New York. The storyboards, characters, layouts, and soundtracks are conceived there, but most of the programs are completed by efficient studios in Asia that handle everything from animation to final shooting. Cable networks are approachable if you have the kind of characters they want. This receptivity follows the rise of programs like *The Simpsons*, *Ren and Stimpy*, *Courage the Cowardly Dog*, and *SpongeBob Square Pants*. The decisions on which ideas or characters are chosen often lie with the advertisers that sponsor these shows, since television basically is an advertising medium.

Commercials

Television commercials appear on such a regular basis that viewers take them for granted, but the bidding to produce them is serious business for studios in major advertising centers.

The good points about working on commercials are that they are short and varied, reflect the newest techniques and solutions, and continually test your ingenuity in keeping them fresh and interesting. On the negative side are the persistent deadlines and quirky revisions. To find out what's going on, read *Advertising Age*, *Ad Week*, *Back Stage Shoot*, *Millimeter*, and other industry trade journals. Find out who views sample reels at specific agencies and send your best samples to them with a letter introducing yourself.

Informational Productions

Many films and videos are made for corporate meetings, schools, and to enlighten audiences on matters of health, science, or the environment. The animation for these productions does not always involve cartoon characters, but requires imaginative graphics and entertaining ways of presenting important information. Most of these subjects originate with business firms, publishers, or public service organizations, and it is possible to approach some of these with original proposals for productions that meet their needs.

Video Cassettes and DVD

With video players in almost every home, a new world for animation awaits the independent producer. Children are the key market here with sales mainly through retailers. Cassettes and DVDs of independent animation are sold to more mature viewers mostly through mail-order. There are distributors who are open to deals if you have anything they can use, and some may extend production capital. But this generally means that you have to share more with them and produce at the lowest possible cost.

The Internet

This is an expanding outlet for information. There is an increasing demand for animated tidbits on the Web. There are thousands of sites and many of them could use animated logos, charts, diagrams, maps, and cartoon characters for added fun or just to hold someone's attention. There are studios that create these items, but the available software makes it ever easier for individual animators with knowledge of Web design to setup their laptops anywhere and pitch right in.

Games

Interactive computer games and video games are a large and still-expanding arena in which animation is highly visible. Gamers play on machines at malls, at home on videogame systems, and with computer software, and they also download from the Internet. Game designs range from near cinematic realism to stylized and cutesy cartoon characters, so in this scheme there must be an area for your special talents.

Computer and videogames are produced by companies of all sizes, from small studios to large enterprises like Disney and ILM, and they are always in

the market for original ideas, or at least new approaches to some good old ideas.

Copyrights

Always place a notice of copyright on works that you create. On storyboards, films, or videos, put your name and the word *copyright*, the abbreviation, *Copr.* or the symbol ©, and the year of its first use. The simple line, "© 2003 Your Name," states all that is necessary.

You are automatically protected at the time you create the work, but submit an application for a copyright anyway for legal establishment of ownership. To obtain applications write to: Library of Congress, Copyright Office, 101 Independence Avenue, S.W., Washington, D.C., 20559, or call (202) 707-3000. The title of a production, its concept, or the ideas it relates to are not copyrightable. Works of authorship such as scripts, plays, or storyboards and accompanying texts are protected by copyright. Characters are also protected if pictorial images of them are submitted with the application. To copyright a film, send the form with your name, address, title of the work, date of its creation, and other pertinent data along with $30 to the Copyright Office. One of the following should also be included: a film print or video copy, script continuity, storyboard, or detailed synopsis. For information about copyright, and to download copyright forms, you can go to the Web address of the copyright office, which is *www.loc.gov/copyright*.

A copyright protects the work without need for renewal for the life of the artist plus seventy years. In the case of joint participation, the copyright extends for life plus seventy years after the death of the surviving author. The copyright is not renewable after the life plus seventy years stipulation. For more information, read the instructions supplied by the copyright office or check your local library for books on copyrights and patents.

Presentations

Whether you are trying to interest someone in a production or merely an idea, you should present your material in a logical way. Include: a brief, typed story outline; storyboard; character designs; capsule background of yourself and your coworkers; an overview of production costs; a description of the target audience and how the production will benefit it; and the advantages for investors. Keep your ideas to the point and arrange them in a logical order; appeal to their interest and make them want to be part of the project.

Check that your name and address are included in more than one place and put everything into a conveniently sized folder or binder. The people who will receive this packet have busy schedules, so the easier it is to read, the better.

Grants

Financing an independent production is done through grants, sponsorships, partnerships, and out of your own pocket. Grants are offered by corporations, foundations, and government agencies for educational projects, health, and the arts. These organizations are

listed in the Grant Index and Foundation Directory at local libraries and grant offices at many universities for use by faculty and students. Some schools give courses in grantsmanship, and each state has a foundation center. Check to see if the grant being offered is for a group or for an individual, since certain organizations make funds available only for schools, theatrical troupes, or symphony orchestras, while others focus on individual artists, painters, sculptors, composers, and filmmakers. The Benton Foundation, (202) 638-5770 or *www .benton.org,* offers information on connecting with nonprofit organizations.

Grants must be applied for and serious research should be done before filling out the applications. First, locate those government, corporate, or foundation entities that relate to your type of work, and then find out about the grants they have given in the past. Write a detailed but clearly defined proposal. Keep it positive and to the point, and rewrite it to eliminate unnecessary items and reinforce your main points. Don't adapt your ideas to ingratiate yourself to the grantor but stick to the subject of your production, stating it as emphatically as you can in your own strong, personal voice.

In planning a proposal, check lab costs, sound-studio rentals, camera service prices, and the hourly rates of coworkers. Once you've got the current prices pinned down, add 30 percent to the total. This is a contingency to cover normal increases in service expenditures.

■ *Be Persistent*

Agencies rarely respond with a grant on an initial submission, but if intrigued they will come through on the second, third, or fourth go-around. It's frustrating, but be prepared to update your information for resubmitting applications and proposals again and again. As in every other endeavor, the pursuit of grants depends on perseverance.

If you do get a grant, it may be for an amount less than you requested. Use the money to begin your production and reapply to the same grantor and to other sources as well. When awarded funds, use it for your production; don't apply the money to other personal expenses, and don't forget to write a sincere thank-you letter to the grantors. Surprisingly, many recipients fail to respond with this basic courtesy.

Sponsors

Sponsorship of a production comes from corporations or any institution or individual that wishes to support the creation of works of art. They may want recognition of some kind, such as credit on the production or its use for advertising and publicity. Television networks and large corporations support independent production to obtain broadcast material and to enhance their image as culturally conscious organizations. This fluctuates, but with research you will discover foundations in existence specifically for the encouragement of artistic works.

Partnerships

Individuals allied in making an animated production can pool their resources and form a legal partnership. In a partnership, the partners agree to invest their talents and capital and spell out terms of participation and distribution of receipts or profits from the completed production. Such concerted effort can result in a showcase for talent for getting jobs, commercial work, or grants. A legal partnership is binding and should be drawn up with the aid of a lawyer, but it needn't go beyond the concerns of one production. If you are planning to become partners with other artists, think it through carefully, since some will pull out for personal reasons and the production will stagger along with just a few people, or just you. It is best to maintain control of a production, delegating certain jobs to others who are paid with cash, screen credit, or a copy of the final work. Whatever the agreement, put it in writing to the satisfaction of all parties.

Shorts

Short animated films haven't been regular parts of theater programs for years, but do reappear occasionally. Their reinstatement could be caused by an increase in theater attendance or simply by the popularity of cartoon characters. To turn out a steady stream of cartoons, each running five to seven minutes, requires a formidable studio, but in recent years occasional low-budget independent productions have found their way to theater screens. There is no guarantee that a time will come when animated shorts made by individuals will have a regular presence in theaters, but what has already proved to be an audience pleaser in the recent past is the packaging of several independent productions put together by astute distributors. These outlets are constantly looking for offbeat shorts to include in programs titled as variously as *The Animation Celebration*, *Outrageous Animation*, and *Sick and Twisted*. A contract with such distributors covers the marketing of the film and specifies what you might earn.

Public broadcasting and cable television outlets use occasional animated pieces as bridges between shows. Another area for short animation is music videos in which the visuals are linked to the sounds of pop recording artists. While still a chancy area of production, there appears to be an increasing demand for short animation.

Features

Can you make your own feature? Well, making a feature is like building an aircraft carrier. It's a large undertaking requiring enormous amounts of supplies, personnel, money, and then, when it's done, it has to be put somewhere. An aircraft carrier requires an ocean and a feature needs an outlet. Long ago, Disney went into feature production because theatrical shorts were becoming increasingly expensive to make and theater-rental earnings were paltry. The seven-minute cartoon, an appetizer for the main show, could easily be jettisoned, but a full-length film held the promise of increased recognition, critical reviews, and larger audiences.

Getting an animated feature into a theater is difficult and has become increasingly so. Part of this is due to the popularity of the Disney product, backed by an accepted trade name and enormous promotional campaigns. Disney's money and resources give it access to marketing strategies unavailable to other animation studios, and it therefore dominates the market. Disney's features are lucrative, not only because of distribution, but equally because of sales of licensed toys, games, books, audio discs, and video spin-offs.

■ *Choice of Subject*

The high risk factor in theatrical production places a burden on the content of feature films. It is foolhardy to spend months or years and untold millions on a film that few would wish to see. Audiences respond to stories or characters that have a familiar ring. The various worlds of children's literature, classic novels, television programs, Broadway musicals, animated shorts, or syndicated comic strips have been mined for the most adaptable subjects. Many of these properties are copyrighted, and any licensing of rights is accompanied by stringent demands from owners who are well aware of the value of what they own. Public-domain fairytales and stories published before the twentieth century are a safer choice for producers.

Undaunted, low-budget, offbeat productions manage to appear, devised to turn the heads of bored moviegoers. Some of these are strictly for mature audiences covering subjects that would have been considered too raw just a short time ago. Feature animation, however, is still thought of as entertainment for child and family audiences.

So, back to the question, "Can you make your own feature?" At various times, small units have obtained distribution for full-length animation. In Europe the British television affiliate Channel 4 and the French Canal+ seem readily interested in funding independent productions of varying lengths.

One independent producer, Bill Plympton (*The Tune*, 1992, and *Hair High*, 2004) was able to interest a distributor of marginal, low-budget films in his venture. Originally, Plympton had approached network television executives about putting his film on as a special, but Plympton's satiric adult humor was considered unsalable in a market where animation is still strictly for kids. However, one distributor agreed to handle the film upon its completion.

Entering a production running over an hour without a promise of distribution is a risky strategy, but Plympton was able to offset his costs by applying money he earned making commercials. The $150,000 production budget, startlingly low for a feature, was also partially funded through screenings of portions of the film while it was still in production. Segments of the uncompleted production were made available to college audiences and these rentals kept him going and also reinforced his following among students, who became his film's potential audience.

Operating Your Own Studio

Among the many things that you must know to operate your own animation business, these three are uppermost:

1. You must be able to *get* the work.
2. You must be able to *do* the work.

3. You must be able to *get paid* for the work.

There are individuals who can do all three, but most people find it easier to fulfill only one or two of these qualifications. Some are good at sales and drumming up assignments, but can't make the film. Others are at a loss getting the work, but are capable of doing it if it comes in. And then there are the insistent ones who demand prompt and proper payment for their efforts, while equally efficient artists fail to go after the money owed to them.

■ *Getting the Work*

Organizations differ in their purposes for producing videos. Music videos publicize new recordings, and videos carry advice on sales training, health information, or equipment repair and maintenance.

To find potential clients, research the trade journals for the names and addresses of companies and organizations to learn what they are doing. Many industry magazines include articles on key personnel and their job titles. When you find a likely prospect, write an inquiry or proposal. Include promotional material about your company and be prepared to show samples of your videos.

You will be expected to discuss costs. Here is a sample breakdown for a demonstration cassette running two minutes. The costs are balanced against the length of the production and the time allotted for its completion, which for this production is eight weeks based on seven-hour days and a five-day week.

Obtain a copy of the latest *Graphic Artists Guild: Pricing and Ethical Guide*; it will add to your confidence and increase your knowledge of what rates some experienced artists and animators are getting.

■ *One Way to Figure a Budget*

Storyboard . . . . 30 hours
Layout . . . . 45 hours
Animation . . . . 70 hours
Assistant animation . . . . 40 hours
Ink and paint . . . . 50 hours
Magnetic track . . . . 200 feet
Backgrounds . . . . 25 hours
Narrator*
Pencil test . . . . 9 hours
Music and effects *
35mm Raw Stock
    (includes excess) . . . . 400 feet
Processing . . . . 400 feet
Final camera . . . . 18 hours
Film editing . . . . 24 hours
Recording studio . . . . 2 hours
Sound transfer . . . . 1 hour
Track reading . . . . 4 hours
Film-to-tape transfer and edit . . . . 2 hours
Overhead (Rent, phones, messengers,
    equipment rental, etc.)*
Unions and guilds*

Salaries are based on rates per hour. The hour totals are arrived at through experience with previous productions or are based on accepted industry stan-

---

*The above breakdown indicates variable cost categories. An actor may agree to do a narration for a reasonable sum, say $500, but if the client suggests the use of a celebrity voice, the price can go a lot higher. Payments to unions, guilds, and associations for actor's benefits and music rights have varying scales. These too should be checked periodically.

dards. Whatever the rate, be on the safe side and figure the hours a little higher. To check the cost of raw stock and lab processing, contact suppliers for their latest prices. Since rates change, keep apprised of them every six months.

Since clients enjoy getting involved in the selection of music and narration, you can suggest that they make their own selection and pay these people directly. Your charges to them will be less and you avoid unnecessary hassles and wasted effort.

■ *Getting the Work Done*

Agreements in writing offer protection and security, so no work should begin until an agreement is signed, whether as a contract or purchase order. Write down anything agreed to orally and have all parties sign it.

The euphoria of getting an assignment will disappear as the job goes into production and problems present themselves. One definition for *producer* is "problem solver," and though many frustrating things are out there to trip you up, keep in mind that production problems *are* solvable. The daily pitfalls become lessons for things to avoid in the next production.

Some difficulties are due to a lack of knowledge or information. Make sure you know all of the requirements of an assignment. Get transcripts of meetings and read them carefully. Always show your clients storyboards and layouts, and character models in line drawings as well as in color. Whenever clients request a change, send them copies of the revised material for their approval and for updating their files.

If you are having trouble with a lab, make sure that you are complying with their guidelines before blaming them, since the errors may be yours. If you feel they are still not giving you quality work, use a different lab. Explain what you expect from them, write out your needs, and emphasize the importance of your requests. Only then will they be able to give you their honest evaluation of a specific task.

Build a coterie of skilled workers and use only the best people and services. Having the most competent people around you will save money and avoid headaches in the long run. In this way, when a client who's unhappy about an aspect of the picture scowlingly points to a perceived error, you can stand behind your people and confidently state that they're the best in the business.

Production Time

Time, not money, is the controlling ingredient in getting most jobs done. Money buys many things, but without the proper amount of time, the chances of success are limited. Allot sufficient hours or days to every phase of production. If an unusually short time is demanded on a job, use limited animation and eliminate excess characters and unnecessary actions. Design the picture for shooting on video and take advantage of instant replay. Television commercial lengths are tightly defined, but general business and promotional productions are not so categorized. (So, it's usually possible to shorten a ten-minute film about the glories of plastic bag ties to seven or eight minutes.) Since each additional minute in a production affects the time needed for finishing it, suggest to your client that a shorter film or video would be just as effective and might even improve the story.

Getting Paid

Clients are billed for payment at specific junctures: One third at the start or signing of the contract; a second payment at the completion of a pencil test or before the inking stage; and a final payment upon delivery of the completed production. It is also possible to be paid half at the beginning and the other half at the end. The important thing is to get some payment upfront; otherwise you are working for nothing and are, in effect, financing their production.

Send out bills promptly and if the client is slow in paying, keep them apprised of your deadline and expenses. Retain a lawyer and an accountant to ensure that financial and legal matters don't become weighty. Record all meetings, client changes, and additions. You can't ask for more money if you find that you figured the budget wrong. That comes out of your pocket, but any new requests from the client are definitely charged as additional work.

The Studio

Don't buy a lot of fancy equipment. There are necessary tools that lighten the daily routine, such as copiers, fax machines, projectors, video players, and computer stuff, but be sure to buy quality equipment that requires little repair. Your studio furniture should be practical but not strive for the apex of office design. The work of architects and interior decorators is reflected in their surroundings, but your efforts go on the screen, so avoid putting money into passing fixture fads that will eat into your profits. Many independent services do editing, camera work, recording, and effects, and they have all the important equipment for these tasks. If your studio does require special machines, rent them from supply houses.

■ *Agency Storyboards*

In the early years of television, advertising agencies expected storyboards to be made at the animation studios. Today, most commercial storyboards are created by agency art departments, and by the time a copy gets to the animator, numerous discussions have taken place. The client, writers, and art directors have all had their say; so with all of the erasures, changes, and paste-overs, the storyboard looks like a discarded paper napkin from the Mad Hatter's tea party. The production of the spot, acquired through competitive bidding, must be completed according to the sense of these meetings. On top of this, if yours is the chosen production company, you are expected to unleash all of the available technical expertise that will give the job the highest quality. The tendency to confuse the purpose of the commercial with glossy production values should be avoided. The clues to what is really expected are in the storyboard, and being able to spot those clues is an extremely important part of producing spots.

No storyboard should ever be accepted by a producer without a panel-by-panel discussion. Agency storyboards do not always reveal the entire story.

You want to avoid discovering that the obscure item in panel nine that you mistook for a flyspeck is the most important part of the commercial. Failure to question every insignificant scribble leads to expenses not spotted at the time of the bidding and frustration after the costs have been set and production is underway.

At one of the many meetings, a suggestion might hang in the air for something to be done in the production to make it more interesting. The clients see it clearly in their heads, but it's up to you to discover what it is they are imagining. Suggest that they make additional storyboard sketches, or do sketches of your own and ask, "How about this?" You are attempting to define the complexities hidden in the spot and learn if you will have to shoot costly tests or expand your staff to get the desired effect. All procedures, such as meetings, new sketches, camera tests, and lab processing are additional costs that might get glossed over at the creative meetings. Only by reading between the pictures does a producer or director discover what incisive questions to ask to uncover hidden costs before taking on an assignment.

Distribution

How a production gets into distribution depends on whether it is meant for general interest, educational, or artistic purposes. Animation on special topics like the environment, health, or other social issues travel a different route than subjects made for entertainment. A video about financing a child's college career will be earmarked for parents' organizations, cable, and public television, but a production made for entertainment, whether silly or poetic, will find its way to theatrical packagers or to the organizers of university screenings.

Television programming is a fiercely competitive area and difficult to break into. Even the extremely successful in this field are the first to warn that rejection is more frequent than acceptance. Though networks and sponsors are constantly looking for new subjects, they tend to go with well-established studios that deliver on time for the agreed price. There are no guarantees here either. Ambitious and well-intentioned productions have failed for one reason or another, and the powers move on to another studio. Some distributors or networks seek new, untried ideas from young animators through open solicitation and contests. This way they see what is going on, and when they do choose the idea they like—and this may be a surprise to you—they expect to own it outright.

Wouldn't it be great if theatrical shorts make a comeback? Here, too, be forewarned. It's hard to know if and when a short has been shown in theaters across the country or around the globe. You can't go to every movie house to check, and so must depend on the distributors accounting. You'll need to do a close reading on what is actually happening to your film and whether the earnings credited to it are true.

■ Making Contact

Check the phonebook under "Distributors" and write or call to see if they are interested in your subject. Advertise your production in one of the many specialized magazines that match your topic. If you have an airplane movie, check the list of advertisers in the many flying-related periodicals. Send a video copy to the editor, since a good review establishes the viability of your production and accents its merits.

■ Animation Festivals

Distributors actively follow festivals in hopes of finding unusual animation. Keep track of international and local screenings and obtain the necessary applications and submission forms. The number and variety of yearly festivals almost guarantees that each production will average about two years on the festival circuit before it is ready to be taken out of competition.

Attending a festival is enjoyable and puts you in direct contact with many distributors, who are easily approached in the event's holiday mood. Naturally, you can't get to every festival, so be sure to furnish stills and information about yourself and where you can be reached.

A Final Word

Imagination is more important than information. —Albert Einstein

In the Preface, I stated that animation depended greatly on the extent of one's imagination, but there is also a lot of just plain "doing" to bring a production to completion. For all the attention given to audience interest, in the end we do animation to please ourselves. To become good at animation, *do* animation—express your imagination and enjoy what you do.

Today, the field is more complicated than in the days when animation was limited to producers in a few cities. Now there are studios in almost *every* corner of the globe, and animators thousands of miles apart share their individual cultures through their art. When you begin a production, your legacy is not just Felix the Cat or Bugs Bunny, but the entire world of art, music, literature, theater, film, and the stories, tales, and experiences of animators around the globe.

You owe a debt to all of the pioneers who blazed trails with pegs, cels, and pixels. In truth, the very nature of the process includes time in the course of

production, where there will be very little call for imagination, a juncture where it is a matter of following the plan, maintaining consistency, and staying on course. This brings up an important point: animated productions are rarely made by one person working alone. Each creator depends on the talents and skills of other artists, editors, musicians, and technicians, as well as family and friends who offer inspiration, advice, encouragement, financing, expertise, or assistance. They are there when you need them most. These are the folks who put up with you while you are wrestling with the creative nuances.

The products of your imagination enrich other people's visions. Animation takes wild and fanciful roads, along which a dinosaur can become a shoe or a shoe can turn itself into a dinosaur. That this transpires is no miracle; the miracle is in how many ways it can be made to happen. One animator, Fred Moore, kept a one-word reminder on his desk: "Appeal." It's a good reminder for any animator, because no matter how offbeat your approach to the medium, the main goal is to give viewers something to take home with them.

Sometimes you will have to settle for less. You'll have to make compromises, but don't be discouraged and don't lose your sense of humor. Here is a paraphrase of some sound advice from the television gourmet Julia Child that applies to animation as much as it applies to the culinary arts: "If you've baked a cake and on the way to the table you drop it, serve it anyway, no one will know what it was supposed to look like in the first place."

Animation history reveals that what appears to be new is often an old technique in a fresh guise. Before the mid-1920s, sound-on-film, stereoscopic movies, and various color systems had all been attempted. Peg registration, cels, pans, rotoscope, matte painting, and scenes combining cartoon characters with live actors were, by then, well-established procedures. This book coincides with a time of great technological advancement. Some of the film processes described here are each day being improved and even supplanted by electronic means. Not too long ago, simple computer animation was being created on slow, clumsy equipment, but now sophisticated images spill from miniscule units that sit on the corner of a desk. Tomorrow, computers may fit in your pocket and television monitors may be built into your eyeglasses. No matter; the emphasis will always be on story, character, and timing.

Storyman Bill Peet once said, "The charm of animation is the obvious appearance of it. It's a drawing come to life. And the living drawing is the charm of it. It always has been, no matter how elaborate you can make it. Animation stands alone."

That, in a nutshell, is the whole story. Good luck.

Time/Frame Calculator

Frames and Feet

FILM SIZE:	Super-8mm				16mm		35mm	
FRAMES PER SEC.:	18		24		24		24	
SCREEN TIME	FEET	FR	FEET	FR	FEET	FR	FEET	FR
I second	0	18	0	24	0	24	I	8
2	0	36	0	48	I	8	3	0
3	0	54	I	0	I	32	4	8
4	I	0	I	24	2	16	6	0
5	I	18	I	48	3	0	7	8
6	I	36	2	0	3	24	9	0
7	I	54	2	24	4	8	10	8
8	2	0	2	48	4	32	12	0
9	2	18	3	0	5	16	13	8
10	2	36	3	24	6	0	15	0
20	5	0	6	48	12	0	0	30
30	7	36	10	0	18	0	45	0
40	10	0	13	24	24	0	60	0
50	12	36	16	48	30	0	75	0
I minute	15	0	20	0	36	0	90	0
2	30	0	40	0	72	0	180	0
3	45	0	60	0	108	0	270	0
4	60	0	80	0	144	0	360	0
5	75	0	100	0	180	0	450	0
6	90	0	120	0	216	0	540	0
7	105	0	140	0	252	0	630	0
8	120	0	160	0	288	0	720	0
9	135	0	180	0	324	0	810	0
10	150	0	200	0	360	0	900	0

Super-8mm: 72 frames per foot • 16mm: 40 frames per foot • 35mm: 16 frames per foot

Exercises

The following are commonplace exercises chosen specifically because they are everyday "problems" animators must solve. See if you can make them interesting.

Character

Create a character that stands upright on two legs and has two arms and a head. It can be a woman, a man, a child, or a humanized animal. Give the character a personality trait, such as timidity, arrogance, impatience, snobbishness, or anything that is typically human. Give the character a name. Use yourself as a model or think of an acquaintance or characters from literature, films, or television. Explore the character in many sketches, from all angles, and in many postures. Take the best of your sketches and make a model chart of the character.

Continuity and Story

Make a series of storyboard sketches of a character losing his or her temper.

1. Establish the locale and the character.
2. Establish the action or something or somebody to annoy the character.
3. Develop the conflict between the character and the annoyance.
4. Create interaction and, if you wish, introduce other elements or characters.
5. Bring the action to a climax.
6. Bring the story to a close.
7. Add an interesting touch just before the end.

Layout

Make several thumbnail sketches of a view from your window or from your imagination. Then simplify the design by eliminating unnecessary elements. Add drama by choosing an interesting angle of the scene. Turn it into a place of fantasy. Make a layout of the scene within an 11-field center and then indicate a move into an interesting area at 4 field, 2 north, 3 east.

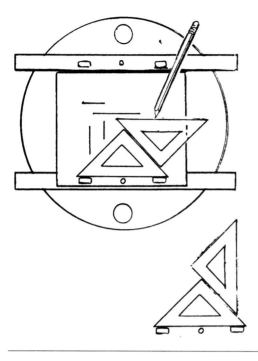

There are convenient methods for drawing straight lines on a revolving animation disc.

Oxberry pegs were designed for aiding in the construction of technical shapes. The square pegs are of sufficient width for balancing a ruler or triangle.

Slide an additional straight-edge alongside the one in contact with the pegs for drawing straight lines in any direction. With Acme pegs, the large center peg interferes with this technique, but a straight edge can be made that fits over the pegs and can then accomodate a triangle.

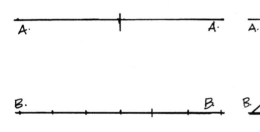

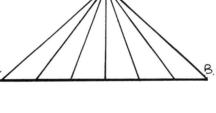

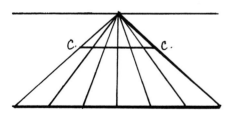

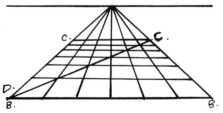

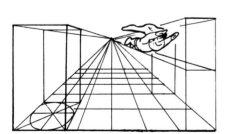

Create a Perspective Grid

(**1**) Draw parallel lines A and B. (**2**) Place a center point on A. (**3**) Mark lines from center point on A to points on B. (**4**) Draw line C. (**5**) Extend diagonal line D from corner of B to corner of C. (**6**) Rule horizontal lines through D where D crosses other lines.

Animation

Use the model chart that you created in the exercise on characters and design a door and doorway. The doorway should express a specific locale such as a restaurant, a dentist's office, a castle, a spaceship, or any other place you wish. Make a short storyboard of your character coming through the door in character. How would an arrogant person enter a room, or someone who is timid or snobbish? Then define the location and the action of the figure coming through the door in distinct poses. Animate the action and add personality touches. Give the drawings numbers and put these on exposure sheets. Shoot the drawings or scan them into a computer.

Special Effects

Shoot video with a camcorder, then design animation to be combined with it. Bring these elements together using a computer compositing program.

Making a Short Film

Pick a subject that calls for one or two characters. Keep it simple. Design it to take place over a simple background.

Make it only thirty seconds to two minutes long. If your story comes out longer, rethink the plot and adjust the story. Decide that you want to do the best thirty seconds or one or two minutes that you can. This will conserve physical and mental energy and keep the costs low.

Tackling a short film allows you to do a better job without the pressure of having to slog out miles of footage to get it done. It is better to do a very good short film than a poorly thought-out, flabbily constructed, and rushed longer production. If you are considering making a film as a sample in seeking a job, a short production is smart, since studio managers have little time to view anything longer than a few minutes.

Film Study

Much can be learned by viewing classic animation. To observe animation and timing, turn off the sound. Study a segment frame-by-frame to see if the animation was done on ones, twos, or threes. Look for the use of cycles and how often holds are used. In well-thought-out animation, movements are simplified to put over the most intricate actions.

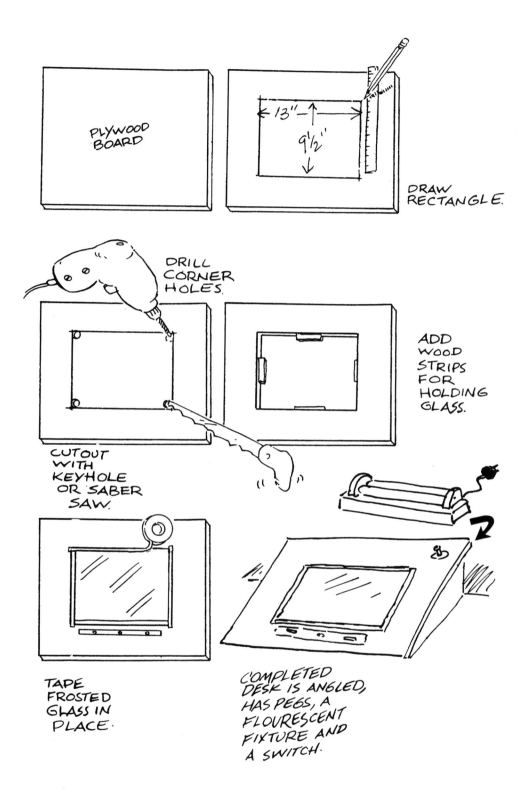

PLYWOOD BOARD

DRAW RECTANGLE.

13"

9½"

DRILL CORNER HOLES.

ADD WOOD STRIPS FOR HOLDING GLASS.

CUTOUT WITH KEYHOLE OR SABER SAW.

TAPE FROSTED GLASS IN PLACE.

COMPLETED DESK IS ANGLED, HAS PEGS, A FLOURESCENT FIXTURE AND A SWITCH.

Build Your Own Lightboard

Resources

Some Schools Where Animation Is Taught

For addresses of schools in other countries, go to *www.ASIFA.net*.

Art Center College of Design
1700 Lida Street
Pasedena, CA 91102
(818) 584-5038
www.artcenter.edu

California College of Arts and Crafts
Film Arts Department
5212 Broadway
Oakland, CA 94618
(510) 594-3600
www.ccac-art.edu

California Institute of the Arts
School of Film and Video
24700 McBean Parkway
Valencia, CA 91355
(805) 255-1050
www.Calarts.edu

California State University—Fullerton
Communications Department
P.O. Box 34080
Fullerton, CA 92834
(714) 278-2011
www.fullerton.edu

Columbia College
Film Department
600 Michigan Ave.
Chicago, IL 60605
(312) 344-7130
www.Colum.edu

Edinboro State College
The School of The Arts & Humanities
Art Department
Edinboro, PA 16444
(814) 732-2799

Harvard University
Carpenter Center
24 Quincy Street
Cambridge, MA 02138
(617) 495-1000
www.harvard.edu

Illinois Institute of Technology
Institute of Design
Animation Department
3300 South Federal Street
Chicago, IL 60616
(312) 567-3793
www.iit.edu

Kansas City Art Institute
4415 Warwick Blvd.
Kansas City, MO 64111
(816) 474-5224
www.kcai.edu

**The Joe Kubert School of Cartoon
    and Graphic Art, Inc.**
37 Myrtle Avenue
Dover, NJ 07801
(973) 361-1327
www.kubertsworld.com

Long Beach City College
Theater Arts Department
Film Program
4901 East Carson Street
Long Beach, CA 90808
(562) 938-4353
www.lbcc.cc.ca.us

Philadelphia College of Art
Department of Photography and Film
Broad and Spruce Streets
Philadelphia, PA 19102
(215) 717-6365
www.uarts.edu

Parsons School of Design
Digital Design Dept.
66 Fifth Avenue
New York, NY 10011
(212) 229-8944
www.parsons.edu

Pratt Institute
200 Willoughby Ave.
Brooklyn, NY 11205
(718) 636-3600
www.Pratt.edu

Rhode Island School of Design
Film Studies Department
2 College Street
Providence, RI 02903
(401) 454-6209
(800) 364-7473
www.risd.edu

San Francisco State University
Film and Creative Arts Interdisciplinary
    Dept.
1600 Holloway Avenue
San Francisco, CA 94132
(415) 338-1111
www.sfsu.edu

School of Visual Arts
209 East 23rd Street
New York, NY 10010
(212) 592-2000
www.schoolofvisualarts.edu

**Sheridan College of Applied Arts &
    Technology**
1430 Trafalgar Road
Oakville, Ontario L6H 2L 1 Canada
(905) 815-9430
www.sheridanc.on.ca

University of California–Los Angeles
Dept. of Film, Television and Digital
    Media
405 Hilgard Avenue
Los Angeles, CA 90095
(310) 825-4321
www.tft.ucla.edu

Vancouver Film School
198 West Hastings St., Suite 500
Vancouver, BC V6B 21H2 Canada
(604) 685-5808
www.vfs.com

Wayne State University
Speech Department
Mass Communications Area
Detroit, MI 48202
(313) 577-4163
www.wayne.edu

Professional Publications & Organizations

Publications

Animation Journal, AJ Press
108 Hedge Nettle Crossing
Savannah, GA 31406
www.animationjournal.com

Animation Magazine
30941 West Agoura Road, Suite 102
Westlake Village, CA 91361
http://animationmagazine.net

Animation World Network
6525 Sunset Boulevard, Garden Suite 10
Hollywood, CA 90028
(323) 606-4200
http://mag.awn.com

Cartoonist Profiles
P.O. Box 325
Fairfield, CT 06430
www.cartoonistprofiles.com

Millimeter, A Penton Publication
826 Broadway
New York, NY 10003
http://millimeter.com

The Hollywood Reporter
55 Wilshire Boulevard
Los Angeles, CA 90036
www.hollywoodreporter.com

Organizations

ASIFA International
Borivoj Dovnikovic, Sec. Gen.
Hrvatskog Projesa B6
41040 Zagreb, Croatia
www.swop.com/animate/asifaint.htm
• This worldwide organization has several chapters in North America. Find the one nearest you at www.asifa.net.

Los Angeles Chapter Siggraph
P.O. Box 6308
Burbank, CA 91510
(310) 288-1148
www.la.siggraph.org

National Cartoonists Society
Columbus Circle Station
P.O. Box 20267
New York, NY 10023
www.rueben.org

Animation Supplies & Services

Supplies

Adobe Systems, Inc.
345 Park Avenue
San Jose, CA 95110
(408) 536-6000
www.adobe.com
• Computer programs: Photoshop,
After Effects, Premiere

B&H Photo and video
420 Ninth Avenue
New York, NY 10001
(800) 947-6628
www.bhphotovideo.com
• Video cameras and sound equipment

Cartoon Colour Company
90324 Lindblade Street
Culver City, CA 90232
www.cartooncolor.com
• Animation field guides, cels, paints,
paper, pegs

CECO International
440 West 15th Street
New York, NY 10011
www.cecostudios.com
• Animation field guides, paper, cels, pegs

Chambles Cine Equipment
RT 1 Box 1595
Higyway 52 West
Ellijay, GA 30540-0231
(706) 636-5210
www.chamblesscineequip.com
• Bolex 16mm cameras, motors, repair

Eastman Kodak Company
343 State Street
Rochester, NY 14650
(716) 724-4000
www.kodak.com
• Motion picture film stock

Linker Systems
13612 Onkayha Circle
Irvine, CA 92620
(800) 315-1174
www.linkersystems.com
• Animation equipment and digital
programs

New York Central Art Supply
62 Third Avenue @ 11th Street
New York, NY 10003
(800) 950-6111
www.nycentralart.com
• Art supplies, animation paper, pegs,
field guides

Services

Deluxe Labs
1377 North Serrano Avenue
Hollywood, CA 90027
(213) 462-5171
www.hollywired.net
• Film processing and video dupes

Du-Art Video & Film Laboratories
245 West 55th Street
New York, NY 10019
www.duart.com
• Film processing and video dupes

Bob Lyons
Liberty Studios
238 East 26th Street
New York, NY 10010
(212) 532-1865
• Animation camera photography and effects

Magno Sound & Video
729 Seventh Avenue
New York, NY 10019

(212) 302-2505
www.magnointernational.com
• Sound recording studio, film, and video editing

Matlin Recording
80 Eighth Avenue, Suite 1500
New York, NY 10011
(212) 206-0350
www.matlin.com
• Sound recording and track mix

Studios

Aardman Features
1410 Aztec West
Business Park
Almondsbury, Bristol B532
www.aardman.com

Blue Sky Studios
44 South Broadway
White Plains, NY 10601
www.blueskystudiois.com

Buzzco Associates, Inc.
33 Bleeker Street
New York, NY 10012
(212) 473-8800
www.buzzzco.com

Calabash Animation
657 West Ohio Street
Chicago, IL 60610
(312) 243-3433
www.calabashanim.com

Klasky Csupo, Inc.
6353 Sunset Boulevard
Hollywood, CA 90028
(323) 468-5978
www.klaskycsupo.com

Dreamworks SKG
100 Universal City Plaza, Building 477
Universal City, CA 91608
(818) 733-7000
dwiwebmaster@ea.com

Walt Disney Pictures
500 South Buena Vista Street
Burbank, CA 91521
http://disney.go.com/disney/careers

Unions & Guilds

IATSE Local 600
80 Eighth Avenue
New York, NY 10011
(212) 647-7300
www.cameraguild.com

Motion Picture Screen Cartoonists
Local 839
4729 Lankershim Blvd.
North Hollywood, CA 91602
(818) 766-7151
www.mpsc839.org

Distributors & Festivals

Distributors

Expanded Entertainment
28024 Dorothy Drive
Agoura Hills, CA 91301

Spike & Mike, MMP Inc.
7488 La Jolla Blvd
La Jolla, CA 92037
(800) 458-9478

Festivals

Annecy International
Animated Film Festival
BP399 74013
Annecy Cedex, France

ASIFA-East Annual Film Festival
c/o Buzzco Assoc. Inc.
33 Bleeker St., 5A
New York, NY 10012

British Animation Film Festival
41B Hornsey Lane Gardens
London N6 5NY, UK

Hiroshima International Animation
Festival
1-1 Nakajima-cho
Naka-ku 730, Japan

Ottawa International Animation
Film Festival
National Arts Center Box Office
P.O. Box 1534 Station B
Ottawa, ON K1P 5W1, Canada
(613) 995-4343

Zagreb World Festival of Animated
Film
Nova Ves 18 41000
Zagreb, Croatia

Glossary

A

Above-the-line: The artistic and creative aspect of a budget. Personnel such as writer and director.

A-B printing: Checkerboard printing of film rolls with alternating footage of picture and lengths of black leader to avoid splice marks in 16mm prints.

Academy aperture: Standard frame dimension of 35mm film, 1.33:1.

Academy leader: Head and tail leaders, each twelve feet in length, standard throughout the industry. The head leader has a countdown of numbers from 8 to 2 for theater projectionists. Established by the Academy of Arts and Sciences.

Action axis: Invisible line that crosses the screen and to which camera viewpoint must adhere. In the case of two characters in conversation the direction that each is facing must be maintained no matter how the angle of view shifts.

Additive principle: Combination of the primaries red, blue, and green that create white light.

Ad-lib: Spontaneous, unrehearsed action or dialogue.

Address code: *See* "SMPTE Time Code."

Aerial image: Image formed at the level of the compound tabletop and recorded by a camera lens focused at that distance to combine cels with processed footage.

Algorithm: Procedure or set of instructions for solving a specific problem.

Aliasing: Stepped or jagged edges of lines in computer images.

Analog: The representation of continuous signals by means of electrical signals by a meter and a needle, as opposed to digital.

Anamorphic lens: Lens that horizontally compresses an image into a standard 1.33:1 frame. When projected through a similar lens, the image expands to normal proportions to form a wide-screen picture.

Animatic: Film or video made from shots of still art, incorporating camera pans, zooms and dissolves to create an illusion of motion. Limited animation is sometimes included.

Answer print: Film with combined

picture and track, for the purpose of checking color and sound quality.

Anti-aliasing: The "cleaning up" of jagged lines by the mathematical filtering of surrounding colors.

Aperture: Adjustable opening in a lens that controls the amount of light passing through.

Aspect ratio: Ratio of width-to-height of a film frame and its projected image.

"A" wind: Single perf 16mm film with emulsion facing inwards. When unwinding clockwise, the sprocket holes are closest to your eye.

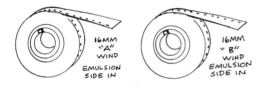

B

Balance stripe: Narrow strip of magnetic material running down one side of a length of film, opposite to the side with a magnetic soundtrack, to ensure that the film winds evenly onto the reel.

Beamsplitter: Split block of glass that allows light from a projector to pass in one direction while a camera, filming on the same axis, records the image.

Beat: Measure of time that sets the tempo for the animator and in frames.

Bi-pack: Raw stock threaded through the camera in combination with processed footage of mattes. Artwork is photographed, along with the mattes, onto the raw stock to make a composite print.

Bit: Basic unit of storage in a digital computer.

Blue screen: Cobalt-blue background against which actors and objects are photographed and which, through laboratory processing, is turned into mattes for combining live scenes with animation and effects.

Buffer: Area of computer memory, disc, or tape for temporary holding of information being transferred.

Burn-in: Photographing high-contrast titles and artwork over previously exposed scenes. When exposed properly the superimposition shows clear white images over a tonal background.

"B" wind: Single perf 16mm film stock in which the sprocket holes face away from you when the film is wound clockwise and the emulsion faces inward.

C

Camera original: Footage, negative or positive, shot in the camera.

Capping shutter: Supplementary shutter used when rewinding for double-exposures and for alternate exposing of cycle cels.

Cathode ray tube: Phosphor-coated glass tube in which electron beams are focused to create an image. Tube in a television set.

CAV: Constant angular velocity. Laserdisc with freeze-frame and slow-motion features.

CC: Close captioned. Titles synchronized with standard television or video screening for the hearing impaired.

Changing bag: A light-tight cloth bag for handling exposed or unexposed film when working far from a darkroom.

CLV: Constant linear velocity. Laserdiscs that can freeze frame only by means of a very sophisticated disc player.

Click track: Audible reference passed through earphones to guide musicians during a recording session. The intervals between the clicks define the tempo.

Collage: Artwork made up of bits and pieces of drawings, diagrams, clippings, photographs, or type.

Color temperature: Scale of degrees of gradations in light.

Complimentary colors: The colors, which when combined with each of the primaries, produce white light. Respectively, they are yellow, cyan, and magenta for blue, red, and green.

Composite print: A length of film, processed in a lab, combining picture and sound.

Computer animation: Sequential graphics composed with or effected by electronic controls.

Crawl title: A title that moves from bottom to top of frame. Employed for a lengthy list of credits.

Credits: The names and specialties of those connected with a production, appearing on-screen at the head or end of the film.

Cue sheet: A master list of sound elements, voice, music, and effects used when mixing soundtracks.

Cutout: Artwork that is not drawn on a cel but is positioned on a cel or a background. A cutout can be still or animated in increments.

Cyan: Blue-green with an absence of red.

D

Dailies: Footage received after overnight processing at a lab. Also called "rushes."

Daylight film: Film emulsion balanced to record colors as they appear in natural light.

Dial numbers: Exposure sheet numbers in the column labeled "dial," which correspond to the frame counters on camera and editing equipment.

Diaphragm: A disc with a variable opening for governing the amount of light passing through a lens. *See* "iris."

Diopter lens: A supplementary lens used in front of a camera lens for close-ups.

Dolby: A noise-reduction system to eliminate hiss during recording and playback.

Dropout: Loss of picture or sound on a video or audiotape due to dust, dirt, or imperfections in its manufacture.

Dub: Adjusting a previously recorded soundtrack to correct slurred dialogue, change a character's voice or add a foreign translation. *See* "looping," "mix."

Dupe: A duplicate of an existing film or video.

DVD: Digital versatile disc or Digital video disc.

E

Echo chamber: An electronic increase in the reverberance of sound.

Edge numbers: Numbers printed along the edge of developed film originals, for matching to an edited workprint. *See "matching."*

Emulsion: A light-sensitive film coating, usually of silver-halide grains, in a thin gelatin layer.

Exponential movement: The speed of an action based on the size of the field.

Exposure meter: A handheld or camera-installed device for calibrating light to determine proper film exposure.

F

Farce: Comedy employing highly exaggerated or caricatured characters.

Field: The area of view encompassed by a lens set at a specific distance.

Foley artist: Operator who creates live sounds during post-recording.

Follow focus cam: An integral part of an animation stand that automatically focuses the lens during field changes.

Foot candle: A measure of illumination equal to the amount of light falling on a surface one square foot in area, each point of which is one foot distant from a light source of one standard candle intensity.

Format: Film, videotape, videodisc, CD-ROM, and their various sizes.

FPS: Frames per second.

Freeze frame: A single frame of film that repeats consecutively on the screen for a length of time.

G

Gels: Clear plastic sheets, in a range of colors, used as artwork overlays or for toning existing lighting.

Grain: Particles in an emulsion that become noticeable and objectionable when enlarged.

Guides: Any diagrams used for the positioning of cutouts and objects during stop-motion filming.

H

Heads: The elements of a tape recorder used for transferring electrical impulses to the tape.

Hi-con: Black-and-white film stock that produces areas that are either dense black or perfectly clear.

I

Insert: Scene added during editing. An animated segment of a live-action production.

Interactive: Immediate reaction to a command.

Internegative: A negative made from a color-reversal original for use in making prints.

Interpositive: Intermediate copy made from an original negative.

Intervalometer: Timing device that exposes single frames at preset intervals.

Iris: The diaphragm that controls the amount of light entering a lens.

Iris out, iris in: A series of sequential mattes that create the effect of a shape getting smaller or larger.

J

Joy stick: Small, vertical arm affixed to some camera stands for manual control of a motorized compound.

Jump cut: A cut in which smooth continuity is purposely disturbed.

K

Key light: Main source of illumination in a lighting setup.

L

Leader: Length of plain film spliced at the head of a reel. *See* "Academy leader."

Logo: The identifying symbol of a company or organization.

Loop: Strand of film prepared for continuous viewing by splicing it end to end.

Looping: Synchronous recording of dialogue by actors as they view projected footage.

M

M & E track: Soundtrack containing no dialogue, only music and effects.

Magenta: Reddish-blue color with a complete absence of green.

Matching: Conforming a negative to a workprint prior to printing.

Match line: On a drawing or cel, the outline of an area of animation or background against which a character will be inked to appear to be on or behind it.

Matte: Black card for masking portions of an image. A subject image shot against black is called a female, and a silhouetted subject against white, a male.

Mix: Re-recording of music, voice, and effects onto a single track. *See* "dub."

Montage: Several images interposed into one composition. European term for editing.

Morgue: A picture reference file relating to variety of subjects.

Multimedia: Any combination of one or more techniques, including: film, slides, video, computer graphics, animation, or live performances in one presentation.

Multiplane: Shooting arrangement with sheets of glass spaced to represent separate levels of view to create an illusion of depth. The level, closest to the lens can be put out of focus while the others remain sharp.

Music editor: Specialist who edits music tracks.

N

N.G.: Ruined footage.

NTSC: National Television Standards Committee; color TV system in the United States, 525 lines, 60 fields, 30 frames a second.

Notch: Indication, next to a frame on a negative, for automatic adjustment of exposure in a color printer.

O

Offline: Isolated, not connected to the line or central system. Preliminary or rehearsal editing of video.

One light print: Untimed print for purposes of editing.

Online: In direct communication with central systems. Final video editing.

Opticals: Special effects made by photography on an optical printer.

Original: Camera negative or positive from which duplicates are made.

Outtake: Any frame or section of a film not used in the final edit.

P

PAL: Phase Alteration Line; European color system, 625 lines, 50 fields, 25 frames per second.

Pan: Short for panoramic. Artwork that is slid in front of the camera.

Pantograph: A field guide, in conjunction with a pointer arm, placed to the right of the compound table as a guide in predetermined moves.

Parallax: Displacement of an image seen through a viewfinder on cameras where the taking lens and the viewing lens are separated.

Peripherals: Any number of devices connected to and controlled by a computer.

Phenakistoscope: Compound Greek name of nineteenth-century slotted disc animation toy, meaning "to deceive the eye."

Pilot-pin registration: The camera element that engages the film sprocket holes to accurately register each frame in the same plane. *See* "process camera."

Pixel: The smallest graphic unit on a monitor screen that can be detected.

Pixilation: Technique of posing live actors for filming as stop-motion subjects.

Platen: Hinged assembly of a frame and a clear glass used for flattening cels and backgrounds during photography.

Polarized light: Vibrations of light moving in one direction.

Polarizing filters: Glass or plastic sheets placed in front of a camera lens and lights to deflect glare.

Polygon: A two-dimensional shape with three or more straight sides.

Print: A positive print made from an original or a dupe negative.

Process camera: A studio camera equipped with pilot-pin registration and a stop-motion motor.

Q

Quartz light: A tungsten lamp bulb, containing a halogen gas (iodine, chlorine, bromine, fluorine, or astatine), which reduces blackening in the lamp and maintains correct color temperature.

R

Ray tracing: Computer method that "traces" indications of light from its origin to a graphic object.

Release print: Copy print from an original, for distribution.

Remaster: Any production previously available in one format, reissued in another format.

Retake: Reshooting a scene.

Reversal film: Film processed by re-exposure or chemical treatment to make a positive original rather than a negative. Typical of 8mm and 16mm film and 35mm slides.

Ride: Unsteady motion of double-exposed image against a background. Frequently occurs when titles are superimposed over a scene shot in a 16mm camera. *See "burn-in."*

Rostrum: British term; an animation camera stand.

Rotoscope: Projection of film footage for tracing or photocopying as a guide in animating life-like motion. For layout of scenes in combining live-action with animation.

Room tone: Recording of the natural sound of any location to maintain a consistent tone when editing soundtracks.

Rough cut: Tryout arrangement of scenes and soundtrack before the final edit.

Rushes: *See "dailies."*

S

Scanning: Systematic exploration of an area, line by line, with an electron beam.

Scratch-off: Economical technique in which portions of a single piece of artwork are removed as a stop-motion camera records each change. Shot in reverse and then projected normally.

Scratch track: Temporary track recorded as a guide for direction, animation, or editing before a final track is available.

SECAM: *Sequential couleur à memoire* (sequential color with memory); French television system.

Shadow board: Black-light barrier positioned in front of the camera lens to eliminate unwanted reflections. Also used for holding special-effects filters and mattes.

Side peg: Portable peg setup with a worm gear attachment to make short vertical pan moves without the necessity of rotating the compound. Also known as a "Rufle," for a device used by animator George Rufle.

Single perf: Film with one row of perforations.

Skip frame: Hurried action created by excising frames through editing or optical printing.

Slit scan: A stretched, smeared image created by trucking or zooming toward the artwork while a mask with a narrow slit pans across the surface of the subject. Done repeatedly for each frame, through computer commands, as the camera shutter remains open during exposure.

Slop print: Test strip for the immediate verification of camera or animation accuracy.

SMPTE Time Code: Society of Motion Picture and Television Engineers' eight-digit address code for editing to identify each frame of videotape by hour, minute, second, and frame number.

Star filter: Glass disc with scribed, intersecting lines for creating a sparkle effect.

Start mark: Usually an *X* made with a grease pencil or marker on the corresponding frames of soundtrack and picture, for synchronization.

Strobing: Stagger or jitter. The effect of animation on twos moving in one direction as the camera trucks to an

off-center field on ones in the opposite direction.

Sync: When picture and sound are in
correct alignment.

T

Take: Character reaction of surprise or
fear. A "double take" is a delayed
reaction. A character looks at something unfazed, looks away, then
looks again and is startled.

A Take

Telephoto: Lens with a long focal
length covering a narrow angle
of view.

Timing chart: A line intersected at
varying points for spacing animation moves.

Timed print: A color-corrected
positive.

Trace back: Drawing made by accurately tracing parts of a previous
drawing.

Trailer: Brief, on-screen announcement
of coming attractions.

Transfer: Recording of film to tape or
photographing tape to film.

Traveling matte: Optical or video
mattes for matching the changing
action in each frame.

Tungsten film: Film stock balanced to
give correct rendering of colors of
subjects under tungsten lights.

TV cutoff: Area along the inside edge
of each frame that is lost during television transmission.

U

U-matic: Trade name of videocassette
system using three-quarter-inch
tape.

V

Variable shutter: Two part shutter
with a cutaway segment that adjusts
for different exposure times by shifting between 0 degrees and 170
degrees without effecting aperture
or frame rate.

Vector: Line connecting x, y, z coordinates on a monitor screen.

Vignetting: Mist-like fading off
around the perimeter of an image.

V.O.: Voice over. Off-screen narration.

VU meter: Gauge for monitoring the
level of sound.

W

Wet-gate printing: Use of a fluid in
optical printing to deflect pits and
scratches on a negative.

Wipe: Series of mattes designed to move
vertically, horizontally, circularly, or
in any other pattern to create the
effect of one scene replacing
another.

Wire frame: Computer-generated
image of structural outline forms.

Workprint: Print used for editing and
serving as guide for matching when
cutting the negative.

X

Xerox: Trade name; electrocopying of animation drawings onto cels.

Y

YCM: Yellow, cyan, and magenta.

Z

Zoetrope: Nineteenth-century animation toy. A slotted drum, open at the top containing strips of sequential drawings. When spun, and the drawings are viewed through the slits, the drawings appear as animation.

Bibliography

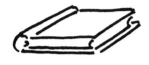

Much has been written about animation, some of it good but much of it publicity for the output of studios. Many interesting works are now out of print, like the 1920 edition of E. G. Lutz's *Animated Cartoons*,* reportedly the book that Disney and Iwerks studied. Also out of print are the first books on the subject that informed me: Nat Falk's *How to Make Animated Cartoons* (1941) and Robert D. Feild's *The Art of Walt Disney* (1942). The following are works that I have found enlightening and useful.

History

Barrier, Michael. *Hollywood Cartoons: American Animation in Its Golden Age.* New York: Oxford Press, 1999. A journey through sixty years of cartoon animation; a solid work derived from the distillation of hundreds of interviews with animators from the period 1911 to 1966.

Bendazzi, Giannalberto. *Cartoons: One Hundred Years of Cinema Animation.* Bloomington: Indiana University Press, 1994. A hefty global history of animation, that details highlights and lesser-

---

*A facsimile reprint was published by Applewood Books in 1998.

known events. Recognizes artists, films, and countries usually ignored in most books on the subject.

Ceram, C. W. *Archaeology of the Cinema.* New York: Harcourt Brace & World, 1965. The prehistory of film. An attempt to put the facts in focus about the many inventions that became the movies. Fully illustrated.

Cohen, Karl F. *Forbidden Animation, Censored Cartoons, and Blacklisted Animators in America.* Jefferson, NC: McFarland, 1997. A panorama of animation in which the content conflicted with perceived morality or which exhibited racial or sexist overtones. Includes a fine account of animators caught in the "red-baiting" politics of the 1950s.

Crafton, Donald. *Before Mickey: The Animated Film 1898–1928.* Cambridge: MIT Press, 1982. The earliest years of film animation, diligently researched and put into perspective. An important work.

Deneroff, Harvey. *Popeye the Union Man: A Historical Study of the Fleischer Strike.* Los Angeles: UCLA, 1985. A doctoral dissertation that delves seriously into the circumstances, personalities, and the attempt to legitimize a New York animation union 1937.

Edera, Bruno. *Full Length Animated Films.* New York: Hastings House, 1977. An exploration of animated features made throughout the world, up to the 1970s.

Holman, Bruce. *Puppet Animation in the Cinema.* New York: A. S. Barnes & Co., 1975. A major contribution to the history of animation. The author's research includes interviews with puppet animators around the world.

Maltin, Leonard. *Of Mice and Magic,* rev. ed. New York: New American Library, 1987. The key American cartoon shorts producers of the 1930s–40s, how they came to be and prospered. With an update on the business since then.

Quigley, Martin, Jr. *Magic Shadows: The Story of the Origin of the Motion Pictures.* Washington D.C.: Georgetown University Press, 1948. The historical development of devices that became the movies.

Robinson, David. *From Peepshow to Palace, The Birth of the American Film.* New York: Columbia University Press, 1996. The very early days of the movies, from penny arcade to the first theaters.

Solomon, Charles. *Enchanted Drawings: The History of Animation.* New York: Alfred A. Knopf, 1989. A large and profusely illustrated history of animation, mostly American. Interesting chapter on animation during World War II.

Biography and Studio Histories

Adamson, Joe. *The Walter Lantz Story.* New York: G. P. Putnam's Sons, 1985. The life of the creator of Andy Panda and Woody Woodpecker.

Barbera, Joseph. *My Life in 'Toons From Flatbush to Bedrock in Under a Century.* Atlanta, GA: Turner Pub., Inc., 1994. The Barbera of Hanna and Barbera, tells of his rise from a Brooklyn boyhood through his trials and successes as producer of hundreds of hours of television animation.

Cabarga, Leslie. *The Fleischer Story*. New York: Crown, 1976; Da Capo Press (paperback) 1988. The author recognizes a need for a book about the Fleischers and does a loving job of assembling available facts and illustrations.

Canemaker, John. *Winsor McCay: His Life and Art*. New York: Abbeville Press, 1987. A large and colorful history of the talented comic-strip creator and distinguished early animator.

Canemaker, John. *Felix, The Twisted Tale of the World's Most Famous Cat*. New York: Pantheon Books, 1991. The hard facts behind the life and times of Felix and his creators.

Crafton, Donald. *Emile Cohl, Caricature, and Film*. Princeton: Princeton University Press, 1990. An in-depth history of the pioneer French animator and his career as a graphic artist. Contains many illustrations and extensive references.

Culhane, Shamus. *Talking Animals and Other People*. New York: St. Martin's Press, 1986. An autobiography of an animation career spanning more than fifty years, written with humor and insight.

Halas, John. *Masters of Animation*. London: BBC Books, 1987. An attempt to honor the key artists in international animation, past and present.

Hanna, William. *A Cast of Friends*. Dallas: Taylor Publishing, 1996. The other half of the duo that created *Tom & Jerry* shorts and hours of popular television cartoons. Includes foreword by Joe Barbera.

Hickman, Gail Morgan. *The Films of George Pal*. South Brunswick: A. S. Barnes and Company, 1977. The life and work of the late producer. Includes his Puppetoon period, but emphasizes his contribution to the sci-fi film genre.

Hollis, Richard, and Brian Sibley. *The Disney Studio Story*. London: Octopus, 1988. Encyclopedic overview of the Disney realm through the decades.

Iwerks, Leslie, and John Kenworthy. *The Hand Behind the Mouse*. New York: Disney Editions, 2001. The Ub Iwerks's story as told by his grand-daughter. Iwerks was the genius behind the technical solutions for many Disney features, and also, as Walt's righthand man in the early years, designed Mickey Mouse and animated his initial exploits.

Maltin, Leonard. *The Disney Films*, rev. ed. New York: Crown, 1984. Each Disney feature described with story synopsis, credits, release dates, and critical response.

Merritt, Russell, and J. B. Kaufman. *Walt in Wonderland: The Silent Films of Walt Disney*. Baltimore: Le Giornate del Cinema Muto/Johns Hopkins Press, 1994. A 164-page work with photos, drawings, and in-depth facts on the Disney studio in the 1920s. Originally published in 1992 in English and Italian.

Peet, Bill. *An Autobiography*. Boston: Houghton Mifflin Company, 1989. Written and illustrated with simplicity and understanding by a story-man turned children's book author. His views on Disney and the studio are perceptive and revealing.

Pilling, Jayne. *Women and Animation: A Compendium*. London: The British Film Institute, 1992. Includes a detailed filmography and considerable biographical information for more than a hundred women animation artists.

Schickel, Richard. *The Disney Version*. New York: Simon & Schuster, 1968. Disney, through the eyes of a critic, who ends up lauding him. The book upset many fans, who had never been exposed to an objective view of Uncle Walt.

Sennett, Ted. *The Art of Hanna-Barbera, Fifty Years of Creativity*. New York: Viking Studio Books, 1989. The team that directed *Tom & Jerry* for MGM and changed the face of Saturday-morning television.

Thomas, Bob. *Walt Disney, An American Original*. New York: Simon & Schuster, 1976. The approved biography of Disney that fills in details of his life.

Drawing and Design

Blair, Preston. *Animation*. Tustin: Walter T. Foster, 1949. A compilation of Blair's earlier paperbacks with additional material. A magnificent guide by a master animator and draughtsman from Hollywood's Golden Age.

Carroll, Lewis. *Alice's Adventures in Wonderland, with David Hall's Previously Unpublished Illustrations for Walt Disney Productions*. New York: Simon & Schuster, Inc., 1986. The original story in tandem with highly imaginative drawings and watercolors.

Finch, Christopher. *The Art of the Lion King*. New York: Hyperion, 1994. Highlights of the story accompanied by character sketches and fully rendered backgrounds from the film. With a foreword by James Earl Jones.

Gilliam, Terry. *Animations of Mortality*. London: Eyre Methuen Ltd., 1978. Unusual and humorous imagery from the animated works of the cartoonist-turned-director, who once upon a time engineered the graphics for Monty Python's Flying Circus.

Johnston, Ollie, and Frank Thomas. *The Disney Villains*. New York: Hyperion, 1993. Some very personable but threatening characters are examined in depth.

Graham, Donald, W. *Composing Pictures*. New York: Van Nostrand Reinhold Company, 1970. Art instruction by the man who conducted classes at the Disney studio for many years. Includes a section on designing for film.

Halas, John. *Design in Motion*. London: Studio Vista, 1962. An overview of the variety of styles that world animators employ. Profusely illustrated in black and white and color.

Hogarth, Burne. *Dynamic Figure Drawing*. New York: Watson-Guptill Publications, 1970. Drawing the figure with emphasis on motion and foreshortening.

Nicolaides, Kimon. *The Natural Way to Draw*. Boston: Houghton-Mifflin Company paperback, 1969. A classic work on drawing that emphasizes observation, form, and action.

Thompson, Frank. *Tim Burton's Nightmare Before Christmas*. New York: Hyperion Roundtable Press, 1993. The story of the film and how it was made.

Includes a foreword by Tim Burton.

Williams, Richard. *The Animator's Survival Guide*. London: Faber & Faber, 2001. Williams's love for the medium is revealed through expressive examples of the most basic animation timing to the exotically advanced approaches employed by classic Disney and Warner's animators.

Music

Bazelon, Irwin. *Knowing the Score: Notes on Film Music*. New York: Arco Publishing, Inc., 1975. Interviews with composers of film music. The composer-author makes some points on music for animation.

Newsom, Iris, Ed. *Wondrous Inventions: Motion Pictures, Broadcasting, and Recorded Sound at the Library of Congress*. Washington, D.C.: Library of Congress, 1985. A very large book with detailed accounts of the musical aspects of Disney's *Bambi* and the UPA shorts. Includes two LP discs of music for film.

Goldmark, Daniel, and Yuval Taylor, Eds. *The Cartoon Music Book*. Chicago: Acapella, 2002. A collection of articles devoted entirely to the music of animation, from the Golden Age classics to the wacky world of television cartoons.

Prendergast, Roy M. *Film Music, A Neglected Art*. New York: W. W. Norton & Company, Inc., 1977. History and aesthetics about music for film. A lengthy chapter on music and animation. Illustrated with cartoon scores.

Story

Adamson, Joe. *Tex Avery: King of Cartoons*. New York: Popular Library, 1975; New York: Da Capo Press, 1985. A run-through of the life and manic animations of the director of Warner and MGM shorts that brightened theater screens in the 1930s and the 1940s. Includes interviews with Mike Maltese and other artists and writers.

Blacker, Irwin R. *Tne Elements of Screenwriting: A Guide for Film and Television Writing*. New York: Collier Books MacMillan, 1986. A handy paperback guide that a filmmaker can turn to when composing a plot or creating a chracter.

Jones, Chuck. *Chuck Amuck*. New York: Farrar, Straus, & Giroux, 1989. The author reminisces about his boyhood and the daily goings-on creating cartoons at Warner Bros.

Jones, Chuck. *Chuck Reducks*. New York: Warner Books, 1996. More reminiscence and wonderful drawings by the articulate Jones, plus a foreword by Robin Williams.

Thomas, Frank, and Ollie Johnston. *Too Funny for Words, Disney's Greatest Sight Gags*. New York: Abbeville Publishers, 1987. Emphasis on what is funny in cartoons, with illustrated gag sequences.

Vale, Eugene. *The Technique of Screen and Television Writing*. New York: Simon & Schuster, 1982. An experienced Hollywood writer shows what to look for when creating a script.

Special Effects

Abbott, L. B. *Special Effects—Wire, Tape and Rubber Band Style.* Hollywood: The ASC Press, 1984. Biography of a veteran special effects artist and how his screen illusions are done.

Culhane, John. *Special Effects in the Movies, How They Do It.* New York: Ballantine Books, 1981. An easy-to-understand overview of various graphic and mechanical film effects.

Fielding, Raymond. *The Technique of Special Effects Cinematography,* Fourth ed. London: Focal Press, 1985. A thorough text on the technical means of creating film special effects, camera operation, exposure, and lighting.

Harryhausen, Ray. *Film Fantasy Scrapbook.* New York: Barnes, 1972. The firsthand experiences of a major stop-motion animator. Includes photos from Harryhausen's adventure films.

Techniques

Culhane, Shamus. *Animation from Script to Screen.* New York: St. Martin's Press, 1988. Culhane explains methods which he employed working at Fleischer, Disney, and Lantz, and in his own studio.

Halas, John, and Roger Manvell. *The Technique of Film Animation.* New York: Hastings House, 1959. A classic work on how animation is done. Includes an interesting roundtable discussion between some animation greats including their speculations on the future.

Laybourne, Kit. *The Animation Book.* New York: Crown, 1979. A fine overview on the many ways to do independent animation. (Revised and enlarged, 1998.)

Madsen, Roy P. *Animated Film: Concepts, Methods, Uses.* New York: Interland, 1969. A technical look on the animation process. Includes a chapter on using an Oxberry camera stand.

Reininger, Lotte. *Shadow Theaters and Shadow Films.* New York: Watson Guptill, 1970. How the author made silhouette movies, including her 1926 feature. Written with refreshing remarks about why she liked working with a wooden animation stand.

Russett, Robert, and Starr Cecile. *Experimental Animation: Origin of a New Art,* rev. ed. New York: Da Capo Press, 1988. Excellent. Articles by important experimental animators with additional material by the authors. Fine for anyone looking for information or inspiration on unusual approaches and techniques.

Thomas, Frank, and Ollie Johnston. *Disney Animation: The Illusion of Life.* New York: Abbeville Publishers, 1981. This is a treasure. Two master animators tell about the workings of the Disney studio. Includes anecdotes about the personnel but the information related to animation is the meat.

Whitaker, Harold, and John Halas. *Timing for Animation.* London: Focal Press, 1981. Solid, basic animation solutions.

White, Tony. *The Animator's Workbook.* New York: Watson Guptill, 1986. Instructions for beginning animators explained with full-color drawings.

Computer Animation

Kerlow, Issac. *The Art of 3D Animation and Imaging.* New York: John Wiley & Sons, Inc., 2000. A guide to the theory and intricacies of creating solid shapes in motion.

Maestri, George. *Digital Character Animation 2, Volume 1: Essential Techniques.* Indianapolis: New Riders Publishing, 1999. A much-admired work on digital computer animation. The author's explanations are concise and clearly written.

Meyers, Trish, and Chris Meyers. *Creating Motion Graphics with After Effects.* San Francisco: CMP Books, 2000, *www.cmpbooks.com.* For the sincere After Effects user. Filled with explanations on how the program works, and practical tips and solutions.

Ratner, Peter. *Mastering 3D Animation.* New York: Allworth Press, 2000. An excellent source that explains all the necessary procedures for anyone wishing to master animation in the round. Fully illustrated and easy to comprehend.

Wands, Bruce. *Digital Creativity: Techniques for Digital Creativity and the Internet.* New York: John Wiley & Sons, Inc., 2002. Wands is thoroughly versed in all areas of animation and digital imaging. Here he explains the basic aesthetics of design, color, music, and the mechanics necessary for creating computer art.

The Business

Curran, Trisha. *Financing Your Film, A Guide for Independent Filmmakers and Producers.* Westport: Praeger Publishers, 1988. How to organize a budget, prepare a presentation, and interest investors in your production.

Gerberg, Mort. *Cartooning, The Art and the Business.* New York: William Morrow & Co., 1989. Reveals the nature of the cartooning field, with a chapter on working in animation.

Lees, David, and Stan Berkowitz. *The Movie Business.* New York: Vintage Books, 1981. How deals are made, budgets are formed, films are distributed, and who does what.

General

Canemaker, John. *The Animated Raggedy Ann and Andy.* New York: Bobbs Merrill, 1977. The making of a feature film, but also a solid book on the art of animation.

Finch, Christopher. *The Art of Walt Disney.* New York: Abrams, 1973. A lavish tome with oversize color art. It details the history of the Disney empire of cartoons, live films, and theme parks.

Halas, John. *The Contemporary Animator.* London: Focal Press, 1990. A concise, contemporary overview of animation theory and practice. Includes color and black-and-white illustrations.

Klein, Norman M. *7 Minutes: The Life and Death of the American Animated Cartoon.* London and New York: Verso, 1993. A serious look at the Golden Age of theatrical cartoons.

The author connects the shorts with the social, economic, and political concerns of those times.

Neuwirth, Allan. *Makin' Tunes: Inside the Most Popular Animated TV Shows and Movies*. New York: Allworth Press, 2003. The author fills us in on the Toon Boom triggered by *Who Framed Roger Rabbit* in 1988. This is a straightforward account of today's popular animation that is heir to that seminal production. The reader learns, through interviews with successful toon creators, what it takes to become one of them.

Thomas, Frank, and Ollie Johnston. *Walt Disney's Bambi, The Story of the Film*. New York: Stewart Tabori & Chang, 1990. Beautifully illustrated with production art revealing the long road of the film's travels from rough sketch to the screen.

Wells, Paul. *Animation: Genre and Authorship*. London: Wallflower, 2002. An exploration of animation as a distinctive language with emphasis on personal expression. Includes interviews with individual animators.

Wilson, Lee. *The Copyright Guide: A Friendly Handbook to Protecting and Profiting from Copyrights, Third Edition*. New York: Allworth Press, 2003. This book covers topics such as what can and cannot be protected under current law; duration and scope of protection; notice and registration; how to avoid infringement and what to do if you suspect infringement.

Wilson, Lee. *Making It in the Music Business: The Business and Legal Guide for Songwriters and Performers, Third Edition*. New York: Allworth Press, 2003. An ideal resource for specific information dealing with the use and protection of music, this book includes helpful chapters on copyright law, protection, infringement and how to avoid it, trademark law, music law and business practices.

Index

h.b.

Books from Allworth Press

Allworth Press is an imprint of Allworth Communications, Inc. Selected titles are listed below.

Makin' Toons: Inside the Most Popular Animated TV Shows and Movies
by Allan Neuwirth (paperback, 6 × 9, 288 pages, 82 b&w illus., $21.95)

Shoot Me: Independent Filmmaking from Creative Concept to Rousing Release
by Roy Frumkes and Rocco Simonelli (paperback, 6 × 9, 240 pages, 56 b&w illus., $19.95)

The Directors: Take Four
by Robert J. Emery (paperback, 6 × 9, 256 pages, 10 b&w illus., $19.95)

The Health & Safety Guide for Film, TV & Theater
by Monona Rossol (paperback, 6 × 9, 256 pages, $19.95)

Technical Film and TV for Nontechnical People
by Drew Campbell (paperback, 6 × 9, 256 pages, $19.95)

Acting for Film
by Cathy Hasse (paperback, 6 × 9, pages, $19.95)

An Actor's Guide: Your First Year in Hollywood, Revised Edition
by Michael Saint Nicholas (paperback, 6 × 9, 272 pages, $18.95)

Creative Careers
by Laurie Scheer (

Directing for Film
by Christopher Lul

Documentary Film
by Liz Stubbs (pap

The Filmmaker's
by Vincent LoBrut

Making Independ
by Liz Stubbs and Ru.....

Please write to requ
to Allworth Press, 1
first book ordered ar
New York State res

heck or money order
and handling for the
·dering from Canada.

w.allworth.com.

To see our complete